Teachings and Philosophy of Maharaja Agrasen

Teachings and Philosophy of Maharaja Agrasen

Editors
Mamta Aggarwal
Sonu Madan

GYAN

Published by

Gyan Publishing House
5, Ansari Road
Daryaganj, New Delhi-110002
Phone: 011-47034999, 9811692060
E-mail: books@gyanbooks.com

Distribution Network
gyanbooks.com
India, USA, Canada, UK, Australia, France

ISBN: 978-81-212-8798-2 (PB)

First Published, 2023

Printed at: Gyan Press, Delhi.

Teachings and Philosophy of Maharaja Agrasen
Editors: Mamta Aggarwal, Sonu Madan

Preface

The book titled Teachings and Philosophy of Maharaja Agrasen is based on the papers received for presentation in the national seminar on 'Socio-Economic and Political Aspects during Maharaja Agrasen Regime: Prospects and Perspectives' rganised by Maharaja Agrasen Chair, Indira Gandhi University, Meerpur-Rewari (Haryana) in collaboration with Haryana Pradesh Vaish Mahasamelan, Sonepat held on 19th February 2022 and thereafter for the purpose of publication in this edited book. The book elaborates on the vision, administrative acumen and legacy of Maharaja Agrasen; a philanthropist, promoter of socialism, and an epitome of good governance. Maharaja Agrasen not only laid *the foundation of the Agrawal community* but also dreamt of a self-reliant society wherein people, with their hard work, should bring social, political and economic progression to their society. The risk-taking ability and strategic managerial skills of Maharaja Agrasen initiated and promoted the inculcation of a sense of social responsibility in society. The book is divided into two broad sections highlighting the Teachings and Philosophy of Maharaja Agrasen and the relevance thereof to facing challenges emerging from a competitive business environment.

Section A illuminates the different aspects of Maharaja Agrasen's life. People today get the message of 'good governance policies for social welfare' and 'there are no communal barriers to do the deeds which are right for the society at large'. This section comprises twelve chapters by Dr Rajesh Gupta, Dr Meera Bamba, Dr Aditi Sharma, Dr Mamta Aggarwal, Dr Bharti, Dr Ishwar Sharma, Prof Sonu Madan, Dr Geetika Malhotra, Dr Samridhi Tanwar, Sh. Rameshwar Dayal Aggarwal, Sh. Durga Dutt Goyal, Pooja Yadav, Arjun Singh Yadav,

Bharti, Monika, Rachna Bansal, Devesh Aggarwal, Bhawna Verma, Manorama, Indu, Komal, Neetu, Sushant Yadav and Ajay Yadav. The articles in this section bring out the vision, principles, philosophy and ideology of Maharaja Agrasen to uplift society. It also highlights the contribution of each capable person to a progressive society.

Section B deals with articles on corporate social responsibility for sustainable growth in the social and economic environments, start-ups in India for developing business models, entrepreneurial skill development and the role of Self-Help Groups. The contributors Dr Sanjay Kumar Hooda, Jyoti, Taruna Sharma, Dr Shivani Arora, Dr Sarika Walia, Dr C.S.Yadav, Sonal Gupta, Sarla Yadav, Dr Samridhi Tanwar, Dr Pooja Vyas, Kanwar Singh, Pushpendra Gothwal, Dr Sonia, Tripta, Dr Garima Dalal, Dr Parul Mittal, Sonal contributed for revealing out the impact of CSR, Startup movements, Skill Development on the society. The section underlines the philosophy of Maharaja Agrasen in practising CSR activities in the modern era. In general, this section presents a theoretical framework for how CSR helps uplift society with particular reference to the *'one brick, one rupee'* concept. Also, it highlights the importance of managerial skills, skill development and self-help groups to handle risk and uncertainty in trade and provide a supportive hand to the growing business.

In brief, articles in this section are dedicated to the unforgettable life stories and incidences of the great king who left his Kshatriya Varna and entered into Vaish Varna for the wellbeing of living beings. The articles provide significant remarks on the gesture of socialism by his 'one brick-one coin' policy which is an unmatched phenomenon.

Mamta Aggarwal

Sonu Madan

Acknowledgements

It was never easy for us to write this section of acknowledgement for the people who consistently stood by us throughout the writing of this edited volume. We must not forget to acknowledge such cooperation and help. It is high time that we acknowledge all those persons whose inspiration and encouragement, and many a times help, and cooperation went a long way in preparing and finishing this work. We are deeply indebted to one and all who gave unflinching support in shaping up our endeavours and thoughts into a perspective to bring out this edited volume. Completing it is a big sense of accomplishment and joy. To start our efforts of this academic journey, it is none other than **Maharaja Agrasen Ji,** a natural source of inspiration for us. His story can inspire others to persevere and strive for their own goals. We see Maharaja Agrasen Ji as a policymaker and the epitome of good governance. The reason behind changing his Varna from Kshatriya to Vaish Varna depicts his concern towards living beings, and the concept of 'One Brick, One Coin' shows his sensitivity towards social issues. With humility and gratitude, we truly dedicate this work to him.

Another great inspirer, who needs to be acknowledged quintessentially as the journey of this book starts with the idea of **Prof S. K. Gakhar**, Former Vice Chancellor of Indira Gandhi University, Meerpur-Rewari. His plan for conducting the National Seminar on Maharaja Agrasen and compiling the presented papers in the form of an edited book paved our way. We are highly indebted to him for his guidance and having confidence in us. Simultaneously, we convey our heartfelt appreciation to **Sh. Rajiv Jain**, President-Haryana Pradesh Vaish Mahasamelan (HPVM), Sonipat; **Sh. Durga**

Dutt Goyal, Secretary-HPVM and their entire team for showing their readiness and ensuring the uninterrupted progress of the work from each dimension very frequently. We also learnt the patience and the spirit of cooperation just for the sake of social welfare from the team. Our words always fall short to mention their role to this academic writing.

The encouragement and unflinching support rendered by **Professor J. P. Yadav**, Vice Chancellor, Indira Gandhi University, Meerpur-Rewari, in providing every support to further the compilation of the articles has been truly enthusing for us. We owe great respect to **Professor Dinesh Kumar**, Vice Chancellor of Gurugram University, for his invaluable advice on staying focused and motivated all the time. His support and guidance have been a fundamental cause of comfort and inspiration for us.

Prof. Parmod Kumar, Registrar, Indira Gandhi University, Meerpur-Rewari, has always encouraged us all the way through his constructive feedback and discussed many points that got reflected in the work for which we are truly thankful to him.

Our acknowledgement will be incomplete if we do not mention the contribution of the authors of the articles. Their keen interest in the literature and endurance while writing the articles and making necessary changes all the time has led us to work consistently and patiently.

Finally, we feel overwhelmed with love and feel emotional to the point of tears for all our friends and family members whose names we cannot mention just because we are one and their impact on our lives is indescribable and can only be felt, not expressed in words.

Throughout this journey, we have taken advantage from different streams of intellectual thoughts and we always felt and learnt that good and intellect people are often driven by a desire to make a positive impact on the society. Their desire to be recognized has totally been vanished, but their supportive work environment encourages us to feel valued and contribute to the greater good.

Mamta Aggarwal

Sonu Madan

List of Contributors

1. Aditi Sharma
Associate Professor,
Indira Gandhi University, Meerpur

2. Ajay Yadav
Ph.D Scholar
Indira Gandhi University, Meerpur

3. Arjun Singh Yadav
Ph.D Scholar,
Indira Gandhi University, Meerpur.

4. Bharti
Ph.D Scholar,
Indira Gandhi University, Meerpur

5. Bharti
Assistant Professor,
Indira Gandhi University, Meerpur.

6. Bhawna Verma
Ph.D Scholar,
Indira Gandhi University, Meerpur

7. C.S. Yadav
Professor,
Shivalik Institute of Professional Studies, Dehradun, Uttarakhand

8. Devesh Aggarwal
Assistant Professor,
Indira Gandhi University, Meerpur

9. Durga Dutt Goyal
General Secretary,
Haryana Pradesh Vaish Mahasamelan

10. Garima Dalal
Associate Professor,
Institute of Management Studies and Research,
Maharshi Dayanand University, Rohtak.

11. Geetika Malhotra
Assistant Professor,
Indira Gandhi University, Meerpur

12. Indu
Ph.D Scholar,
Indira Gandhi University, Meerpur

13. Ishwar Sharma
Assistant Professor,
Indira Gandhi University, Meerpur

14. Jyoti
Research Scholar,
IMSAR, MDU

15. Kanwar Singh
Assistant Professor,
Indira Gandhi University, Meerpur-Rewari

16. Komal
Ph.D Scholar,
Indira Gandhi University, Meerpur

17. Mamta Aggarwal
Assistant Professor,
Indira Gandhi University, Meerpur

18. Manorama
Ph.D Scholar,
Indira Gandhi University, Meerpur

19. Meera Bamba
Assistant Professor,
Indira Gandhi University, Meerpur

20. Monika
Ph.D Scholar,
Indira Gandhi University, Meerpur

21. Neetu
Ph.D Scholar
Indira Gandhi University, Meerpur

22. Parul Mittal
Assistant Professor,
Kishan Lal Public College, Rewari

23. Pooja Vyas
Assistant Professor,
IMSAR, MDU-ROHTAK

24. Pooja Yadav
Ph.D Scholar,
Indira Gandhi University, Meerpur.

25. Priya Rani
Research Scholar,
Institute of Management Studies and Research,
Maharshi Dayanand University, Rohtak.

26. Pushpendra Gothwal
Research Scholar, Amity Business School,
Amity University, Gurugram, Haryana

27. Rachna
PGT(Commerce),
Govt. Sr Sec School Carterpuri 0750 Gurugram

28. Rajesh Gupta
Principal,
Hindu Kanya Senior Secondary School, Sonipat

29. Rameshwar Dayal Aggarwal
New Anaj Mandi,
Rewari, Haryana

30. Samridhi Tanwar
Associate Professor,
Indira Gandhi University, Meerpur

31. Sanjay Kumar Hooda
Associate Professor,
Indira Gandhi University, Meerpur

32. Sarika Walia
Assistant Professor,
Department of Management Studies, Gurugram University, Gurugram

33. Sarla
Research Scholar,
Faculty of Management and Commerce,
Baba Mastnath University, Rohtak

34. Shivani Arora
Assistant Professor, PDP Department, Graphic Era Hill University, Dehradun, Uttarakhand

35. Sonal Gupta
Research Scholar (JRF)
Faculty of Management and Commerce,
Baba Mastnath University, Rohtak

36. Sonia
Associate Professor,
Institute of Management Studies and Research,
Maharshi Dayanand University

37. Sonu Madan
Professor,
Chaudhary Bansi Lal University, Bhiwani

38. Sushant Yadav
Assistant Professor,
Indira Gandhi University, Meerpur

39. Taruna Sharma
Research Scholar,
University of Engineering and Technology Roorkee,
Haridwar, Uttarakhand

40. Tripta
Research Scholar, Institute of Management Studies and Research,
Maharshi Dayanand University

Contents

SECTION-A

1

HFIS: Maharaja Agrasen's Philosophy of Income Management and Satisfaction of Needs

Bharti[1], Arjun Singh Yadav[2], Pooja Yadav[2]

Abstract

Income is what one earns in the form of wages, salaries, compensation, commission, gains and profits etc. It is the earnings received against physical or mental work. The paper focuses on income management based on the teachings and principles of Maharaja Agrasen. Maharaja Agrasen, a socialist emperor, focused on trade or business for the prosperity of his kingdom. His focus was on development of all sections of the society. Maharaja Agrasen proposed the principle of disposal of income in a way that not only prospers the individual or his business but also to society (Lai and Tan, 2019). As per the philosophy of Maharaja Agrasen, income should be divided into four parts. First part of income should be used to meet household expenses, second part should be saved for future, third part should be invested into the business, farming or in any other occupation one carries and fourth part should be used for welfare of society and others (Gupta, 2019). This philosophy of Maharaja Agrasen fulfils the different kinds of needs of an individual through income management.

Key Words: Income, management, saving, household expenses, investment, social welfare.

---

1. Assistant Professor, Department of Management, Indira Gandhi University, Meerpur-Rewari, Haryana.
2. PhD Scholar, Department of Management, Indira Gandhi University, Meerpur-Rewari, Haryana.

Introduction

Income is the monetary value that people get in exchange for their work, or producing a product or service or investing capital. Income is earned in different forms like wages, salaries, incentives, commissions, profits and gains etc. for the physical, mental work or as a reward for the risk (Scott, 2021). A major portion of income gets consumed in basic necessities and rest is saved for emergency funds (Shah & Bhatt, 2014). After paying the taxes on this earned money, the individual is left with the disposable income at his/her end that can be utilised for different purposes. Income is essential for the survival and growth of any person, society, state and nation (Kenton, 2022). As every person has different needs and income levels, they need to plan their finances effectively and efficiently to get the maximum satisfaction and to achieve their desired goals. This process of managing the personal income or finance according to individual needs is also known as personal financial planning (Beramendi and Cusack, 2009). In India, domestic saving is highly influenced by the household sector and its contribution is about three-fourth in domestic savings (Krishnamurty & Saibaba, 2014).

An individual has different kinds of needs to fulfil with his income. Everyone has different motives to be fulfilled with the limited income they earn. Abraham Maslow gave a sequence of fulfilment of needs based on these motivations and it increases the potential of a human to the maximum (Zalenski & Raspa, 2006). This sequence doesn't have any scientific reason behind it but study of human nature has supported this fact as people can easily recognise this in themselves and in others too (Oleson, 2004). The basic physiological needs of the individual and his family comes first. It is the basic nature of every human being that one will think of his and his family's survival first (Abulof, 2017; Chai et al., 2014). Once the basic necessities are fulfilled, then one thinks of the financial security of himself and his family. Ming & Tan (2009) showed that the attitude of people towards saving is primarily affected by the job status and secondarily by the demographics. They think of their future and growth prospects. Then they think of their responsibilities towards the society they live in. Humans have a tendency to fulfil the 'deficit needs' firstly and then they try to fulfil the 'growth needs' in any country of the world (Poduska, 2015). The deficit needs are the needs related to basic life survival necessities and growth needs are related to the power or popularity a person wants. According to The Business World (2020) & The International Monetary Fund Organisation (2021), Indians have a tendency of saving money more than any other country. The saving rate in India was 6.5 percent in the first plan period (1951-52 to 1955-56) which was raised to 22 percent till 1976-77 to 1978-79 (Krishnamurty & Saibaba, 2014). They save money broadly for the education and marriage of their children. With time the pattern of disposing of income has also changed. It has shifted from the traditional method of investing money into materialistic assets to investments into third parties that can give them continuous growth in their savings (Messey & Basem, 1992). Money is required for unforeseen future needs, to meet the expected and unexpected expenses like education, marriage, asset purchase, medical emergency etc. Individuals also want to grow in their respective careers, so they need to invest in their business, profession and career to make it big (Agarwal et. al, 2015). It enhances their self-esteem and status in the society. Every individual owes a responsibility towards the society they live in. It is the duty of every human being to make the society a better place to live. Contributing to the upliftment of the vulnerable and marginal sections of the society gives a sense of self fulfilment. It satisfies the need of self-actualisation (Asimakopulos, 2020). Oishi et al. (1999) shows that the satisfaction can be taken differently depending on the external conditions. In developed countries it can be related to high predictors such as love while in underdeveloped countries it is more about safety (Pahl, 2008). The disposal of income is not the same for all the individuals in the society (Dickman et al., 2016). It depends on the economic as well as political condition of that area. There are rules made by the governing body so that every individual can give their contribution for the betterment of the society while fulfilling their own needs. For example, people pay taxes based on their income level and this is further used for development of the society (Beramendi & Cusack, 2009).

Money is not everything, but it is needed for everything. Money earned in the form of income is spent by the individuals in a way that satisfies their different needs. Money is needed for satisfying their physiological needs like food, clothing and shelter. When these needs get satisfied then for upper hierarchy too money is needed such as for getting designer clothes, delicious food or having home at a desired location etc. For security needs, they invest in different kinds of insurances or safety tools then they need money for their personal goals either related to their personal life or professional life (Oleson, 2004; Oldfield & Levell, 2011). Nations should also follow the sequence of fulfilling needs created by Maslow following from physiological needs to security, belongingness, esteem and self-actualisation for the development of quality life in nations (Hagerty, 1999). Maharaja Agrasen has proposed a philosophy of income management by which an individual can satisfy many of his needs at the same time and also relates to the Need Hierarchy given by Maslow that fulfils their personal, family, growth and societal needs. It shows the similarity in the theory of disposing of an individual's income for getting maximum satisfaction.

Maharaja Agrasen and His Systems

Maharaja Agrasen was a Suryavanshi emperor from the dynasty of Lord Rama. He was the icon of non-violence, peace, prosperity and a true socialist. According to available literature, Maharaja Agrasen was born during the later years of Dwapar Yug. Maharaja Agrasen established his new kingdom at Agroha in North India. Agroha soon became a prosperous kingdom as agriculture and trade flourished there during his regime (Gupta, 2019). His interest in trade resulted in the growth of businesses and commerce in his kingdom which brought prosperity, peace and happiness in the state (Gupta, 2021).

Maharaja Agrasen was against any kind of discrimination in the society. Any discrimination on the basis of income, occupation, birth, money, religion etc. was unacceptable in his kingdom. All human beings were treated with equality and justice. Maharaja Agrasen has restricted animal killing in his kingdom and refused to slaughter animals for *yajnas*. Cows have been worshiped in India since time immortal. Maharaja Agrasen built many cowsheds in his state for cow rearing which increased the percentage of cows in his kingdom (Madhup, 2017). The people of his kingdom also contributed to this noble cause. Maharaja Agrasen's focus was on trade and commerce. He took many steps for the establishment of trade and business in his state. He provided the finance, security and market for trade and business. He also ensured that every business is carried out with honesty and integrity. He gave equal importance and respect to the farmers (Gupta, 2021). He was of the belief that we can earn and grow only when our stomach is full and the farmers are the *'Annadata'* who grow grains and make the state self-sufficient in food (Aggarwal, 2019). During his regime, many big and small traders came to his kingdom for their business and livelihood. As a king, he alone could not bear the responsibility of all the new entrants who were needy. So, he asked every household of his state to donate one brick and one coin to the new chum for their shelter building and business. Many times, people lose their business and try to start their business again. People help them by giving one brick and one coin from every house.

Research Methodology

This research paper is exploratory in nature. Different books, research papers from journals, websites, e-newspapers, articles etc. were studied to understand the principles and philosophies of Maharaja Agrasen ji and their contribution in need satisfaction.

Objectives of the study

The main objective of the study was to understand the philosophies and practices of Maharaja Agrasen for income management, the following sub-objectives were framed for the same:

- To understand the philosophy of Income Management laid by Maharaja Agrasen; and
- To explore the satisfaction of needs through the income management philosophy of Maharaja Agrasen.

Maharaja Agrasen Philosophy of Income Management: HFIS (For Household, For Future, For Investment and For Society)

Income is essential for the survival and economic growth of any person, society, state and country. People can utilise their income in different ways. Maharaja Agrasen has proposed a philosophy to divide and utilise the income in four parts: one part on household expenses, second part to save for future, third to invest in business, farming or occupation and fourth on social welfare (Gupta, 2019). This income management philosophy was the key for economic stability and growth of his people and kingdom.

Part I- Household expenditure (H): Maharaja Agrasen guided that one part of income should be used as household expenditure. Money is required to meet the daily expenses of food, education, medicines etc. The household expenses of self and family are to be met with the income earned.

Part One	**Part Two**
Household Expenditure (H) (Food, Shelter, clothing and other basic amenities)	Savings for Future (F) (Children education, marriage, Investment in assets, unforeseen events)
Part Four	**Part Three**
Social Welfare (Donations to poor and vulnerable sections of society, animal welfare)	Investment (Investing in business for growth)

Figure 1: HFIS: Income Management based on Maharaja Agrasen's Philosophy.

Part II- Savings for future: In India, people have a tendency of saving since ages. Maharaja Agrasen also proposed that one part of income should be saved for the future of self and family. Savings can be utilised at difficult times and also to meet the planned expenses in future. It gives a sense of security to the family.

Part III- Investment: Maharaja Agrasen ji also recommended investing a part of one's earnings in business, occupation, farming etc. The investment in the business, occupation or farming is essential for its growth. Money begets money, so income invested will yield more income. It is a method of wealth creation and prosperity.

Part IV- Social Welfare**:** People live in the society and work with society. Maharaja Agrasen urged the people of his kingdom to donate a part of their income for the welfare of animals, others and society.

The income management philosophy of Maharaja Agrasen was for the welfare of self, family, business and society.

Satisfaction of Needs through Income Management Philosophy of Maharaja Agrasen

***Household expenditure on Basic Needs*:** Survival is the basic objective of one's life. One can think of all other things later but of survival first. A human being will also first spend money on the basic things that are needed for one's survival. Firstly, individuals use their income for the household expenses such as the amount paid for food, daily utilities, electricity bill, rent of shelter etc. In other words, we can say that one part of income, firstly, is used for fulfilling the physiological or basic needs of an individual that are essential for their survival. The household expenses satisfy or fulfil individuals' psychological needs (Maslow, 1948). Maharaja Agrasen also proposed to spend one part of income on household expenditure.

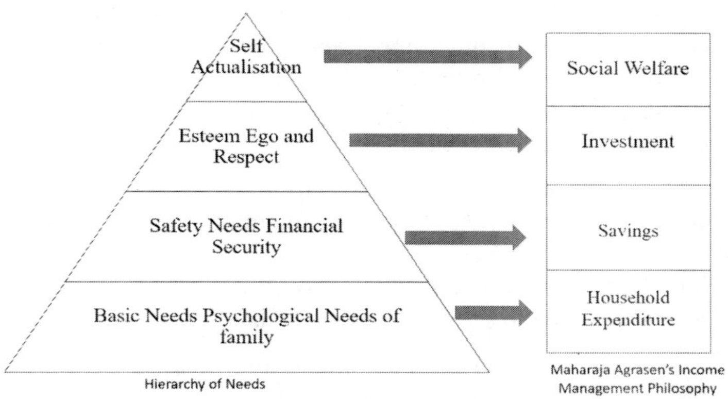

Figure 2: Need Satisfaction and Maharaja Agrasen's Philosophy of Income Management.

***Savings for Financial Security Needs*:** People always save one part of their income to meet their future needs. In India, people have a tendency of saving money for future needs such as children's education, marriage, insurance, medical expenses, asset purchase and unforeseen events etc (Krishnamurty and Saibaba, 2014). Savings meet the security and safety needs of a person. Everybody wants to be financially secure and they also ensure their financial security of their loved ones. Government also promotes savings by providing a good interest rate on accounts open under different saving schemes such as Sukaniya Samridhi Yojana, Jan Dhan yojana, Public provident Fund, Kisan Vikas Patra, National saving certificates etc. Investment in real estate, gold and other assets also give a sense of financial security to the individuals and their families. Different institutions like banks, insurance companies, post offices etc. provide a platform for savings and secure their future.

Maharaja Agrasen also asked the people of his state to save a portion of their income for their future. He encouraged them towards savings for the future of their families.

Investment for Self-esteem Needs: People strive for growth and progress in their lives. They dream to grow their business and make it bigger. It satisfies their ego and enhances their self-esteem. It is not possible to make it big without money. So, it is needed to invest a part of income in business, occupation, farming etc. a person is in. Money makes money, so it becomes important to invest some part of income to harvest returns in future. Investment is a medium of increment in their future income. When a person and his business grow, a sense of accomplishment is achieved.

Maharaja Agrasen also proposed to invest a portion of income on business or farming etc. He was visionary to foresee that to grow the business money is needed, so a part of income should be invested back in the business (Gupta, 2019). It is also needed for the survival of the business and to overcome the bad phase.

Social Welfare for Self-actualisation Need: People live in the society and owe many things to society. People use public and natural resources. So, people have some responsibility towards their society and environment. One should contribute in social welfare, conservation of the environment and Ecosystem. We all should make the planet Earth a better and beautiful place to live. Nowadays, the government has bound the big corporations to contribute two percent of their profits in social responsibility activities under Corporate Social Responsibility (CSR). Many Non-Government Organisations provide food to the hungry, education to the illiterate or poor children's, provide shelter to the homeless persons and animal rearing etc. Government also plays a big role in social welfare by providing free education, grain at cheaper rate to the below poverty line peoples, cylinders at subsidized rates, shelter to the homeless under the Pradhan Mantri Awas Yojana etc. Individuals, corporates and governments spend their one part of income on social welfare.

Income management philosophy of Maharaja Agrasen also proposes to donate a part of income on social welfare and animal welfare.

Conclusion

Maharaja Agrasen was a socialist emperor having knowledge about business and good managerial, financial skills with philanthropist attitude. He worked a lot for prosperity in his kingdom in every field. For managing finances and accomplishing needs in his kingdom, he had a philosophy about income. According to him, income should be divided into four parts- household expenditure, savings for future, investment and social welfare. First part, household expenditure includes the daily living expenses (e.g., for food, shelter and clothing), then the second part covers savings that can be used as an emergency fund. Third part includes investment in one's occupation for its growth and enhancing finances. Fourth part should be kept for social welfare that includes helping others in society, animals etc. This philosophy is applicable in today's era too, as explained in Maslow's hierarchy of needs. At present time also, one focuses on his basic survival needs at first (food, shelter and daily utilities etc). Then, they try to save some part of their income for future needs such as education, marriage, emergency medical expenses etc. Next, they run after achieving their self-esteem needs (their personal or professional goals, desire for recognition, social status etc) by investing in their occupation expecting future returns. At last, they work for social welfare to attain self-actualisation needs by accomplishing efforts towards environment, society and ecosystem. Thus, we can say that the philosophy behind Maharaja Agrasen's income management is still successful for division of income, as it satisfies all human needs at the same time in today's era.

References

Abulof, U. (2017). Introduction: Why we Need Maslow in the Twenty-first Century. *Society, 54*(6), 508–509. https://doi.org/10.1007/s12115-017-0198-6

Agarwal, S., Amromin, G., Ben-David, I., Chomsisengphet, S., and Evanoff, D.D. (2015). Financial Literacy and Financial Planning: Evidence from India, *Journal of Housing Economics*, doi: http://dx.doi.org/10.1016/j.jhe.2015.02.003.

Aggarwal, M. (2019). *Agarwal Samaj Ki Virasat*, Gulibaba Publication House Pvt. Ltd, Kanahiya Nagar, Trinagar, Delhi-10035.

Aggarwal, M. (2019). *Haryana ka Gorav- Aggarwal Samaj*, Mohit Agarwal and Lala Narumal Garg Welfare Organisation, Hansipura road, *Tripura,* Delhi-110035.

Asimakopulos, A. (2020). A Kaleckian Theory of Income Distribution. *Investment, Employment and Income Distribution*, 23–46. https://doi.org/10.4324/9780429033193-2.

Beramendi, P., and Cusack, T.R. (2009). The Politics and Economics of Wage, Market, and Disposable Income Inequalities, *Political Research Quarterly, 62* (2), pp. 257-275. doi:10.1177/1065912908319220.

Business World (2020). Indian Savings Culture - Will the History Repeat? Retrieved from https://www.businessworld.in/article/Indian-Savings-Culture-Will-The-History-Repeat-/05-06-2020-194349/.

Chai, A., Rohde, N., & Silber, J. (2014). Measuring the diversity of household spending patterns. *Journal of Economic Surveys, 29*(3), 423–440. https://doi.org/10.1111/joes.12066

Dickman, S. L., Woolhandler, S., Bor, J., McCormick, D., Bor, D. H., & Himmelstein, D. U. (2016). Health spending for low-, middle-, and high-income Americans, 1963–2012. *Health Affairs, 35*(7), 1189–1196. https://doi.org/10.1377/hlthaff.2015.1024

Gupta, A. (2021). "*Maharaja Agrasen Aur Agrvansh*". Trident Enterprises, Noida.

Gupta, K. (2019). *"Maharaja Agrasen: Agravansh Ka Sanshipt Itihaas"*. GenNext Publication.

Investopedia. (2021, January 22). *What is Disposable Income, and Why is it Important?* Investopedia. Retrieved January 29, 2023, from https://www.investopedia.com/terms/d/disposableincome.asp

Kenton, W. (2022). Disposable Income, Investopedia.com, retrieved on 12 Dec., 2022. URL:https://www.investopedia.com/terms/d/disposableincome.asp

Krishnamurti, K. and Saibaba, P. (2014). Determinants of Saving Rate in India, *Indian Economic Review, New Series, Vol. 16*, No. 4 (October-December 1981), pp. 225-249.

Lai, M.M. and Tan, W. (2009). An Empirical Analysis of Personal Financial Planning in an Emerging Economy, *European Journal of Economics, Finance and Administrative Sciences,* Issue 16, pp. 99-111.

Madhup, O. (2017). *Ek Eant Ek Rupya*, Omprakash Garg Madhup and Agroha Vikas Trust, Agroha Dham, Hisar, Haryana.

Maslow, A.H. (1948). "Higher" and "Lower" Needs, *The Journal of Psychology: Interdisciplinary and Applied, 25:*2, 433-436, DOI:10.1080/00223980.1948.9917386.

Massey, D., and Basem, L. (1992). Determinants of Savings, Remittances, and Spending Patterns among U. S. Migrants in Four Mexican Communities, *Sociological Inquiry, Vol. 62*, No. 2, Spring 1992, University of Texas Press, P.O. Box 7819, Austin, TX 78713.

Oishi, S., Diener, E., Lucas, R. E., & Suh, E. M. (2009). Cross-cultural Variations in Predictors of Life Satisfaction: Perspectives from Needs and Values. *Social Indicators Research Series*, 109–127. https://doi.org/10.1007/978-90-481-2352-0_6

Oldfield, Z., & Levell, P. (2011). The Spending Patterns and Inflation Experience of low Income Households over the Past Decade. https://doi.org/10.1920/co.ifs.2011.0119

Oleson, M. (2004). Exploring the Relationship between Money Attitudes and Maslow's Hierarchy of Needs". *International Journal of Consumer Studies, 28*(1), 83–92. https://doi.org/10.1111/j.1470-6431.2004.00338.x

Pahl, J. (2008). Family Finances, Individualisation, Spending Patterns and Access to Credit. *The Journal of Socio-Economics*, *37*(2), 577–591. https://doi.org/10.1016/j.socec.2006.12.041

Poduska, B. (2015). Money, Marriage and Maslow's Hierarchy of Needs, *American Behavioral Scientist 1992, 35*, pp. 756-770. DOI: 10.1177/0002764292035006010

Scott, M. P. (2021). Income, Investopedia.com, retrieved on 26 Feb, 2022. URL: https://www.investopedia.com/terms/i/income.asp

Shah, S. and Bhatt, A. (2014). An Insight into Personal Financial Planning: An empirical study in Ahmedabad. https://ssrn.com/abstract=2813478

Zalenski, R. J., & Raspa, R. (2006). Maslow's Hierarchy of Needs: A Framework for Achieving Human Potential in Hospice. *Journal of Palliative Medicine, 9*(5), 1120–1127. https://doi.org/10.1089/jpm.2006.9.1120

2

The Contemporary Relevance of Philosophical tenets of Maharaja Agrasen's Rule

Samridhi[1]

Abstract

The era of some ancient Indian rulers was often characterised as the "ideal" conditions to live in. The concepts and ideologies over which the ruling policies of that time were framed are equally relevant today. Maharaj Agrasen is one of such ancient Indian rulers who emphasised equally on different diverse aspects of a state's growth. Drawing on folklore stories and anecdotal evidences, this study investigates the philosophical foundations of Maharaja Agrasen's rule and ponder upon their relevance in current times. Particularly, the ideologies associated with socio-economic and political areas will be explored to draw out some implications for current times.

Keywords: Social, economic, Political, Philosophies, Maharaja Agrasen

"In order to live in heaven after death, we shall have to live in heaven before death"

Introduction

India's rich history is replete with examples of such great rulers that have transformed the way one could look at ruling and

1. Associate Professor, Department of Management, Indira Gandhi University, Meerpur-Rewari, Haryana.

thus immensely contributed, not only to the society but also to the disciplines of politics, economics and sociology by illuminating their ideal practical sides. Lord Rama, Ashoka, Chandragupta Maurya, Prithviraj Chauhan are few of such rulers who are revered for their valor, wisdom, and astuteness. Maharaja Agrasen is another such ruler who had transformed the economical and social face of Indian rule. He was considered to be an innovator, a great patriarch, a promoter of trade and business, and a revolutionary who raised voice against several societal dogmas.

Maharaja Agrasen is mostly recognised as Vaishya ruler who was the predecessor of the Aggarwal community. However, anecdotal evidences and stories from Indian folklore illuminates different dimensions of Maharaja Agrasen's life and rule that seems to be very relevant, even for current times. This study examines, different social, economic, and political aspects of Maharaja Agrasen's rule and tries to unveil the underlying philosophies and assess its relevance in present times of unrest and disruption.

History of Maharaja Agrasen

Maharaja Agrasen was a Suryavanshi Kshatriya ruler who lived during the later stages of the Dwapar Yuga in the Mahabharat epic era, and was contemporary with Lord Krishna, according to Bharatendu Harishchandra's narrative (Singhal, 2017). He was the son of King Vallabha Dev, a Kush (Lord Rama's son) descendant. He was also a Suryavanshi King Mandhata descendent. Gunadhi and Mohan were King Mandhata's two sons. Maharaja Agrasen was the eldest son of King Vallabh of Pratapnagar, a descendant of Mohan. Maharaja Agrasen had 18 offspring, which gave rise to the Agrawal Gotras (Pathak, 2019; Tanwar, 2021).

According to the current calendar, Maharaj Agrasen was born around 5185 years ago. Prince Agrasen was recognised for his compassion even when he was a child. He never prejudiced against anyone, and the subjects praised him for his professionalism.

When Agrasen was a young man, he went to the Swayamvara of King Nagaraj's daughter, Princess Madhavi. Indra, the King of the Devas, was among the many kings who attended from all across the universe. Princess Madhavi chose Prince Agrasen in the Swayamvara by placing the garland on him. Because Prince Agrasen was a Suryavanshi and Princess Madhavi was a Naagavanshi, this marriage brought together two separate family cultures. Indra, the Devas' King, had fallen in love with Princess Madhavi's beauty and intended to marry her. However, he became enraged and envious of Agrasen for thwarting his schemes. Indra, commonly known as the Lord of Rain, ensured that Pratap Nagar did not receive any rain and that famine devastated the Pratap Nagar kingdom in order to exact revenge on Agrasen. Emperor Agrasen then launched war on Indra, and because he had dharma on his side, his army defeated and defeated Indra's armies. Indra asked Narada (the celestial sage) for help in resolving the conflict between him and Emperor Agrasen. Narada was able to reach an agreement with them (Pal, 2021).

Agrasen became concerned with establishing a long-term peace in order to put an end to the hostility. As a result, Agrasen travelled to Kashi and began penance in order to appease Lord Shiva. Lord Shiva appeared in front of Agrasen, pleased with his extreme penance, and advised him to propitiate Shri Mahalakshmi. Maharaj Agrasen began to contemplate Shri Mahalakshmi. Maharaj Agrasen's commitment pleased Goddess Mahalakshmi, who came before him. Goddess Mahalakshmi blessed Agrasen and advised him to abandon his Kshatriya lineage and follow the Vaishya business tradition for the sake of his people's prosperity. In exchange for her immortal presence with his progeny, she also required that he construct a new empire.

Social Dimension of Maharaja Agrasen's Rule

Maharaja Agrasen was a doer (a Karmyogi) who wished for everyone's prosperity. He established a one-of-a-kind guideline to ensure an egalitarian society as a Socialism devotee. He decreed that everyone wishing to stay permanently in Agroha be granted one rupee, or one brick, by each Agroha resident. He could build a home with the bricks he had collected, and he could start his own business with the money he had amassed. This way, each person may achieve equal status in the society of equals by providing a tiny amount of assistance.

Another anecdotal evidence establishes that Maharaja Agrasen was a staunch supporter for women empowerment. While earning his education in gurukul, he came across an ascetic lady who was being kidnapped and forced by a king named Ratindra. Agrasen, not only freed the lady but also punished Ratindra publicly to set an example for the society.

During the 18th Yagna, he saw the futility of animal sacrifices and adopted the principle of Non-Violence. The Yagna was held to commemorate the founding of the 18th Gotra. His philosophy about non-violence reflects very well in his words:

"Instead of targeting a crane with an arrow, I wish to see it flying; Instead of eating away a nightingale, I wish to hear it singing".

His commitment in nonviolence, however, did not imply non-resistance to injustice; rather, he advocated for self-defence. Self-defence and national defence, he claimed, were not solely the responsibility of Kshatriyas, but rather it was the responsibility of every citizen to protect and safeguard his motherland.

The spirit of the current Indian Constitution is based on Maharaj Agrasen's 5000-year-old beliefs of equality, socialism, and nonviolence. We Indians, on the other hand, have not been able to incorporate these ideas into our daily life; they remain just words in our constitution. As a monument to our forefather, it is now up to us to live up to these principles.

Economic Dimension of Maharaja Agrasen's Rule

Maharaja Agrasen acknowledged the value of self-reliance and promoted agricultural, industrial and trade related activities under his reign. He was also an innovator since he was the first to adopt artificial irrigation methods such as rivers, canals, baolis for agricultural activities (Agarwal, 2021). He also understood the roles and duties of state in promoting the entrepreneurial and trade related activities. For agricultural empowerment, the innovative irrigation resources were available to everyone for free. Also, the beautiful policy through which every citizen is encouraged to donate a brick and a rupee to anyone who is unable to earn their livelihood underlies the value of collaboration and collective effort.

Also, once while inspecting the jails in his state, Maharaja Agrasen came across his childhood friend Shaakunt. With utmost, surprise and dismay, Agrasen asked his friend about the reason for his present condition. Shaakunt explained that poverty and starvation forced him to become a thief (Garg, 2021). On hearing his friend's plight, Agrasen being a responsible ruler, looked upon it as state's responsibility to provide enough opportunities to everyone to earn their daily bread and butter. This event also drove him towards the enactment of 'one brick, one rupee' policy.

Maharaja Agrasen also extended some innovative ideas related to management of personal finances. He believed that one should divide his earning in four parts such that one part should be spent to meet family's day-to-day's requirements, one part for his business development, another part should be used developing public utilities and welfare and fourth part should be saved for future and state development works (Bhandari, 2021).

Political Dimension of Maharaja Agrasen's Rule

Maharaja Agrasen was considered to be a pioneer who introduce the concept of socialism in India. He emphasised on the importance of community efforts for the betterment of all. He also established robust defence policies, according to which each and every citizen of the state should be well trained in arts of war and everyone is free to fight for their state in the hour of need. Furthermore, he inculcated the concept of social cooperation among his people (Nagrath, 2017). He provided various infrastructural and economic assistance to his citizens to grow and become self-reliant. He built several dharamshalas, hospitals, schools, and libraries as his infrastructural development plans. The deeds of Maharaja Agrasen shows that true socialist democratic society can be built only on the foundations of social cooperation, community efforts and a sense of collaboration.

Relevance of Maharaja Agrasen's Philosophies in Current times

The recent pandemic situation has disrupted both personal and professional lives of people. Evidences of migrant exoduses, high rates of unemployment and layoffs, management failures at cremation grounds, sheer dearth of self reliance among citizens highlight the areas where the governance needs to fix its mechanisms. These are the areas where Maharaja Agrasen's regime not only did well but established certain examples and extended various methods to build a state where cooperation is revered, where all the citizens are concerned and took responsibility about the economic conditions of the nation, and where governance assumes the responsibility to nourish the citizens like family.

Conclusion

The current study explored the social, economic, and political aspects of Maharaja Agrasen's regime and an effort has been made to relate their relevance with current times. Anecdotal evidences and insights from folklore stories showed that Maharaja Agrasen was one of those great rulers who laid the foundations of an ideal nation. The policy and projects that were functional under his regime were build upon the philosophies of socialism, social cooperation, self-reliance, egalitarianism, and non-violence. All these abstract concepts are equally relevant in present times as continuous efforts on the part of citizens and authorities is required to build a society based on these ideals. Although it has been more that 5000 years since the reign of Maharaja Agrasen, his ideologies and his philosophies could provide a guiding light to make a better nation.

References

Agarwal, S. (2021, November 27). Maharaja Agrasen : जानिए युग प्रवर्तक महाराजा अग्रसेन के जीवन की कहानी और उनके कार्य. Prinsli.com. Retrieved February 16, 2022, from https://prinsli.com/maharaja-agrasen-story-history-biography-in-hindi/

Bhandari, N. (2021, October 7). Maharaja Agrasen Jayanti 2021: ये महाराजा अग्रसेन से जुड़ी महत्वपूर्ण जानकारी. punjabkesari. Retrieved February 17, 2022, from https://www.punjabkesari.in/dharm/news/maharaja-agrasen-jayanti-1469636

Garg, K. (2021, December 19). महाराजा अग्रसेन जयंती इतिहास एवम् अनमोल वचन 2022 Agrasen Maharaj Jayanti in Hindi. Deepawali. Retrieved February 15, 2022, from https://www.deepawali.co.in/agrasen-maharaj-jayanti-jeevan-parichay-history-quotes-in-hindi.html

Nagrath, R. (2017, September 22). People still carry out Maharaja Agrasen's ideals. The Pioneer. Retrieved February 17, 2022, from https://www.dailypioneer.com/2017/state-editions/people-still-carry-out-maharaja-agrasens-ideals.html

Pal, S. (2021, September 27). महाराजा अग्रसेन का इतिहास। जीवन परिचय। अग्रसेन जयंती शायरी. Ajab Gajab Jankari | Hindi - अजब गजब जानकारी. Retrieved February 17, 2022, from https://ajabgajabjankari.com/maharaja-agrasen-jayanti-in-hindi/

Pathak, A. (2019, July 2). महाराजा अग्रसेन इतिहास जयंती: Maharaja agrasen history Jayanti in Hindi. Viral Facts India. Retrieved February 16, 2022, from https://www.viralfactsindia.com/maharaja-agrasen-jayanti-history-in-hindi/

Singhal, D. G. (2017). Maharaja Agrasen Biography. I am Agarwal. Retrieved February 17, 2022, from https://iamagarwal.com/maharaja-agrasen-biography

Tanwar, R. S. (2021, March 23). महाराजा अग्रसेन जीवन परिचय व इतिहास - Maharaja Agrasen history in Hindi. The SimpleHelp. Retrieved February 17, 2022, from https://thesimplehelp.com/maharaja-agrasen-history-in-hindi/

3

A Study of Life and "One Brick and One Rupee" Philosophy of Maharaja Agrasen

Aditi Sharma[1], Neetu[2]

Abstract

Maharaja Agrasen was regarded as the founder of the Agrawal or Vaishya Samaj or Agrawal Samaj. The Agrawal or Vaishya Samaj or Agrawal Samaj was said to have its origins with Maharaja Agrasen. Agrasen Ji was a Kshatriya by birth, but he switched to the Vaishya religion because he detested animal sacrifice and other Kshatriya religious practices. Maharaja Agrasen, who was renowned for his generosity and compassion, established the kingdom of merchants Agroha. At the same time, the 18 gotras of the Agrawal Samaj were named after these 18 sons. Maharaja Agrasen is regarded as a genuine socialist, a promoter of peace, an advocate of nonviolence, a symbol of benevolence, and a model of selflessness. Because of his one brick and one-rupee economic ideology, Maharaja Agrasen is often referred to as the Father of Socialism.

Gaining a deeper knowledge of Maharaja Agrasen's life and social and economic ideas is the purpose of this research. The paper analyses the life of Maharaja Agrasen and his one brick and one rupee economic and social equality concept using secondary sources. Also examined was how Maharaja Agrasen taught us about corporate social responsibility.

---

1. Associate Professor, Department of Commerce, Indira Gandhi University, Meerpur-Rewari, Haryana.
2. Research Scholar, Department of Commerce, Indira Gandhi University, Meerpur-Rewari, Haryana.

Maharaja Agrasen's life has a number of equally significant aspects. As a result, there is a vast spectrum of research accessible in all other subjects.

Keywords: Socialism, trusteeship, non-violence, economic equality.

Introduction

According to Bharatendu Harishchandra, Maharaja Agrasen was a Suryavanshi Kshatriya ruler who was contemporaneous with Lord Krishna and was born in the last phases of the Dwapar Yuga, the era of the Mahabharat epic. He was the offspring of King Vallabha Dev, a lineal descendant of Kush (Lord Rama's son). He was also a descendant of Suryavanshi King Mandhata. The two sons of King Mandhata were Gunadhi and Mohan. The eldest child of King Vallabh of Pratapnagar, a lineal descendant of Mohan, was Maharaja Agrasen. The 18 children of Maharaja Agrasen gave origin to the Agrawal Gotras. Solar Dynasty Vaish King Maharaja Agrasen converted to Vanika Dharma for the sake of his subjects.

As a result of this realisation, he became a major proponent of 'Non-Violence.'

The name Agrawal, which means Children of Agrasen or People of Agroha, refers to the ancient Kuru Panchala city that is said to have been founded by Maharaja Agrasen and is located close to Hisar, Haryana. Maharaja Agrasen longed for everyone's success and was a doer (a Karmyogi). As a supporter of Socialism, he created a unique set of rules to maintain an equitable society. He ordered that each Agroha inhabitant donate one rupee, or one brick, to anyone willing to live there permanently.

He accepted the idea of non-violence after realising the futility of animal sacrifices during the 18th Yagna. In remembrance of the 18th Gotra's establishment, the Yagna was held. This insight led him to become a leading advocate of non-violence.

Maharaja Agrasen's belief in nonviolence did not imply that he did not support opposition to injustice; rather, he supported self-defence. He asserts that every citizen has a duty to defend and secure his country, not just the military caste known as the Kshatriyas.

Married life and penance of Lord Shankar and Mata Lakshmi

In his first union, Maharaja Agrasen Ji wedded Princess Madhavi, a child of King Nagraj. A swayamvara, in which King Indra also took part, conducted their wedding. This made him feel ashamed and enraged, so he gave the order that Pratapnagar be spared from rain. Due to the severe famine that had been induced in Pratapnagar, people started to experience hunger and thirst, and there was panic all around. When they realised this, Maharaj Agresan and his brother Shurasen made the decision to use their mighty and heavenly abilities to engage in a bloody battle with King Indra in order to retake their domain of Pratapnagar. decided to flee a catastrophe, such as a terrible hunger.

Even after Maharaja Agrasen's victory was certain, the gods and Naradamuni reconciled Maharaja Agrasen and Indra, despite the fact that Maharaja Agrasen had the upper hand at the moment. Despite this, the issues facing the residents of Pratapnagar did not appear to be getting any better. Maharaja Agrasen was determined to protect his kingdom Pratapnagar, which is situated on the banks of the Saraswati River between Haryana and Rajasthan. Indra was making life difficult for the residents of Pratapnagar by creating new issues one after another. To avoid Indra's wrath, Agrasen gave strict alms to Lord Shankar and Mata Lakshmi. While Maharaja Agrasen was performing his penance, Indra tried to give him a lot of hardship, but Goddess Lakshmi was pleased with his strict penance.

Maharaja Agrasen told Goddess Lakshmi about Indra's situation in the meantime. Then, Goddess Lakshmi told Agrasen Ji that he would acquire all of his abilities if he wed the daughter of Kolapur's King Mahirath (Nagvanshi). Indra would therefore have to carefully weigh his alternatives before speaking to Maharaja Agrasen. Maharaja Agrasen shielded Pratapnagar from danger by remarrying Princess Sundaravati. He was also instructed to establish a new dominion without fear by the goddess Lakshmi.

Precursor of Socialism and One Brick and One Rupee philosophy of Maharaja Agrasen

Socialism was supported by Maharaja Agrasen. He wanted there to be no gap between the affluent and the poor in his kingdom. They will all be similar. He created the one brick, one rupee concept for that reason. This states that every home in the city shall provide a brick and a rupee to an outside family that is visiting the city.

The one brick and one rupee credo of Maharaja Agrasen is well known. In reality, there have been periodic famines, severe crises like starvation, and widespread epidemics in Agroha. Agrasen Maharaj changed into a different set of attire while traversing the city to deal with this serious issue.

Agrasen Maharaj also saw that there was chaos all around him as he moved throughout the city in various attires to find a solution to this dire issue, how I was acting. He saw that just four individuals in a household had cooked the meal, and when the visitor arrived, the family had to decide what to eat, so they each took a modest portion from their plates. A fifth plate was displayed. The guest's food issue was thus rectified. This had an impact on Maharaja Agrasen, the Agrawal Samaj's founder, who devised the idea of one brick and one rupee. This had an impact on Maharaja Agrasen, the Agrawal Samaj's founder, who devised the idea of one brick and one rupee.On the basis of this concept, he asked every new family that moved to the city to donate a brick and a rupee on behalf of every other family in the city. As a consequence, every family in the city—both those going in and those already living there—collects bricks to build their homes and uses the proceeds to launch a company. A person might achieve equality in the community of equals in this manner with a little assistance from each. They'll use bricks to construct the homes and cash to do commerce. There will be happiness and prosperity for everybody.

Following the proclamation of this ideology, Maharaja Agrasen ji acquired a new identity as the founder of socialism. Maharaja Agrasen ji is known for his kind disposition, as a supporter of Ram Rajya, and as a socialist. He will be revered for a very long time due to the incredible things he accomplished for society.

Ideals of Maharaja Agrasen

- **Democratic government:** A committee made up of elected members from all spheres of society was created by Maharaja

Agrasen, and it was with their approval that state policies and laws were developed. The first ruler in history to establish democracy on this continent. Maharaja Agrasen thought that every member of the kingdom should be prepared to protect it if required and that the right to defend the state should not be restricted to the Kshatriya caste. As a consequence, the state made receiving an education in firearms a requirement, and he was given the right to carry weapons.

- **Economic equality and equity:** The first king to build irrigation infrastructure including canals, bawris, and other similar structures as well as offer free irrigation to farmers in his state was Maharaja Agrasen.
- **Social equality:** No discrimination was present based on caste, social standing, or religion. Under the guise of socialism, a class-based caste-vote war is currently raging, but Maharaja Agrasen rose above it all and offered a new path to the country, releasing his states from suffering and poverty. He is acknowledged as the socialist and secular leader.
- **Emphasis on industries:** He always highlighted industrial endeavour as a means of obtaining Lakshmi. His counterargument to repeatedly doing Lakshmi's penance was that Lakshmi is constantly gained by the enterprising man, thus man should always make an effort to accomplish the same. His teachings have had the result that the Agrawal caste is renowned for its entrepreneurship and is capable of succeeding even in challenging situations without assistance.
- **The spirit of trusteeship:** From Gandhiji's perspective, Maharaja Agrasen embodied this sentiment; one for all, all for one served as the cornerstone of his life; his idea of one coin, one brick was also a living example of this philosophy; and Sarve Bhavantu Sukhin: Sarve Santu Niramaya was infused with the spirit of living and letting live. In one way or another, his state upheld the values we discuss today, such as democracy, Antyodaya, secularism, and peaceful coexistence.
- **The rendering of non-violence religion:**

“Ended the practice of animal sacrifice - gave the message of love to animals”.

Maharaja Agrasen was very fond of animals. At the period, animal sacrifices were a regular practise in the Yagyas. At the beginning of each of the 18 yagyas, animals were sacrificed. Thus, 17 yagyas were performed.

Maharaja Agrasen saw a horse being led to be sacrificed try to escape the altar of sacrifice during the 18th yagnas. This moved Maharaja Agrasen, who questioned what type of riches could be attained via the sacrifice of mute creatures. The idea of ahimsa enthralled Maharaja Agrasen. The King and his ministers then discussed it at a meeting. Following that, the ministers prophesied that if Maharaja Agrasen accepted ahimsa, neighbouring kingdoms would perceive it as a sign of weakness and be inclined to attack Agroha.

Maharaja Agrasen asserted that putting a stop to injustice and violence does not signify weakness. He halted the practise of sacrifice right away and declared that no one in his realm would offer sacrifices or eat meat. All living things shall be safeguarded. Then he stated that under his rule, no acts of violence or the killing of animals would be permitted.

Instead of targeting a crane with an arrow,
I wish to see it flying;
Instead of eating away a nightingale,
I wish to hear it singing.

As a result, Maharaja Agrasen abandoned the Suryavanshi Kshatriya religion and converted to Vaishya. In the Vaishya religion, no one eats meat. Maharaja Agrasen was a gentle and animal-loving ruler, as seen by this.

CSR (Corporate Social Responsibility) Lessons from Maharaja Agrasen

The 2013 Companies Act, as amended, mandates that businesses contribute 2 percent of their average net profit to CSR, with a rider of ₹ 5 crore or more profit in the prior three years. They have to spend money on CSR in a way that stakeholders would approve of, which includes self-regulation, transparency, and compliance.

However, they ought to draw inspiration from Maharaja Agrasen, who vigorously advocated donating 25 percent of one's wealth to the health and wellness of socially significant living things. He also asserted that in order to deal with financial crises of any kind, one must set away 25 percent of one's salary for the future. This is especially true now, when inflation is out of control and people's quality of life is getting more and more expensive.

Honours and awards received by Maharaja Agrasen

Through his extraordinary ideas and accomplishments, Maharaja Agrasen of Pratapnagar not only established the Agrawal or Vaish civilisation, but also gave it a new direction. On the other side, Maharaj Agrasen taught everyone the virtues of capitalism and socialism.

Maharaja Agrasen is regarded as a genuine socialist, a promoter of peace, an advocate of nonviolence, a symbol of benevolence, and a model of selflessness. He is one of the well-known people whose recognition by the Indian government resulted in the creation of a postage stamp in his honour.

The Indian government released a 25-paise postage stamp in his honour on September 24, 1976. Additionally, in 1995, the South Korean government sold the Indian government the battleship "Maharaja Agrasen" for 350 crores. Agrasen Ki Baoli was a postal paper published by India Post in 2012.

Maharaja Agrasen's last moments on earth - Maharaja Agrasen's death

After over a century of rule and the establishment of Agrawal Samaj and Agroha Dham, King Agrasen abdicated to his eldest and most intelligent son Vibhu and went to the bush, free from his duties. Because of his love, generosity, diligence, action, and justice, he was given the rank of God in society. In addition, Bharatendu Harishchandra ji published a number of novels about notable leaders including Maharaja Agrasen ji.

Bharatendu Harishchandra ji was such a monarch who not only taught the people the importance of economic policies but also established Agroha a sacred abode on September 29, 1976, which is now frequented by a sizable number of people. Bharatendu Harishchandra ji worked tirelessly for the betterment of the people. The temple of Agrasen ji, which was founded on Basant Panchami in 1959, was also built here.

Conclusion

Our collective path should be that of Maharaja Agrasen. At all costs, violence should be avoided. Love is required for animals. The practise of animal sacrifice was outlawed and replaced with a message of respect for all living things. No discrimination was present based on caste, social standing, or religion. Under the guise of socialism, a class-based caste-voting system is at war, but Maharaja Agrasen rose above it all and offered a new path to the country, releasing his kingdoms from suffering and destitution. He is acknowledged as the socialist and secular leader. The socialism of Maharaja Agrasen is a threat to modern politicians, especially those who identify as socialists and secularists.

They remained here for 108 years, and during that time they led lives free of sin and darkness, even in the persona of Lord Rama thanks to Sita Preeta. Maharaja Agrasen had a reputation, although he was constantly illuminated by a bright light.

Teachings of Maharaja Agrasen

- It is a sin to kill a living being. Stop the sacrificial practise of murdering animals.
- Never do violence; instead, promote nonviolence.
- Be a socialist, neither rich nor poor.
- Conduct business and industry in a way that benefits everyone.
- Treat everyone equally.
- Promote democracy.
- Love the people.
- Look after cows.
- Develop moral ideals.

Bibliography

Agrawal, O. (2016, September). *Agradhara*. 5 to 7. Shri Agrawal Sabha.

Bansal, K. K. (1992). Virta Ki Virasat, वीरता की विरासत. Hisar: Agroha Vikas Trust.

Gupt, C. (2017). श्रेष्ठ समाज यशस्वी भारत. Agroha Vikas Trust.

Gupta, S. K. (2019). *Maharaja Agrasen: A Brief History of Agra descent.* Gyan Book Pvt Ltd.

Mittal, J.P. (2006). *History of Ancient India (4250 BC to 637 AD)* page 675, ISBN 978-81-269-0616-1

https://www.1hindi.com/essay-on-maharaja-agrasen-jayanti-in-hindi/

https://www.snehpost.com/2019/09/agrasen.html#:~:text=The%20Birth%20of%20Maharaja%20Agrasen,Kalyug%20was%20at%20its%20beginning.

https://www.1hindi.com/essay-on-maharaja-agrasen-jayanti-in-hindi/

https://www.gyanipandit.com/maharaja-agrasen-history-in-hindi/

https://www.snehpost.com/2019/09/agrasen.html#agrasen

https://web.archive.org/web/20170222184750/http://agarwalsabha.org/agradhara/2016/sep16.pdf

https://mamc.edu.in/about-maharaja-agrasen/

4

Contribution of Maharaja Agrasen and Reliance Industries in promoting social security among underprivileged sector of society

Meera Bamba[1], Sonu Madan[2], Monika[3]

Abstract

Maharaja Agrasen is recognised as a real socialist, a peacemaker, a nonviolence representative, a symbol of compassion, and an inspiration for sacrifice. He motivated many with his distinctive ideas like "No to mute animal killing for sacrifice" and "support to peace and non-violence". His life has been an inspiration to many for being at the forefront of social welfare efforts. People were really delighted with his actions, which was consistent with his attitude of promoting equality. This paper highlighted the resemblance in initiatives taken by Maharaja Agrasen and Reliance Industries Limited for uplifting the underprivileged sector. The purpose is the same to provide as much development to individuals and underprivileged communities as possible.

Keywords: Maharaja Agrasen, society, underprivileged, Reliance.

1. Assistant Professor, Department of Commerce, Indira Gandhi University, Meerpur- Rewari, Haryana.
2. Professor, Department of Economics, Chaudhary Bansi Lal University, Bhiwani, Haryana.
3. Research Scholar, Department of Commerce, Indira Gandhi University, Meerpur-Rewari, Haryana.

Introduction

Maharaja Agrasen was a pioneer of socialism and non-violence and his ideas are relevant even today. According to Bharatendu Harishchandra's account, Maharaja Agrasen was a Suryavanshi Kshatriya ruler who reigned during the last phases of the Dwapar Yuga, the time of the Mahabharat epic, and was contemporaneous with Lord Krishna. He was a Kush (Lord Rama's son) descendent and the son of King Vallabha Dev. Maharaja Agrasen, the founder of the Agrahari and Agrawal families, was born almost 5,000 years ago, yet his ideas of socialism and economic equality in society are still carried out by his descendants (Aggarwal, 2012). He was a good king whose major goal was to make his kingdom affluent. He was a capable administrator who built his royal beliefs on equality, socialism, nationalism, and nonviolence. He was a visionary king with strong administrative skills who was concerned about his citizens' economic well-being. In 1976, the Indian government released a postage stamp honouring Maharaja Agrasen.

Initiatives taken by Maharaja Agrasen

Maharaja Agrasen is regarded as a true socialist, a peacemaker, a nonviolent advocate, a symbol of kindness, and a sacrifice inspiration. People got the rites of service to the country and society from Maharaja Agrasen. People were really delighted with his actions, which was consistent with his attitude of promoting equality. He never discriminated and, in fact, instilled in many people the desire to be indiscriminate.

Prohibited Animal Killing

Maharaja Agrasen used to do a lot of Yagna for the people of his kingdom. Yagna was viewed as a sign of wealth throughout ancient times. When Maharaja Agrasen witnessed a horse attempting to get away from the sacrifice platform during one of these Yagnas, his heart broke with sadness and he felt terrible for the animal and the system (Gupta, K., 2019). Many historical traditions claim that the entire horse sacrificing incident took place during the 18th Yagna, the last of the Great 18 Yagnas, Maharaja Agrasen destroyed the tradition of sacrificing a horse for good luck. He took the effort to end the practice of slaughtering silent and innocent animals as sacrifices during the Yagna, and he became a shining example of kindness in the process (Gupta, 2019). From Prince Agrasen to Maharaja Agrasen, his life has been an inspiration to many for being at the forefront of social welfare efforts. People are attracted towards Maharaja Agrasen's selfless and kind beliefs.

"One Brick and One Coin by Each to New": Amazing, Indeed Unique Welfare Policy

Maharaja Agrasen was a legendary monarch of the epic ages who constructed a perfect empire that would set an example for upcoming kings. Maharaja Agrasen introduced the idea of "One Brick, One Rupee". Every existed citizen is told to have donated 1 brick and 1 coin to anybody who came to his empire to become a citizen. He is said to have issued an order granting one rupee and one brick to everyone who want to stay in Agroha. The funds a new resident receives would be used to launch a new business that would guarantee his income, and the bricks would be used to build his home. The above-mentioned idea of gathering resources from many to one is the foundation of business (Garg, 2017). This manner, each person may attain equal status in the society of equals by providing a tiny amount of assistance. Maharaja Agrasen's ideas were carried on by his descendants after him (Gupt, 2017).

Some philosophies for society given by Maharaja Agrasen

- Benefits received by the business are used to promote the prosperity of the whole public community
- Promote agriculture and trade
- Cow protection and kindness for all animals
- Adherence to non-violence
- Serving the poor or helpless people
- Having faith in one's own religion and not criticising other religions
- All programmes for the underprivileged with a meaningful vision should be based on brotherhood
- With courage and determination, inspire your power for good work.

- Follow the social organisation's rules and have complete faith in it.

Reliance Industries Limited

Reliance is helping in the implementation of change on the ground level across the country, with a focus on the most vulnerable and marginalised communities. Dhirubhai Ambani, India's most famous entrepreneur, founded Reliance Industries Ltd. in 1973. He is known for his rags-to-riches narrative. The corporation owns businesses in the energy, textiles, petrochemicals, retail, natural resources and telecommunications sectors (People, planet, prosperity, 2022). At the time of India's liberalisation, The Reliance Group was already one of the country's main business groups, and throughout time, it has only strengthened its position at the top of the corporate ladder in India. Reliance Industries Limited (RIL) had a good influence on society and the community at large through its responsible actions.

Reliance Industries Limited established the Reliance Foundation (RF) as a non-profit organisation to bring about change in Indian society. Reliance Foundation is dedicated to improving the lives of the poor by focusing on several sectors such as education, sports for development, disaster relief, arts, culture, and rural transformation. The Reliance Foundation was established in 2010 and is run by Mrs. Nita Mukesh Ambani. More than 12 million individuals in 10500 villages across India have benefited from the organisation and its humanitarian projects (Naye India ka Naya Josh, 2020). They take aggressive measures to enhance the quality of life of the marginalised parts of society.

Initiatives taken by Reliance Industries Limited (RIL)

They take aggressive measures to enhance the quality of life of the underprivileged parts of society. The programme includes helping the community in times of need as well as longer-term initiatives in fields including education, health, and social improvement. The goal is to give people and communities with as much holistic development as possible.

Animal care and welfare

Reliance runs the Reliance Veterinary Hospital in Padana, Gujarat, which is dedicated to animal care. A pharmacy, an animal mobile van, an isolation room, a major animal operation theatre, an indoor animal shed, an x-ray unit, an animal laboratory, an animal ambulance, and an animal shed have all been added to the hospital's animal healthcare facilities during the last year. Through its 'People for Animals' initiative, Reliance also shows its unconditional love and care for animals. This wonderful project helps street animals and birds. They promoted vegetarianism and animal welfare by raising awareness. Through 300+ camps, they have impacted 46,500 livestock and treated about 75,000 animals. The Reliance Veterinary Hospital in Padana handled over 15,000 animals, with over 13,000 receiving medical care, 376 receiving surgery, and 1,298 receiving gynaecological therapy (Chandra, 2019). Reliance sponsored organisations that engage with societies to safeguard wildlife and avoid human-animal clash in the sake of wildlife conservation and animal welfare. Fifty volunteers from communities around the reserves were taught in camera traps, GPS and managing human-animal conflict occurrences as part of this effort.

Craft Training Centre

To educate rural people skills like welding, grinding, scaffolding, and fitting, a craft training Centre has been created in Jamnagar, Gujarat. As a corporate citizen, Reliance industries has always believed in developing "employability" in addition to delivering jobs. It is working to develop a World Class Craft Training Institute in this direction. This world-class facility, which will be located in Jamnagar, will feature the newest generation of equipment and machinery purchased from world-class manufacturers. Thousands of young people - skilled, semi-skilled, partially skilled, and unskilled from all across the nation were enrolled in the plan, and contractors provided temporary labour accommodation with complete utilities. Reliance believes that these abilities, which are in high demand, will have a limitless market and provide these young people earning prospect around the globe. The institute will teach students in their particular trades with "Certification". In order to enhance the quality of life for local residents, Reliance has carried out community service initiatives in the neighbourhoods surrounding its Jamnagar complex. The actions carried out in Jamnagar included giving free fodder, regular health check-up camps, mobile dispensary services, setting up blood donation camps, rebuilding temples and helping various volunteer organisations to perform cultural and social festivals.

Skill and employment programme

Reliance has made contributions to the government's National Skill Development Mission by putting an emphasis on employment and skilling through the use of technology, skill development, and encouraging micro-enterprises. Individuals can get information about skilling courses and career prospects using digital technologies. By offering marketable skills and job placement support through its skilling and employment programme, Reliance aims to make the youth employable. Reliance has used technology to connect potential youth with skills training and job opportunities. Agriculture, mushroom farming, horticulture, animal husbandry, fisheries, mobile repairing skills, and other farm and non-farm industries have developed links with skilling training institutes for business growth. 9,400 young people were connected to numerous job possibilities in a variety of industries, including retail, finance, and telecommunications. The project helps the government of India's Skill India Mission.

Education

Reliance want to improve educational quality, promote sports development, grant scholarships and increase access to higher education. Every year, more than 14,500 kids receive an excellent education from Reliance Foundation Schools in Jamnagar, Mouda, Vadodara, Dahej, Lodhivali, Surat, Nagothane and Koparkhairane. The Dhirubhai Ambani Scholarship Programme was established in 1996 with the goal of empowering the youth by granting scholarships to deserving students. The scholarship is available to students in class 12th who wish to continue their education in fields such as medicine and engineering. The Reliance Dhirubhai Ambani Protsahan Scheme helps financially underprivileged kids in class 10 to attend college. A total of 12,000 students have benefited from the programme, with 2263 of them being differently abled students.

Rural Development

The Rural Transformation Initiative is an ongoing project that concentrates on all significant development indicators, including rural livelihoods, food, water, women's empowerment, nutrition, and access to knowledge resources. Reliance hopes to strengthen disadvantaged communities, and enable leadership to collaborate with local authorities by doing so. In order to provide water security, Reliance Foundation has worked with more than 500 communities. They aid rural residents in getting access to water for both drinking and agricultural use. RF has created more than 10,000 structures, including wells, ponds for farming, check dams, earthen dams, and masonry dams (Report on Corporate Social Responsibility, 2018). For successful water management, they have formed 'water usage groups' for farmers. To support against uncertainty, Reliance Foundation offers and encourages other sources of income. If agricultural activities and sources of income are affected due to catastrophes, Reliance assists small farmers to develop poultry, vermicomposting nurseries and goat-rearing. Till date, Reliance foundation have facilitated over 10,000 rural households. In order to improve governance at the Gram Panchayat (GP) level, Reliance supports local leadership. By emphasising a participatory approach to planning, the GPs are helped to create Gram Panchayat Development Plans that are successful and implementable.

Conclusion

Maharaja Agrasen and Reliance Industries both are taken various initiative towards development of underprivileged community. Many enterprises continue to be motivated to promote social security by the teachings and values of Maharaja Agrasen. The protection of animals was important to Maharaja Agrasen. Today, when we study the route he has shown, we find that reliance industries have taken a number of initiatives to preserve animals. Reliance also exhibits its unconditional love and care for animals through its 'People for Animals' project. The Reliance Foundation and Animals SOS have partnered to promote kindness, compassion, and social responsibility toward wildlife in order to advance animal welfare, animal conservation, and nature and environment protection. Legendary ruler Maharaja Agrasen built an ideal kingdom that served as a model for upcoming kings. He lived a life of dedication, devotion, and compassion that was ideal. "It was said that one who came to his kingdom, to be a citizen, was given one brick and one coin by every other resident. The coins he would end up with would provide money to set up a new business and the bricks would help him build his house". This thought instilled confidence in his kingdom's citizens, inspiring them to become self-sufficient. Reliance Industries also inspired from this thought and they established Craft Training at Jamnagar, Gujarat, to teach rural people skills such as welding, grinding, scaffolding and fitting. Reliance believes that these in-demand skills would have an endless market and present these young people with opportunities to make money all around the world. Maharaja Agrasen always promoted business and believed that the benefits received by the firm are utilised to benefit the whole public community. Reliance industries follow the ideas of Maharaja Agrasen and places a great value on enhancing the standard of living in the areas where its manufacturing facilities are situated. Reliance has its own schools on its production locations, providing high-quality education to employees' children as well as youngsters from the surrounding community. All of these institutions have modern amenities, such as computers, well-stocked libraries, labs, sports facilities, and playgrounds. So the life of Maharaja Agrasen and working of Reliance industries has been an inspiration to many for being in the forefront of social welfare efforts.

References

Aggarwal, S. (2012). *Agrasen Agroha Aggarwal.* Agroha: Agroha Vikas Trust.

Chandra, A. (2019). *Reliance Industries CSR Activities in India.* https://www.avinashchandra.com/reliance-csr

Garg, O. (2017). *Ek Int Ek Rupayaa.* Agroha: Agroha Vikas Trust.

Gupt, C. (2017). *Shreshat Samaj Yashsavi Bharat.* Agroha: Agroha Vikas Trust.

Gupta, A. K. (2019). *Aggarwal Samaj And Swadhinta Sangram.*

Gupta, K. (2019). *Maharaja Agrasen.* New Delhi: GenNext Publication.

Naye Indparulia ka Naya Josh. (2020). Retrieved on March 2, 2022, from Reliance India Limited.

People, planet, prosperity. (2022). Retrieved from Reliance Industries Limited: www.ril.com

Report on Corporate Social Responsibility. (2018). Retrieved from Reliance Industry Limited.

5

महाराजा अग्रसेन का जीवन, कार्य और सामाजिक दर्शन

राजेश गुप्ता[1]

अग्रकुल प्रवर्तक, समाजवाद के प्रणेता, वैश्य शिरोमणी, अहिंसा के पुजारी, शांतिदूत महाराजा अग्रसेन का जन्म मर्यादा पुरुषोत्तम श्रीराम के पुत्र कुश की 34वीं पीढ़ी में सूर्यवंशी क्षत्रिय कुल के प्रतापनगर (वर्तमान में अग्रोहा हरियाणा–राजस्थान की सीमा पर सरस्वती नदी के किनारे स्थित) के राजा बल्लभ व महारानी भगवती देवी के सबसे बड़े पुत्र थे। इनका जन्म अश्विनी शुक्ल प्रतिपक्ष को लगभग 5175 वर्ष पूर्व हुआ था। महाराजा बल्लभ ने यमुना नदी के किनारे एक नए नगर की स्थापना की जिसका नाम अग्रपुर रखा गया, जो बाद में आगरा नाम से प्रसिद्ध हुआ। अग्रसेन के जन्म के समय गर्ग ऋषि ने महाराजा बल्लभ से कहा था कि यह बालक बहुत बड़ा राजा बनेगा। इसके राज्य में एक नई शासन व्यवस्था उदय होगी और इसका नाम अमर होगा। महाराजा बल्लभ सेन के दो पुत्र थे। अग्रसेन और शूर सेन। अग्रसेन का लालन–पालन बड़े लाड़–चाव के वातावरण में हुआ।

शिक्षाः– वे बचपन से ही बड़े प्रतिभाशाली थे। बड़े होने पर प्राचीन शिक्षा प्रणाली के अनुसार उनकी शिक्षा उज्जैन में आगर नगर में संदीपन ऋषि के आश्रम के पास तांडव्य ऋषि के आश्रम में सम्पन्न हुई। अग्रसेन ने वेदशास्त्र, अस्त्र–शस्त्र, राजनीति, अर्थनीति आदि का ज्ञान प्राप्त किया। वे सभी विद्याओं में पारंगत थे।

महाभारत के युद्ध में भागः– महाभारत के युद्ध के समय श्री अग्रसेन 15 वर्ष के थे। युद्ध हेतु सभी मित्र राजाओं को दूतों द्वारा निमन्त्रण भेजे गए थे। पाण्डव दूत ने वृहत्सेन (अग्रसेन के दादा) की पाण्डु महाराज से मित्रता स्मरण कराते हुए राजा

1. प्रधानाचार्य, हिन्दू कन्या वरिष्ठ माध्यमिक विद्यालय, काठमण्डी, सोनीपत।

बल्लभ से अपनी सेना सहित युद्ध में सम्मिलित होने का निमन्त्रण दिया। महाभारत के इस युद्ध में महाराजा बल्लभ सेन अपने पुत्र अग्रसेन तथा सेना के साथ पांडवों के पक्ष में लड़ते हुए दशवें दिन भीष्म पितामह के बाणों से बिंध कर वीरगति को प्राप्त हो गए थे। अग्रसेन व्याकुल होकर विलाप करने लगे तभी भगवान श्री कृष्ण ने उन्हें सांत्वना देते हुए संसार की असारता का पाठ पढ़ाया। अग्रसेन ने पूरे 18 दिन युद्ध लड़ा।

विवाहः— सब प्रकार से सुयोग्य होने पर महाराजा अग्रसेन का विवाह हुआ। एक समय नागलोक से नागों का राजा कुमुद अपनी कन्या माधवी को लेकर भूलोक में आया। इन्द्र ने उसे चाहा और उसने नागराज से वह कन्या मांगी पर नागराज ने सब प्रकार से अग्रसेन को सुयोग्य जानकर उसका विवाह अग्रसेन से कर दिया। महिधर ने विवाह की खुशी में अग्रसेन के नाम का एक नगर बसाया जिसका नाम अगरतला रखा जो आजकल त्रिपुरा राज्य की राजधानी है। महाराजा अग्रसेन का विवाह एक महान वैभवशाली नागवंश में अत्यन्त ही रुपवान, गुणशील कन्या के साथ हुआ। इस वैवाहिक संबंध के कारण महाराज अग्रसेन और देवराज इंद्र के मध्य शत्रुता हो गई। यह विवाह दो संस्कृतियों का मिलन था। अग्रसेन सूर्यवंशी थे और महिवर नागवंशी थे। इस पर महाराजा अग्रसेन ने इन्द्र पर चढ़ाई कर दी। महाराजा अग्रसेन के पास जो नैतिक बल था, उसके सामने इंद्र की सेना टिक नहीं पाई और वह घबरा कर युद्ध से भाग गया। ऐसी अवस्था में इन्द्र ने देवर्षि नारद को महाराजा अग्रसेन के पास संधि करने भेजा। नारद जी ने महाराजा अग्रसेन और इन्द्र के बीच संधि करायी।

महालक्ष्मी वरदानः— इस बीच अग्रसेन के मन में अनेक विचार पैदा हुए। उनके मन में यह विचार सबसे अधिक उथल—पुथल मचा रहा था कि इन झगड़ों से हमेशा के लिए कैसे बचा जाए। उन्होंने काशी जाकर भगवान शिव की आराधना प्रारम्भ की। उनकी कठिन तपस्या से प्रभावित होकर भगवान शंकर ने दर्शन दिए। भगवान शंकर के आदेशानुसार महाराजा अग्रसेन ने महालक्ष्मी की आराधना प्रारम्भ की। महालक्ष्मी ने उन्हें दर्शन दिए और उनकी तपस्या से प्रभावित होकर महाप्रतापी होने का आशीर्वाद दिया। साथ ही महालक्ष्मी ने यह भी कहा कि वे क्षत्रिय वर्ण त्याग कर वैश्य वर्ण अपनायें। महालक्ष्मी ने उन्हें आशीर्वाद दिया और कहा कि वे हमेशा उनके वंशजों के साथ रहेंगी। महालक्ष्मी ने अग्रसेन को यह भी कहा कि वे अपना अलग राज्य स्थापित करें।

अग्रोहा की स्थापनाः— महालक्ष्मी के आशीर्वाद का कवच पहनकर अग्रसेन ने पूरे भारत की यात्रा की। एक स्थान पर उन्होंने देखा कि एक सिंहनी उसी समय प्रसव कर रही थी। अग्रसेन जी के लाव लश्कर से उसके प्रसव में बाधा पड़ी। सिंह के क्रुद्ध बच्चे ने जन्म लेते ही राजा के हाथी पर प्रहार किया और अकल्पनातीत शौर्य को प्रदर्शित किया। यह देखकर राजा को बहुत आश्चर्य हुआ। महारानी माधवी और अग्रसेन ने सोचा कि यह भूमिवीर प्रसूता है। उन्होने वहीं पर अपना राज्य बनाने का निश्चय किया। वहां पर बसाये नये नगर का नाम ही अग्रोहा रखा गया। अग्रोहा के सुनियोजित विकास से अग्रोहा की तरफ लोगों का आकर्षण बढ़ा और देखते ही देखते

यह राज्य का सबसे समृद्धशाली नगर बन गया। व्यापार, कृषि और उद्योग के विकास से महाराजा अग्रसेन की कीर्ति चारों ओर फैलने लगी।

न्यायप्रियः— महाराजा अग्रसेन ने शासन की बागडोर संभालते ही न्याय, समानता व समय की आवश्यकता को देखते हुए निर्णय लिया कि अपने अनुज भ्राता शूरसेन जी को पृथक राज्य का शासक बनाते हुए अग्रजनपद में एक पृथक राज्य स्थापित किया।

यह नगर महाभारत युद्ध के 51 वर्ष पूर्व स्थापित हो चुका था। श्री शूरसेन को समान अधिकार प्रदान करते हुए राजा के पद से सुशोभित किया गया तथा उनकी राजधानी वर्तमान आगरा (अग्रनगर) शहर को बनाया।

अहिंसाः— अहिंसा को उन्होने राज्य धर्म का आधार बनाया। महाराजा अग्रसेन ने 18 यज्ञ आयोजित किये। उस युग में यज्ञ करना और उसमें सफलता प्राप्त करना, सम्पन्नता का प्रतीक माना जाता था। एक यज्ञ के समय महाराजा अग्रसेन ने देखा कि बलि के लिए घोड़े लाये जा रहे थे। घोड़े बलि स्थान की ओर बढ़ने की बजाय पीछे हटना चाह रहे थे। महाराजा अग्रसेन के मन में घोड़ों के प्रति करूणा के भाव पैदा हुए और उन्होंने सोचा कि इन मूक पशुओं की बलि से क्या मेरा कल्याण हो सकता है। उस यज्ञ में उन्होंने पशु बलि नहीं दी और अपने राज्य में हिंसा रोकने का आदेश दिया। इस भावना से उनके मन में अहिंसा का एक तूफान उठा और उन्होंने अपने मंत्रिमण्डल से इस बारे में विचार—विमर्श किया। अधिकतर लोगों को मानना था कि हिंसा बंद कराने से पड़ोसी राज्यों पर असर पड़ेगा और वे कहीं अग्रोहा पर हमला ना कर बैठें। इस पर महाराजा अग्रसेन ने कहा कि समाज में पर्याप्त विषमता को दूर करने के लिए आवश्यक कदम उठाएंगे लेकिन हिंसा बंद कराने का यह अर्थ नहीं था कि हम अपने राज्य की भी रक्षा नहीं कर सकेंगे। उन्होंने लोगों को शस्त्र (तलवार) तो पकड़ाई लेकिन अपनी रक्षा के लिए राज्य की सुरक्षा के लिए उन्होंने अति प्राचीन परम्परागत नियमों की अवहेलना कर एक नया नियम लगाया। प्रत्येक गृहपति बालक, वृद्ध, युवती शस्त्र धारण करें और अपनी रक्षा करें। प्राचीन युद्ध के नियमों के अनुसार केवल क्षत्रिय ही युद्धों में भाग लेते थे। इस नियम से देश की तीन—चौथाई जनता एकदम अकर्मणय हो गई थी। राजा की जय—पराजय केवल क्षत्रियों पर निर्भर रहती थी। इस कारण महाराजा अग्रसेन ने इस नियम का विरोध किया और उनके राज्य में शस्त्र चलाना अनिवार्य हो गया। यही कारण था कि अग्रवाल जाति ग्यारहवीं शताब्दी तक अग्रोहा में अपना अस्तित्व बनाए रखने में सक्षम रही।

लोकतंत्र के संस्थापकः— अग्रोहा राज्य को 18 जनपदों में विभाजित कर अपने पुत्रों को एक—एक जनपद का अधिशासी बनाया। यज्ञों में 18 राजकुमारों के साथ बैठे गुरुओं के नाम पर गौत्रों की स्थापना की। यही गौत्र आज अग्रवंश को गीता के 18 अध्याय की भांति अलग—अलग होकर भी एक दूसरे से जोड़े हुए हैं। इस व्यवस्था से अग्रोहा का चहुँमुखी विकास हुआ। अपने जीवन के उत्तरार्ध में 133 वर्ष की आयु में

(कलयुग सम्वत् 108) महाराजा अग्रसेन ने अपने बडे पुत्र विभु को राजगद्दी सौंप दी और स्वयं वानप्रस्थ को चले गये। 193 वर्ष की आयु में ब्रह्मलीन हो गए।

महाराजा अग्रसेन का कार्य और सामाजिक दर्शन :—कुशल शासकों की कीर्ति किसी एक युग तक सीमित नहीं रहती। उनका लोक हितकारी चिंतन, युगों—युगों तक समाज व देश का मार्गदर्शन करता है। ऐसे शासकों से न केवल जनता, बल्कि सभ्यता और संस्कृति भी समृद्ध बनती है। ऐसे शासकों की दृष्टि में सर्वोपरि हित सत्ता का न होकर समाज एवं मानवता का होता है। ऐसे ही महान शासक थे महाराजा अग्रसेन। वे कर्मयोगी लोकनायक तो थे ही, संतुलित एवं आदर्श समाजवादी भी थे। अग्रकुल प्रवर्तक समाजवाद के प्रणेता, वैश्य शिरोमणी, गणतंत्र के संस्थापक, अहिंसा के पुजारी व शान्ति के दूत थे। वे एक प्रकाश स्तंभ थे।

समाजवादी शासन तंत्रः— महाराजा अग्रसेन को समाजवाद का अग्रदूत कहा जाता है। महाराजा अग्रसेन हजारों वर्ष पूर्व उत्पन्न हुए परन्तु आज भी अपनी प्रजा वत्सलता, धार्मिक, न्याय, दानशीलता, लोकोपकारी प्रवर्तियों और श्रेष्ठ आदर्शों के कारण अमर है। आज के इस प्रगतिशील और विश्व बन्धुता की ओत—प्रोत वैज्ञानिक युग में विकसित शासन प्रणालियां भी नवागन्तुक को एक रूपया, एक ईंट देकर अपने समान बना लेने की शासन प्रणाली को विकसित करने की क्षमता नहीं हो सकी है, जबकि उस युग में महाराजा अग्रसेन ने सहकारिता और क्षमता के आधार पर भेद—भाव रहित एक आदर्श समाज और राज्य की रचना कर इतिहास में अपना गौरवान्वित स्थान बनाने में सफलता प्राप्त की।

एक बार अग्रोहा में अकाल पड़ने पर चारों ओर त्राहि—त्राहि मच गई। ऐसे में समस्या का समाधान ढूंढने के लिए अग्रसेन जी वेश बदलकर नगर भ्रमण कर रहे थे। उन्होंने देखा कि एक परिवार में सिर्फ चार सदस्यों का ही खाना बना था। लेकिन खाने के समय एक अतिरिक्त मेहमान के आने पर भोजन की समस्या हो गई। तब परिवार के सदस्यों ने चारों थालियों मे से थोड़ा—थोड़ा भोजन निकालकर पांचवी थाली परोस दी। मेहमान की भोजन की समस्या का समाधान हो गया। इस घटना से प्रेरित होकर उन्होंनें 'एक ईंट और एक रूपया' के सिद्धांत की घोषणा की। जिसके अनुसार नगर में आने वाले हर एक परिवार को नगर में रहने वाले हर परिवार की ओर से एक ईंट और एक रूपया दिया जाए। ईंटों से वो अपने घर का निर्माण करें एवं रूपयों से व्यापार करें।

इस तरह महाराजा अग्रसेन के राजकाल में अग्रोदय गणराज्य ने दिन—दूनी रात—चौगुनी तरक्की की। कहते हैं कि इसकी चरम समृद्धि के समय वहां लाखों व्यापारी रहा करते थे। वहां आने वाले नवागत परिवार को राज्य में बसने वाले परिवार सहायता के तौर पर एक रूपया और एक ईंट भेंट करते थे, इस तरह उस नवागत को लाखों रूपये और ईंट अपने को स्थापित करने हेतु प्राप्त हो जाती थी। जिससे वह चिंता रहित होकर व्यापार शुरू कर लेता था।

महाराजा अग्रसेन का मूल मंत्र था–परिश्रम और उद्योग से अर्थार्जन और उसका समान रुप से वितरण। वे कहते थे कि उत्पादन का कुछ भाग पूंजी के रुप में परिवर्तित करो। आय से अधिक खर्च करना न केवल पाप अपितु घातक भी है। किसी भी देश के आर्थिक विकास और प्रगति के लिए यह नितांत आवश्यक है कि देश की संचित पूंजी में निरन्तर वृद्धि होती रहे क्योंकि यह संचित पूंजी ही वितरण और नये–नये उद्योग संचालन का आधार बनती है। फिर भी वे अपना निर्णय किसी पर नहीं थोपते थे।

महाराजा अग्रसेन ने समाजवादी व्यवस्था की स्थापना की जिसमें कभी किसी भी व्यक्ति की कोई भी आर्थिक हानि होती तो वह राजा से ऋण ले सकता था और सम्पन्न होने पर वापस दे सकता था। समाजवाद और मानवता का इस से बड़ा सिद्धांत व्यवहार में कुछ हो ही नही सकता था। नियम अत्यन्त सरल एवं व्यावाहारिक होने के कारण जनसामान्य के लिए जीवन का एक अंग बन गए थे क्योंकि लेना और देना दोनों ही राज्य का नियम था। अतः देने वाले के मन में न अहं का भाव आता था और न ही लेने वाले के मन में कृतज्ञता का भाव आता था। महाराजा अग्रसेन के समाजवाद में 'समृद्ध व्यक्तियों की ओर निठल्ले बैठे ललचाए जाने का कोई स्थान न था। उनके समाजवाद की व्याख्या थी–"प्रत्येक नागरिक परिश्रम करता हुआ राष्ट्र के सामूहिक उत्थान में योगदान दे। प्रत्येक व्यक्ति सबके लिए जिए और सब एक के लिए जिएं। उनका आदर्श था– "कर्मण्येवाधिकारस्ते मा फलेषु कदाचन" जिस राज्य की जनता अपनी क्षमता एवं योग्यता के अनुरुप कर्म करती हुई फल की चिंता न करे, उस राज्य में कैसा अभाव, कैसी विषमता ? जीओ और जीने दो–उनका आदर्श था।

क्षत्रिय से वैश्य वर्णः– महाराज अग्रसेन ने तंत्रीय शासन प्रणाली के प्रतिकार में एक नई व्यवस्था को जन्म दिया, उन्होंने पुनः वैदिक सनातन आर्य संस्कृति की मूल मान्यताओं को लागू कर राज्य की पुर्नगठन में कृषि–व्यापार, उद्योग, गौ–पालन के विकास के साथ–साथ नैतिक मूल्यों की पुनः प्रतिष्ठा का बीड़ा उठाया।

आग्रेयगण भी इसी प्रकार वार्ताशस्त्रीपजीवी जनपद था। यहाँ के लोग कृषि, पशुपालनव व्यापार के साथ शस्त्र संचालन में भी कुशल थे।

महाराजा अग्रसेन इन्हीं वैश्यकुलोत्पन्न शासकों में थे, जिन्होंने अपनी सूझबूझ, तपस्या और लगन से क्षत्रियों के समान ही वैश्यों के एक गणराज्य की स्थापना की, वैश्यों में इस गणराज्य की रक्षा हेतु क्षत्रियोचित गुण भरे और महाराजा की उपाधि धारण की। जिससे वे उद्योग–व्यवसाय धर्म–पालन एवं उत्तम संस्कारों के साथ राष्ट्र की रक्षा में भी योगदान दे सके। इसके लिए उन्होने वैश्यों को शस्त्र विद्या में भी निपुण किया।

महाराजा अग्रसेन पहले वैश्य थे, जिन्हें वैश्य होते हुए भी महाराजा की पद्वी से विभूषित किया गया तथा क्षत्रिय राजाओं के समान छत्र, चंवर रखने की अनुमति दी गई। उन्होंने यह प्रमाणित किया कि वर्ण और धर्म की अपेक्षा कर्म ही मनुष्य के जीवन

में महत्वपूर्ण हैं। इसलिए वे जन्म से वैश्य होते हुए भी कर्मणा क्षत्रिय बन गए थे। प्राचीन काल में जबकि राजा की पदवी का अधिकार केवल क्षत्रिय को ही हो सकता था, इसी कारण वैश्य होते हुए भी महाराजा अग्रसेन को क्षत्रिय समझने की भ्रांति हो जाती है।

महाराजा अग्रसेन की विदेश नीति पारस्परिक समानता, शान्ति एवं सद्भाव पर आश्रित थी। उन्होंने न कभी किसी पर आक्रमण ही किया और न कभी विजेता बन चक्रवर्ती सम्राट बनने की इच्छा की। उनकी शक्ति बलपूर्ण दूसरे राज्यों पर अधिकार करने की अपेक्षा अपने राज्य के आर्थिक विकास की योजनाएं बनाने की ओर अधिक केन्द्रित रहती क्योंकि वे अर्थ को राज्य की सुव्यवस्था का मूल केन्द्र समझते थे। उनका विश्वास था कि उत्पादन का चक्र हर समय चलता रहना चाहिए। ताकि अभावों से जूझती जनता की आवश्कता पूर्ण कर उनके जीवनस्तर को ऊंचा किया जा सके।

गोत्र स्थापना:– राज्य स्थापना यज्ञ आदि से निवृत्त होकर अग्रसेन जी ने वैश्य वर्ण की उत्कृष्टता कायम करने के लिए गोत्रों की स्थापना पर बल दिया। महाराजा अग्रसेन के समय वंशानुगत शासन था किन्तु उन्हें अपने राज्य को 18 गणों में विभक्त कर दिया। एक–एक निर्वाचित प्रतिनिधि शासन परिषद् में लिया तथा उनकी सलाह से राज्य का प्रशासन चलाकर लोकतांत्रिक गणराज्य की नींव डाली। अपनी प्रजा को पुत्रवत प्यार करने के कारण ही सभी 18 गण गणपति महाराजा अग्रसेन को पितृतुल्य मानते थे। यही कारण है कि कभी–कभी इन गण प्रतिनिधियों को उनका पुत्र मानने का भ्रम हो जाता है। विवाहित नियमों को उन्होंने अनुशासन में बांटकर वैश्य वर्ण को अठारह गौत्रों में ही विवाह करने का नियम बनाया। अन्य जातियों में होने वाले विवाहों को वर्जित कर दिया।

वैश्य जाति को उन्होंने तराजू प्रदान करने के साथ वार्ताशस्त्रोपजीवी भी बनाया। ये वैश्य लोग सामान्य समय में व्यापार–व्यवसाय करने के अतिरिक्त युद्ध एवं शस्त्र संचालन में भी दक्ष होते थे और आवश्यकता पड़ने पर अस्त्र हाथ में उठा आत्मरक्षा के साथ देश की रक्षा भी करते थे। उनकी गणना भी मार्शल कौमों में की जाती है।

आग्रेयगण पर जब–जब भी संकट आया अथवा उसके कल्याण की बात आई, महाराजा अग्रसेन ने राज्य सुखों को त्याग तपश्चर्या का मार्ग अपनाया और भगवान शंकर, महालक्ष्मी आदि की कठोर साधना करके प्रजा के कल्याण की कामना की। इस प्रकार के आदर्श इतिहास में बहुत कम मिलते हैं। उन्होंने आदर्श प्रस्तुत किया कि राजा को प्रजा, जन एवं देशहित के लिए सर्वस्व न्यौछावर करने के लिए तत्पर रहना चाहिए। राजा का सुख प्रजासुख में ही निहित है। उन्होंने अववर्षण से पीड़ित प्रजा की भलाई के लिए जो कठोर तपस्या की, वह उनके लोकानुराग को प्रकट करने के लिए पर्याप्त है। यही वह आदर्श है, जिसे अपनाकर आज भी राष्ट्रहित की साधना की जा सकती है।

धार्मिक उत्थान:– उन्होंने धर्म एवं जनकल्याण को अपने राज्य का आधार बनाया। किसी भी राज्य की नींव सुविचारों एवं अच्छे आदर्शों पर ही निर्भर होती है।

जहाँ सदाचार होता है, वहां, चोरी, डकेती, छलकपट, लूटमार, हत्या जैसे जघन्य कर्म पनप ही नहीं सकते। सदाचार तभी पनपता है जबकि पेट भरा हो। भूखे व्यक्ति को सदाचार और नैतिकता के उपदेश व्यर्थ ही सिद्ध होते हैं। अतः महाराजा अग्रसेन ने एक रूपया और एक ईंट के आदर्श द्वारा जहाँ एक ओर अपने राज्य को बेकारी, बेरोजगारी, निर्धनता जैसे अभिशापों से मुक्त कर दिया, वहाँ सदाचार की भी गहरी नींव रखी।

महाराजा अग्रसेन के राज्य में प्रत्येक को अपने विश्वास के अनुसार धर्म पालन की पूर्ण स्वतंत्रता थी। कोई शिव की उपासना करता तो कोई लक्ष्मी की। वहाँ सभी जातियों, धर्मों के लोग सुख–शांतिपूर्वक जीवन व्यतीत करते थे। स्वयं महाराजा अग्रसेन उन्हें माला के धागे की तरह एकता के सूत्र में पिरोये रखते थे।

उन्होंने अपने राज्य में 18 यज्ञ कराए। उस समय यज्ञ धार्मिक एवं नैतिक भावनाओं के प्रचार के श्रेष्ठ माध्यम थे। महान मुनियों के सान्निध्य में किए जाने वाले इन यज्ञों में अग्रोहा की भूमि को भी यज्ञमय बना दिया। महाराजा अग्रसेन ने यज्ञों में होने वाली पशुबलि को भी बन्द करा दिया और घोषणा की, कि उनके राज्य में भविष्य में हिंसा न होगी। इस प्रकार उन्होंने अपने राज्य में जीवमात्र के प्रति करूणा, प्रेम एवं सहानुभूति का नया नारा दिया। धर्म में अहिंसा का पालन करवाकर सम्पूर्ण जाति को उन्होंने सात्विक वृत्ति से आपूर कर एक नया मानवतावादी पाठ पढ़ाया, जहां मांसाहार, अनाचार का निषेध था, जहां पशु–पक्षियों तक को राजकीय संरक्षण प्राप्त था। उसी का परिणाम है कि आज भी अग्रवाल जाति हिंसा से दूर है। जीवमात्र के प्रति दया एवं करूणा भाव से प्रेरित होने के कारण यह समाज न केवल असंख्य निराश्रितों और असहायों के लिए आश्रय की व्यवस्था करता है अपितु चींटियों के लिए दाना, पक्षियों के लिए चुग्गा और असहाय पशुओं के लिए चारे की व्यवस्था कर आत्मीय सुख शान्ति का अनुभव करता है। यह अग्रसेन की प्राणि–मात्र के प्रति करूणा एवं स्नेह भावना का ही प्रसार है।

यदि कहा जाए कि महाराजा अग्रसेन ने अपने राज्य में भारतीय संस्कृति के चार तत्वों–धर्म, अर्थ, काम, मोक्ष को समान महत्व दिया तो कोई अतिश्योक्ति नहीं होगी। उनका यह धर्म किसी प्रकार के वैराग्य अथवा अनासक्ति भाव पर आधारित नहीं था। उन्होंने जीवन में कर्म को ही सदैव धर्म माना और अपने राज्यवासियों को कर्म करने की प्रेरणा दी। उनकी इस प्रवृति का परिणाम है कि अग्रवाल जाति कभी निठल्ले बैठना पसंद नहीं करती। कर्म में ही लक्ष्मी का निवास होता है और यही अग्रवाल वैश्य जाति के वैभव एवं उत्कर्ष का मूल कारण है। इसके अलावा महाराजा अग्रसेन ने सरलता, सादगी आदि पर बल दिया।

महाराजा अग्रसेन ने एक ऐसे आदर्श राज्य की नींव रखी, जहाँ न कोई गरीब था और न कोई अमीर। सब व्यक्तियों को जीवन की सुख–सुविधाएं समान रूप से उपलब्ध थीं। इस प्रकार इतिहास में उन्हें एक ऐसे आदर्शलोक कल्याणकारी राज्य की स्थापना का श्रेय प्राप्त है, जहाँ वर्ग संघर्ष के बिना स्वतंत्रता, समानता, लोकतंत्र,

भाईचारे जैसे आदर्श साकार रूप में विद्यमान थे। यह दृष्टव्य है कि वर्ग, संघर्ष एवं हिंसा जैसे आदर्शों पर आधारित साम्यवाद जहाँ रूस में टुकड़े–टुकड़े होकर बिखर गया और अन्य देशों में अंतिम सांसे ले रहा है, वहाँ महाराजा अग्रसेन का समाजवाद आज भी अपनी यशोपताका फहरा रहा है।

आज सम्पूर्ण जाति युद्धों से त्रस्त है। विभिन्न गुटों में विभक्त देश एक दूसरे के खून के प्यासे बने हुए अस्त्र–शस्त्रों के निर्माण पर भारी धन खर्च कर रहे हैं। ऐसे समय में महाराजा अग्रसेन का यह प्राणीमात्र के प्रति करूणा, स्नेह, अहिंसा का भाव ही युद्ध–त्रस्त मानवता की रक्षा का अमोघ साधन सिद्ध हो सकता है।

अन्य उपलब्धियांः– आज हम पर्यावरण शुद्धि की चर्चा करते हैं। जलवायु–प्रदूषण को रोकने के लिए करोड़ों अरबों रूपयों की योजना प्रतिवर्ष बनाते हैं परन्तु प्रदूषण बढ़ता ही जाता है। रूकने का नाम नहीं लेता। महाराजा अग्रसेन ने यज्ञों द्वारा मानव मन की शुद्धि के साथ–साथ वातावरण शुद्धि की ओर भी ध्यान दिया था। यज्ञों में धृत एवं सुगंधित कीटनाशक द्रव्य की हानि से वातावरण शुद्ध होता। उससे परमाणुविहीन बादल बनते। बादल शुद्ध जल की वर्षा करते। परिणामस्वरूप नदियों, नहरों का जल शुद्ध होता। पेड़–पौधे, फल, वनस्पतियां प्रदूषण रहित होकर अपनी स्वच्छ, शीतल, सुगंधित वायु से वायुमण्डल को शुद्ध बनाते हैं। इससे सभी का स्वास्थ्य अच्छा रहता। लोग हष्ट–पुष्ट होते। यही कारण है कि वहां के वीरों ने हर आक्रमणकारी का दृढ़ता से मुकाबला किया। यज्ञ उनके लिए आत्म शुद्धि के साथ–साथ वातावरण शुद्धि का भी श्रेष्ठ साधन था।

महाराजा अग्रसेन जी का शासन काल चारों ओर शान्ति और अमनचैन का काल रहा। महाभारत की युद्ध विभीषिका से त्रस्त लोग शान्ति की खोज में जहां जिसे स्थान मिला वहां जीवनयापन कर रहे थे। ऐसे समय में महाराजा अग्रसेन जी का प्रादुर्भाव हुआ। उन्होंने चारों ओर घूम–घूम कर लोगों को संगठित किया और एक चहुंमुखी शान्तिपूर्ण धार्मिक, अहिंसावादी राजनीति की छत्रछाया में प्रजा का पालनपोषण कर उन्हें सुख चैन प्रदान दिया।

इस प्रकार का साम्यवाद व विश्वबंधुत्व का सही तथा प्रत्यक्ष उदाहरण सर्वप्रथम महाराजा श्री अग्रसेन जी ने ही प्रतिपादित किया। यह निर्विवाद रूप से कहा जा सकता है कि महाराजा अग्रसेन विश्व में सहकारिता एवं समाजवाद के प्रणेता एवं जनक थे।

जग में मिसाल है, अग्रोहा का राज, एक ईंट की मदद से लक्षाधीष समाज।

6

Maharaja Agrasen in the Context of Economic Development and Social Work in India

Geetika Malhotra[1]

Introduction

"To live in Heaven after death, we must live in Heaven before death"

Agroha's name is associated with Maharaja Agrasen. He is not only the founder of Agroha, but also a great leader who works tirelessly for the good of society. Vanika Dharma was adopted by Vaish King, Maharaja Agrasen for the welfare of his people. Actually, Aggrawal refer to "children of Agrasen" / "People of Agroha", Kuru Panchala town near Hisar, Haryana have been founded by Maharaja Agrasen. He was the practitioner (Karmyogi) praying for prosperity to all. As adherent of Socialism, he created a special policy to achieve equality and democratic society. Agrasen announced that everyone who comes to Agroha to stay permanently, each resident of Agroha must give one rupee, one brick. With the money he collected, he was able to build a brick house and start his own business. In this way, everyone can reach an equal place in an equal society with a little help from everyone. This paper tries to address Maharaj Agrasen's ideas on equality, socialism, non-violence, economic development

1. Assistant Professor, Department of Social Work, Indira Gandhi University, Meerpur-Rewari, Haryana.

and social work. This chapter analyzes the prominent initiatives and contributions of the descendants of Maharaja Agrasen for the upliftment and development of humanity as well as society. In fact, this research paper will be a theoretical paper based on secondary data.

Objective

The present paper focuses to study Maharaja Agrasen and relevance of Social Work

- To objectively examine the background and vision of Maharaja Agrasen.
- To examine the prominent initiatives and the contribution for upliftment and development of society by descendants of Maharaja Agrasen.

Methodology

In this paper, an attempt has been made to emphasize the initiatives and the contribution for upliftment and development of society by Maharaja Agrasen and his descendants. The study used a qualitative approach and did two things to identify and describe initiatives and the contribution of Maharaja Agrasen – firstly, analyses the relevance of Social Work and Maharaja Agrasen- Secondly, used secondary sources used in the study, including published government publications, newspapers, and blogs.

Role of Maharaja Agrasen in Social and Economic Development

Vanika Dharma was adopted by Vaish King, Maharaja Agrasen for the welfare of his people. Actually, Aggrawal refer to "children of Agrasen" / "People of Agroha", Kuru Panchala town near Hisar, Haryana have been founded by Maharaja Agrasen. Maharaja Agrasen is the one who creates prosperity for all (Karmyogi).

Bharatendu Harishchandra said that Maharaja Agrasen had eighteen Children from Agrawal Gotras. The Agrawal background can be traced back to "Origin of the Agarawals and Agrahari", in 1871 text by the famous Agrawal writer and poet Bharatendu Harishchandra (1850-1885). It is alleged that he wrote "traditions" and legends from "ancient literature", in particular Shri Mahalakshmi Vrat ki Katha.

In 1976, "Ancient History of the Agrawal Caste" was written in Mahalakshmi Vrat Ki Katha by Satyaketu Vidyalankar. Maharaja Agrasen was the practitioner (Karmyogi) praying for prosperity to all. He announced that everyone who comes to Agroha to stay permanently, each resident of Agroha must give one rupee, one brick. With the money he collected, start his own business and he was able to build a brick house. In this way, with a little help from everyone, an equal place in an equal society can be achieved.

Initiatives and Contribution

The initiatives and contributions of Maharaja Agrasen and his descendants for the upliftment of society are mention below:

- **Socialism**: As a supporter of socialism, he passed special laws to ensure equality among people. He declared that everyone who comes to Agroha to live permanently, every resident of Agroha should receive **one rupee, one brick**. With the money he collected start his own business and he was able to build a brick house. Thus, with a little help from everyone, everyone can have an equal place in an equal society. In this era, Aggrawal Community open community halls (Aggrawal's Bhawan) and parks for people form any community as part to serve society. Example, Mr. Ramesh Aggrawal owner of Aggrawal Movers and Packers Group, Jaipur who dedicatedly participated in Ekal Vidyalaya yojna, Driver Seva Kendra, Beti Padhao Campaign, blood donation camps and natural resource conservation, etc. as he believes to serve nation is biggest nationalism.
- **Non-Violence:** At the time of the 18th Yagna, when he vainly knows about animal sacrifice. For origin of eighteenth gotra, Maharaja Agrasen performed Yagna and this awareness made him of the powerful heroes of "non-violence". His descendants follows same principle of truth and non-violence by educating young soul though running Bhavans Usha and Lakshmi Mittal Institute of Management.

- **Nationalism:** However, Maharaja Agrasen believes in non-violence does not mean, he is against to oppression, it encourages self-defence. According to him, self-protection and defence of the country is not only work of kshatryas – the warrior caste, but also the responsibility of citizen to protect and defend his motherland. Apart from this, Lala Lajpat Rai who participated in freedom struggle of India.
- "Instead of targeting a crane with an arrow, I wish to see it flying; Instead of eating away a nightingale, I wish to hear it singing"

- **Education:** In Aggarwals, the literacy rate is high as well as they were in most professional occupation like doctors, engineering, government officials and runs there own business too. Example, Mr Ramesh Aggrawal owner of Aggrawal Movers and Packers Group, Jaipur who dedicatedly participated in Ekal Vidayalaya yojna, Driver Seva Kendra, Beti Padhao Campaign, blood donation camps and natural resource conservation, etc. as he believes to serve nation is biggest nationalism.
- **Economic Development:** They have been important trade and business communities who suppor the economic development of India in earlier and today's times. The Aggarwals family is considered one of the most respected businessmen and entrepreneurs prominent in business, commerce and industry in Punjab. In Punjab cities and neighbouring states like Rajasthan, Uttar Pradesh and Delhi their economies are growing by Aggarwals, the economy is fully controlled and many people are migrating from far away. His descendants are now totally very successful in this field and Laxmi Mittal is specially mentioned here (Arcelor Mittal), O.P. Jindal (Jindal Business Group), Anil Agrawal (Vedanta).

Social Work

Social Work Profession establishes ethical rules. Ethics refers to the Social Worker's values, standards and moral judgments that guide the behaviour. Social work is a professional practice and discipline that contributes to change and growth, relationships, and empowerment and independence of people. The principles of justice, human rights, responsibility and respect for differences are the basis of social work. It brings people and organisations together to solve problems in social work, life and health improvement based on social work, social science, humanities and local knowledge theories. (IFSW)

The core principle of social work includes non-judgment, acceptance, confidentiality, individuality, self-awareness, and self-determination. The Code of Ethics for Social Work aims to promote service, social justice, respect for worth and dignity, and the development of the people. Social work deals with the limitations, injustices

Maharaja Agrasen and the Approaches to Social Work

- Agrasen approach that social workers should be social, personal, **non-exploitative, and non-manipulative relationship with clients.** This is a disciplinary relationship, not a management relationship.
- The Approach is important for the construction of a society based on truth, non-violence, and for the welfare of all the lower class, the poor.
- His way of supporting social practice is the principle of the unity of all or the harmony of the world.

Conclusion

In entire life, Maharaja Agrasen works vigorously for welfare of people. He gives wonderful approach to society for creation of we feeling among people and to run buisness, as to contribute economic development of nation. Maharaja Agrasen was the practitioner (Karmyogi) praying for prosperity to all. As a socialist, he created a special policy to achieve equality. Maharaja Agrasen and his descendants are great leaders for equality, harmony, non-violence, excellent growth of jobs and education, and their contribution to social development. The influence of social work and Maharaja Agrasen has promoted the relationship with ethical standards, social development and human relations through its methods.

References

Bhattacharya, Sanjay. (2012). *Social Work: An Integrated Approach*. New Delhi: Deep and Deep Publication.

Cabot, Richard C. (2020). *Social Work: Essays on the Meeting-Ground of Doctor and Social Worker.* New Delhi: Momentum Publishers Distributors.

Gupta, Ashok. (2021). *Maharaja Agrasen and Agravansh*. Haryana Pradesh Vaish Mahasammelan.

Kumar, Janardan. (2015). Mahatma Gandhi in the Context of Enhancement of Rural and Economic Development in India. *International Journal of Creative Research Thoughts*. Volume 3, Issue 3 August 2015 | ISSN: 2320-2882. pp. 485-492.

Tatiya, Harpitray. (2015). *Bharat Ka Gaurav.* Haryana: Agroha Vikas Trust.

7

CSR helping in Upliftment of Society: with special reference to 'One Brick, One Rupee' concept given by Maharaja Agrasen

Devesh Aggarwal[1], Rachna Bansal[2]

Abstract

This is a theoretical study about how Corporate Social Responsibility is beneficial in uplifting the society. The study is done keeping in mind the special reference to the great Maharaja Agrasen who was a real pioneer of the Indian society and did many things which helped in the betterment of it. His 'One Brick, One Rupee' rule laid down the foundation of socialism. This study followed the descriptive design research approach. Information from many magazines, journals, books and websites also gathered in completing this study. It was concluded in the study that the CSR is not only the responsibility of big companies, individuals who can afford to help the society should definitely help for the betterment of the society. With the help of CSR, quality of life, ecological environment, sustainability, promotion of diversity and equality can also be achieved. Strong relationship among the companies, communities and government can also be developed.

Keywords: Corporate Social Responsibility (CSR), Transparency, Social Responsibility, Self Help Groups (SHG).

1. Assistant Professor, Department of Commerce, Indira Gandhi University, Meerpur-Rewari, Haryana.
2. PGT(Commerce), Govt. Sr Sec School Carterpuri 0750, Gurugram.

Introduction

The corporate social responsibility is a significant activity whether nationally or globally. The CSR is related to economic and social environment and affects the both. The transparency is increasing in corporate due to CSR. Companies are required to act morally and responsibly toward the many stakeholder groups in society and the environment. Companies began including their CSR initiatives in their yearly reports as well.

Corporate Social Responsibility (CSR) activities help in society upliftment by:

- *Improving quality of life:* CSR initiatives aimed at improving access to healthcare, education, and clean water can enhance the standard of living for communities.
- *Economic development:* By investing in local communities, companies can create job opportunities and stimulate economic growth.
- *Environmental sustainability:* CSR programmes that focus on environmental conservation and sustainability can protect natural resources and promote long-term ecological health.
- *Building community:* CSR programmes can foster strong relationships between companies and communities and improve community well-being.
- *Promoting equality and diversity:* CSR initiatives aimed at promoting gender and social equality can help to address social and economic imbalances in communities.

Overall, CSR can play a critical role in creating positive social and economic impact and contribute to the sustainable development of communities.

Above explained points are very much significant and we should be aware that all these were covered by the Maharaja Agrasen in the form of 'One Brick, One Rupee' concept.

One Brick, One Rupee concept

According to this, when a new family came to the city Agroha, which was ruled by Maharaja Agrasen at that time, a custom was made to offer them One gold coin and One brick from each house so that they can easily settle themselves in the Agroha city. One rupee from each house collectively formed capital for the newly arrived family and they can use it to start business and one brick from each house helps them to build their home so that they have place to stay. This was a very clever step of Maharaja to help the needy people. This concept of Maharaja is also passes to the present time and followed by the Aggarwal community. The Aggarwals prefer business over jobs because the business is based on gathering the resources from many persons while job is based on one to one. The community not only gathers resources but also provide the resources to needy people. This all is happening even today only because of the trend started by the Maharaja Agrasen.

Big corporate are also following the CSR concept to uplift the poor and backward section of the society. Many big companies like ONGC, Indian Oil Corporation, SAIL, BHEL, Indian Airlines, Coca-Cola, Reliance, Bajaj, Mahindra & Mahindra, etc. are spending huge amount for the sake of improvement in Health, Sanitation, Education, and Employment sector of our country.

Significance of the study

This study is very important for all the sections of our society. It tells about the ancient king Maharaja Agrasen's concept 'One brick, One rupee' concept which started a wave of CSR and it was a great concept for the sake of development of society. All the companies or individuals who can spend a decent amount for CSR should contribute accordingly.

Review of related literature

To better understanding of the concept, some past studies have been selected to obtain the information. Some of the major previous studies are included in literature review, which are as follows:

Kapoor, S. (2019) revealed in the study that the companies should be encouraged to accept the CSR for Self Help Groups (SHG). It was also concluded in the study that the SHGs can help in promoting the awareness in the society if they are provided the opportunities which can be done by the CSR. The women can be empowered with the help of CSR. The CSR can also help in fighting the poverty.

Maan, P. (2014) did a study based on the secondary data and concluded that the aim of any company should not only to increase the profits rather trust building and social relationships are equally important and it is the only key to long term survival. This research also studies about many giant companies who follow CSR on primary basis.

Sahoo et. al. (2012) in their study analysed that the awareness in increasing about the CSR nowadays. In this study the major focus is towards the banking industry. The Indian banking sector is adopting many CSR strategies. Twelve major banks are chosen in this study with the help of simple random sampling method, data of which collected from many secondary sources. The research covered the period of 2007-10. It was concluded that the government of India should make good relations with the financial institutions so that they can adopt good strategies of CSR.

Research methodology

This paper describes the evolution of the concept of Corporate Social Responsibility. It is a theoretical study, information of which is sourced from websites, journals, magazines and books etc. The descriptive design of research is followed in the current study. History of Maharaja Agrasen, who was king of Agroha, currently situated in Hisar, Haryana, also studied to contribute in this research.

Findings and conclusions

It was found in the study that the concept of CSR was initiated in the ancient times and the society also has expectations from the corporates. The companies who can afford or legally bound should help in development of backward sections. The great Maharaja Agrasen started the great principle of 'One Brick, One Rupee' which is equal to CSR. Earlier it was done by the villagers of Agroha but now big companies are doing this. Some companies are also following the concept to increase their goodwill among the general public. It can also be concluded that the CSR should not only done by companies but it should also done by the individuals who can afford this. The government of India also legally binds companies under CSR which falls under the eligible criteria. The Corporate Social Responsibility can also helps in achieving the economic development, improved life quality, promotion of equality, accepting diversity and good environment and many more.

References

Chaudhury, S. K., Das, S. K., & Sahoo, P. K. (2012). Practices of corporate social responsibility (CSR) in banking sector in India: An assessment. *Research Journal of Economics, Business and ICT,* 4.

Kapoor, S. (2019). Entrepreneurship for economic and social empowerment of women: A case study of a self help credit program in Nithari Village, Noida, India. *Australasian Accounting, Business and Finance Journal,* 13(2), 123-142.

Maan, P. (2014). CSR-key issues and challenges in India. *International Journal of Science, Environment and Technology,* 3(6), 2038-2045.

www.bhaskar.com

www.google.com

www.quora.com

8

Maharaja Agrasen: Life, Thought and Accreditation

Ajay Yadav[1], Sushant Yadav[2]

Abstract

India is a land of great souls and great people. Over the years many great people have been born in this country who worked for social justice and the upliftment of weaker sections of society. Maharaja Agrasen is one of the greatest souls of India who work for socialism and nonviolence. In today's scenario, geopolitics around the globe face huge conflicts. It is the need of the hour to follow and implement the ideology and principle of welfare and equality of the great king Agrasen. The great kingdom was established and nourished where the root foundations build with strong and prosperous ideas and values. The knowledge and thoughts of king Agrasen are as much realistic in the present. His life and thoughts can inspire billions of people across the world, this paper attempts to exhibit the life, thoughts, and accreditation of the great son of India Maharaja Agrasen.

Keywords: Socialism, Nonviolence, Economic and Social equality.

Introduction

Maharaja Agrasen is a legendary figure in Indian history, revered for his philanthropy and social justice. He is believed to have lived

1. Research Scholar, Department of Commerce, Indira Gandhi University, Meerpur-Rewari, Haryana.
2. Assistant Professor, Department of Management, Indira Gandhi University, Meerpur-Rewari, Haryana.

in the early centuries and is the founder of the Agrawal community, a prominent merchant class in India. Maharaja Agrasen's life and thoughts have been the subject of numerous studies, which have sought to understand his impact on Indian society and culture. This research report aims to explore Maharaja Agrasen's life and thoughts, with a focus on his contributions to social welfare and economic development. This research study is based on a review of existing literature on Maharaja Agrasen and his legacy. The sources used in this report include academic articles, books, and online resources. Maharaja Agrasen is remembered as an epithet of a peacemaker. He is the first Vaishya king and is idealised as a spirit of socialism and self-reliance. Agreyen is the kingdom of Agrasen where over one lakh people lived and every citizen of that prosperous kingdom was self-dependent and associated with entrepreneurship.

Maharaja Agrasen was born in the kingdom of Pratapnagar, which is believed to have been located in present-day Haryana. He was the son of King Ballabh and Queen Madhavi, and was known for his wisdom and compassion from an early age. According to legend, Maharaja Agrasen was a great warrior who fought for justice and equality. He is said to have established the first democratic state in India, based on the principles of equality and social justice. Maharaja Agrasen had eighteen sons, who went on to become the rulers of eighteen different states in North India. He is believed to have been a wise and just ruler, who was loved by his subjects.

Maharaja Agrasen (The prince of Pratap Nagar) was a very well-known personality from an early young age for his compassion. The conduct of his behaviour with his nature of supporting equality was very pleasing among people. He never discriminated against and indeed inspired indiscrimination to many. The Agrasen attended the Swayamvar of King Nagaraj Kumud's daughter. She was a beautiful Princess named Madhavi. In the preceding *Swayamvara*, Princess Madhavi chose King Agrasen among various participants including Indra by the gesture of her selection and will. The wedding was a combination of different cultures as King Agrasen was a Suryavanshi and Princess Madhavi was a Naagvanshi. Agrawals worship snakes as the queen Madhavi belongs to the Nagvanshi family background. In the *swayamvara,* even the gods of the god Indra were there to marry princess Madhvi. He was impressed with the splendid beauty of the princess and badly wanted to marry her. When he wasn't able to marry her, he got annoyed and jealous of Agrasen. He is furious with him and decides to take revenge by taking undue advantage of his power.

Maharaja Agrasen fought the epic battle of Mahabharata at the age of 15 from the side of Pandavas. Lord Krishna was also impressed with the wisdom, bravery and dedication of young Agrasen. He also predicted that Agrasen will be admired and remembered as Yug Purush in the future. On the advice of Lord Shiva, Agrasen prayed for goddess Mahalaxmi and pleased her with his strong dedication and determination. Mahalaxmi blessed Agrasen with prosperity and goodwill. She ordered him to leave the warrior section and adopt Vaishya Dharma. And soon Agrasen became the first Vaishya king.

Literature Review

Maharaja Agrasen was a legendary king and a Hindu icon who lived in India during the tenth century. He is known for his immense contributions to society, particularly for his philosophy of "simple living and high thinking." Agrasen believed in the importance of integrity, honesty, and the well-being of others. He believed that a leader should be responsible for the welfare of his subjects and that wealth should be distributed equally among all. In this note, we will explore Agrasen's thoughts and their significance in contemporary society. Agrasen believed that a leader's primary duty is to serve their people. He argued that rulers should not only be concerned with their personal interests but should also strive to promote the well-being of their subjects. He believed that a ruler should be compassionate, empathetic, and just, and should work tirelessly to create a society that is prosperous and harmonious (Pandey, 2017). According to Agrasen, wealth should be distributed equally among all members of society. He believed that no one should be allowed to accumulate an excessive amount of wealth, as this would create inequality and foster feelings of envy and resentment. Agrasen believed that wealth should be used to improve the lives of others, and that those who are fortunate enough to have wealth should use it for the benefit of society as a whole (Singh & Gautam, 2021). Agrasen also believed in the importance of education. He argued that education was essential for the well-being of individuals and society as a whole. He believed that everyone should have access to education, regardless of their social status or economic background. Agrasen believed that education was the key to unlocking one's potential and achieving success (Saxena & Sharma, 2019). Agrasen's philosophy of "simple living and high thinking" emphasizes the importance of leading a simple and modest life. He believed that material possessions should not be the primary focus of one's life, and that true happiness and fulfilment could only be achieved through spiritual and intellectual pursuits. Agrasen believed that individuals should strive for excellence in all aspects of their lives and should work tirelessly to achieve their goals (Bala & Bala, 2021). In contemporary society, Agrasen's thoughts are still relevant and valuable. His emphasis on the importance of serving others, promoting equality, and pursuing education is particularly important in a world that is facing numerous challenges. Agrasen's philosophy of simple living and high thinking is also relevant in today's society, which is increasingly materialistic and focused on consumerism. In conclusion, Maharaja Agrasen's thoughts and philosophy have had a significant impact on Indian society and culture. His emphasis on the importance of serving others, promoting equality, pursuing education, and leading a simple life is still relevant and valuable today. Agrasen's ideas continue to inspire people around the world, and his legacy is a testament to the power of positive leadership and social responsibility.

Managerial Skills, Relevance and Implementation in the Present Era

Maharaja Agrasen is idealised as a peacemaker and a supporter of non-violence. He is the icon and inspiration for sacrifices and compassion. Above all, He was a doer who produced prosperity for all. He upholds the ideology as a true socialist and is remembered for his greatness and kind behaviour. Apparently, there are many more insights of king Agrasen which enlighten the path even in today's world. He was the originator of many innovative ideas like "One Brick One Coin" and many others. He was also an entrepreneur by his ideas and a leader by birth. He led the Agreyen community of more than one lakh people on the path of prosperity and indulged them in business activities. He is also remembered as a visionary leader who was beyond his time. He was an extraordinary communicator and visionary leader. An icon of compassion and prosperity, King Agrasen was also remembered as a true socialist. His lessons and knowledge will continue to enlighten the path in various dimensions of recent times also. Leadership, entrepreneurship, and welfare of the community (social service) are key dimensions where his life and knowledge were able to influence many initiators and doers.

One Brick and One Coin Initiative

The innovative step is also named the "One brick, one rupee" initiative. It is a welfare programme in order to ensure an egalitarian society. The unique rule promulgated that any inhabitant reaching the land of Agroha to settle down permanently shall be given one rupee, one brick, by each resident of Agroha irrespective of his other demographic features. As the immigrant collected more bricks that helped him build a house and start any business and venture with the money received from the citizens of Agroha in terms of coins. This way through a small help each person could attain equal status in society equals which shows the greatness and kindness of king Agrasen.

Leader by birth

The great king Agrasen built a kingdom named "Agrayen". Where more than one lakh people lived and indulged in business activities in any possible aspect. He helps his associates and followers to be an entrepreneur. This is the ultimate remark of his business thinking and innovative mindset. King Agrasen was a doer who nourished prosperity in the kingdom through his effective leadership and business skill. He laid down the foundation of the prosperous state of Agroha.

Exceptional administrator by work

King Agrasen was a pioneer of such a great and prosperous kingdom. The people living in the community were highly skillful and engaged in various types of business activity. King Agrasen had a rare and special managerial skill that led to infrequent growth during his time period. His values and thoughts are much more reliable in today's scenario. A prosperous and growing kingdom "Agreyen" depicts his administrative capabilities. He was also an administrator of the highest category and brought us various ideas and principles of being a good administrator. In today's scenario, geopolitics around the globe face huge conflicts. It is the need of the hour to follow and implement the ideology and principle of welfare and equality of the great king Agrasen. The great kingdom was established and nourished where the root foundations build with strong and prosperous ideas and values. The knowledge and thoughts of king Agrasen are as much realistic in the present.

A true socialist

King Agrasen was not only a true socialist but also a huge supporter of non-violence. He banned animal sacrifices in "*Yagya*". King Agrasen had 18 sons, and the kingdom was segregated into 18 substrates. The representative from each substrate formed governing council to administer the kingdom. The democracy in his kingdom is the ultimate evidence that he was a true socialist.

Legacy and Impact of Maharaja Agrasen

Maharaja Agrasen is revered as a legendary figure in North India, and his legacy continues to inspire people to this day. Many institutions and organisations have been named after him, including the Agrasen ki Baoli, a historical stepwell in Delhi. The Agrawal community, which traces its origins to Maharaja Agrasen, is one of the most prominent and prosperous communities in India today. Maharaja Agrasen's impact on Indian society and culture has been significant. He is revered as a symbol of social justice and equality, and his legacy has inspired numerous social reform movements in India. The Agrawal community, which he founded, has played an important role in India's economic development, particularly in the areas of trade and commerce. Today, the Agrawal community is one of India's most prosperous and influential communities.

Conclusion

Maharaja Agrasen was a legendary king who is remembered for his wisdom, courage, and philanthropy. His principles of equality, justice, and education continue to inspire people to this day. Maharaja Agrasen's legacy serves as a reminder of the importance of values such as compassion, generosity, and community spirit. Maharaja Agrasen's life and thought have profoundly impacted Indian society and culture. His commitment to social justice and equality and his emphasis on community and philanthropy continue to inspire generations of Indians. The Agrawal community, which he founded, has played an important role in India's economic development and continues to be a significant force in Indian society today.The thought of economic and social equality and non-violence was propounded by Maharaja Agrasen almost 5000 years back. They are such inspirational and splendid thoughts and accreditation that they are present in the soul and spirit of the present Constitution of India. However, at some stage, we Indians have not been able to nurture these ideals into our lives. They remained as words written on our constitution despite the proper implementation and practice. It is the fundamental duty of every Indian to adopt these ideals in our lives as a tribute to the pioneer of such great thought and accreditation. Establishing individual responsibility as it lies upon us now to adopt these ideals in our lives as a tribute to our progenitor.

References

Agrawal, S. K. (2012). Maharaja Agrasen: A legendary hero of India. *International Journal of Social Science and Humanity*, 2(5), 391-395.

Bala, N., & Bala, P. (2021). Maharaja Agrasen's simple living and high thinking. *Journal of Human Values,* 27(1), 21-28. https://doi.org/10.1177/0971685820978347

Bhandari, M. L. (2005). *Agrawal history: A study of thirty-three agrawal kuldevi temples.* New Delhi: B.R. Publishing Corporation.

Gupta, A. (2013). *Agrasen: The legendary king.* New Delhi: Diamond Pocket Books.

Gupta, A. K. (2004). *Agrasen ki baoli: Delhi's unique monument.* New Delhi: D.K. Printworld.

Gupta, R. K. (2008). *Maharaja Agrasen and his ideals.* Agrawal Vikas Trust.

Jain, S. K. (1996). *Maharaja Agrasen and his times.* New Delhi: Radha Publications.

Jha, R. (2020). Maharaja Agrasen's vision of inclusive society. *International Journal of Innovative Research in Social Sciences & Strategic Management,* 7(1), 1-6.

Kolli, S. K., & Srikanth, A. (2020). The Participation of Indian Firms During Covid-19 Pandemic-A Corporate Social Responsibility Perspective. *European Journal of Molecular & Clinical Medicine, 07*(08).

M, S. B., & S, U. P. (2021). CSR contribution towards the normalcy and upliftment of the society during COVID-19 pandemic. *PalArcg's Journal of Archaeology of Egypt/Egyptology, 18*(9).

Mishra, L. (2020). Corporate social responsibility and sustainable development goals: A study of Indian companies. *Wiley*. https://doi.org/10.1002/pa.2147

Mitra, N., & Chatterjee, B. (2020). India's Contribution to the Sustainable Development Goals (SDGs) With Respect to the CSR Mandate in the Companies Act, 2013. *The Future of the UN Sustainable Development Goals: Business Perspectives of Global Development in 2030*, 383-396. https://doi.org/10.1007/978-3-030-21154-7_19

Pandey, S. K. (2017). Maharaja Agrasen: A paradigm of leadership, sacrifice and devotion. *International Journal of Research and Analytical Reviews,* 4(4), 370-377. https://doi.org/10.21474/IJRAR17/5245

Patil, V., Jauhari, S., & Maheshwari, D. (2017). CSR Activities and its Impact on Socioeconomic Upliftment: An Integrated Review. *Learning Community, 8*(2), 65-69. https://doi.org/10.5958/2231-458X.2017.00009.4

Saxena, P., & Sharma, R. (2019). Role of Maharaja Agrasen in spreading education in ancient India. *Asian Journal of Management,* 10(3),

Singh, M. P. (2005). *Agrasen: The first republican hero of the world.* Book Palace.

Singh, P. (2015). *Maharaja Agrasen and the Agrawals: Origin, history and culture.* New Delhi: V & S Publishers.

Thakur, N. K. (2018). Maharaja Agrasen: A social reformer. *International Journal of Research in Social Sciences,* 8(3), 470-476.

Verma, M. L. (2010). Agrasen ki baat: A study of Agrasen's life and philosophy. Shri Agrasen Kanya P.G. College.

9

Philosophy of Maharaja Agrasen and Corporate Social Responsibility practices in the modern era

Ishwar Sharma[1], Bhawana Verma[2]

Abstract

Companies can contribute to the betterment and upliftment of the society by contributing a part of their profit to CSR activities. The idea of socialism is not new. It was practiced by Maharaja Agrasen about 5000 years back and this concept is replicating in the present time as "Corporate Social Responsibility". The present study examines the role of CSR in the upliftment of society. This study is descriptive and is supported by secondary data taken from the National CSR Portal. The study finds that nearly ₹ 20,360 crores had been spent by 8,633 companies during financial year 2020-21. The healthcare and education sectors are the sectors that received the highest CSR amount. Healthcare sector received nearly 34 percent and the education sector received nearly 32 percent of the total CSR contribution.

Keywords: Maharaja Agrasen, Sustainability, Corporate Social Responsibility.

1. Assistant Professor, Department of Commerce, Indira Gandhi University, Meerpur-Rewari, Haryana.
2. Research Scholar, Department of Commerce, Indira Gandhi University, Meerpur-Rewari, Haryana.

Introduction

According to the World Business Council for Sustainable Development (WBCSD), CSR is "the continuing commitment by business to behave ethically and contribute to economic development while improving the quality of life of the workforce and their families as well as of the community and society at large". In modern business practices, corporate social responsibility (CSR) has gained significance as companies strive to balance their financial objectives with their obligations towards society and the environment. Section 135 of the Companies Act 2013 mandates companies with a turnover of ₹ 1,000 crores or more, a net worth of ₹ 500 crores or more, or a net profit of ₹ 5 crores or more in the preceding fiscal year to spend a minimum of two percent of their average net profits earned during the three immediately preceding fiscal years on designated CSR initiatives. The concept of social responsibility is not new. One such tradition is Maharaja Agrasen philosophy, which is rooted in the principles of social responsibility, ethical behaviour, and community service. The idea of socialism was practiced by Maharaja Agrasen about 5000 years back in the form of one brick and one rupee principle in his dynasty. He was the king of Agroha and the founder of the Agrawal community in India. The word 'AGRAWAL' is made up of two words 'AGRA' and 'WAL'. Agra means 'Agrasen' and Wal means 'Son' so Agrawal means 'son of Agrasen'. As per the principle of one brick and one rupee, one brick and one rupee should be given by every family living in the Agroha to every new family coming to Agroha so that they can conveniently build their house with bricks and do business with the money given to them. He was a proponent of spending 25 percent of the income on social welfare. The traditional concept of social responsibility is replicating in the present time in the form of Corporate Social Responsibility. The principles of dharma in Hindu philosophy, which emphasize social responsibility, ethics, and duty, are closely aligned with the goals of CSR (Singh and Ahmed, 2018). CSR is the ethical behaviour of the corporate sector for the upliftment and betterment of society.

Literature Review

Patil et al. (2017) examined the impact of Corporate Social

Responsibility on Socio-Economic Development. They concluded in their study that the CSR concept helps in the upliftment of society and economic development to an extent. The involvement of the corporate sector in CSR activity is still limited.

Kolli and Srikanth (2020) examined the participation of Indian companies during COVID-19. They collected secondary data and found that many Indian companies contributed during Covid. By practicing CSR activities companies also benefitted along with the nation. It helps companies in building customer loyalty.

Mishra (2020) analysed the CSR policies used by Indian businesses. Companies were found to have made significant contributions to the social, educational, and healthcare sectors, but relatively little was made to address environmental challenges. The study found no company was contributing to SDG No. 13 i.e., "Climate Action" and SDG No. 14 i.e., "Life below water".

Mitra and Chatterjee (2020) explored how Indian companies' CSR efforts contributed to Sustainable Development Goals. They discovered that 5097 businesses spent ₹ 98.22 billion on CSR initiatives in the 2015–16 fiscal year. Out of which ₹ 93.36 billion were spent in those areas which are related to Sustainable Development to achieve Sustainable Development Goals (SDGs).

M and Priyadarshini S (2021) examined the contribution of Corporate Social Responsibility towards the upliftment of society during the COVID-Pandemic. They discovered that businesses spent money on purchasing technological devices for school children who couldn't afford them. Jack Ma, a co-founder of Alibaba, gave coronavirus testing kits and other medical supplies to other countries. During COVID-19 Pandemic, Tata Sons contributed ₹ 1000 crore and many other companies had also contributed during COVID-19.

These are some studies that suggest the principles of social responsibility, ethical behaviour, and community service promoted by this philosophy are highly relevant to modern CSR practices.

Objective of the study

The primary goal of the present study is to evaluate the significance of CSR for social development.

Research Methodology

The present study is descriptive and is supported by secondary data taken from the National CSR Portal (https://csr.gov.in). Line chart has been utilised for data analysis.

Data Analysis and Interpretation

Table 1: CSR contribution by top Indian companies during the financial year 2020-21

Name of company	CSR contribution
Reliance Industries Ltd.	Spent ₹ 922 crores on training to promote sports, Health Care, Education, Rural Development Project and Environmental Sustainability.
Tata Consultancy Services Ltd.	Spent ₹ 674 crores on Health Care, Education, Environment Sustainability, Art and Culture, Prime Minister's National Relief Funds and Other Central Government Funds.
HDFC Bank Ltd.	Spent ₹ 634.91 crore on Health Care, Environment Sustainability, Eradicating Poverty and Rural Development Project.
Oil and Natural Gas Corporation Ltd.	Spent the amount of ₹ 538.77 crores on Education, Environment Sustainability, Vocational Skills, Health Care, Prime Minister's National Relief Funds and Training to Promote Sports.
NTPC Ltd.	Spent ₹ 418.87 crores on Rural Development Projects, Swachh Bharat Kosh, Vocational Skills, Health Care, Training to Promote Sports, Livelihood Enhancement Projects, Eradicating Poverty, Women Empowerment, Environmental Sustainability, Art and Culture.
Infosys Ltd.	Spent ₹ 361.82 cr. on setting up homes and hostels for women, Health Care, Eradicating Poverty, Livelihood Enhancement Projects, Swachh Bharat Kosh, Rural Development Projects, Education, Senior Citizens Welfare, Environment Sustainability, Animal Welfare and Vocational Skills.
ITC Ltd.	Spent ₹ 335.43 crores on Education, Livelihood Enhancement Projects, Sanitation, Vocational Skills, Environment Sustainability, Health Care, Rural Development Projects, Art and Culture, Vocational Skills, Women Empowerment and Education.
Wipro Ltd.	Spent ₹ 246.99 crore on Health Care, Education, Prime Minister's National Relief Funds, Environment Sustainability, Art and Culture, Rural Development Projects.
Tata steel limited	Spent ₹ 221.98 crores on Training to promote sports, Animal Welfare, Vocational Skills, Education, Health Care, Livelihood Enhancement Projects, Sanitation, Rural Development Projects, Art and Culture, Socioeconomic Inequalities, Environment Sustainability and Eradicating Poverty.

Source: https://csr.gov.in

Table 2: CSR spent: Development sector-wise (FY 2020-21)

Sr. No.	Development sectors	Amount Spent (in ₹ cr.)
I.	"Clean Ganga Fund"	7.21
II.	"Education, Differently Abled, Livelihood"	6,463.81
III.	"Encouraging Sports"	212.56
IV.	"Environment, Animal Welfare, Conservation of Resources"	1,035.58
V.	"Gender Equality, Women Empowerment, Old Age Homes, Reducing Inequalities"	322.90
VI.	"Health, Eradicating Hunger, Poverty and Malnutrition, Safe Drinking Water, Sanitation"	6,920.08
VII.	"Heritage Art And Culture"	396.96
VIII.	"Other Sectors (Technology Incubator And Benefits To Armed Forces And Admin Overheads)"	116.73
IX.	"Prime Minister's National Relief Fund"	1452.94
X.	"Rural Development"	1,671.50
XI.	"Slum Area Development"	16.63
XII.	"Swachh Bharat Kosh"	148.13
XIII.	"Any Other Central Government Fund"	1,327.85
XIV.	"NEC/ Not Mentioned"	267.29
Grand Total (in INR cr.)		**20,360.25**

Source: https://csr.gov.in.

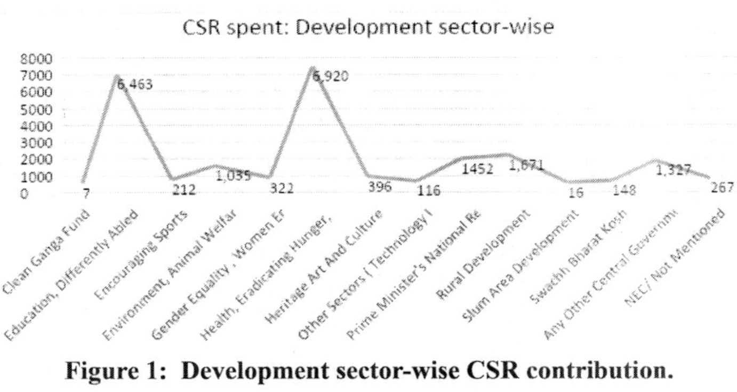

Figure 1: Development sector-wise CSR contribution.

Table 1 presents the CSR contribution by Top Indian Companies. It shows that Reliance Industries Limited spent ₹ 922 crore on training to promote sports, healthcare, education, rural development project and environmental sustainability and is the top spender in the CSR activities. Table 2 present development sector-wise CSR contribution and Figure 1 is the graphical presentation of it. Table 2 reveals that total amount of ₹ 20,360.25 cr. have been spent on different sectors. Table 2 and Figure 1 show that the highest amount (i.e. ₹ 6,920.08 Cr.) spent on Health Care, Eradicating Hunger, Safe Drinking Water, Sanitation Sectors, Poverty and Malnutrition. The second highest amount (i.e. ₹ 6,463.81 Cr.) was spent on the Education Sectors. The least amount (i.e. ₹ 7.21 Cr.) spent on Clean Ganga Fund.

Conclusion

The present corporate social responsibility can be linked to the 'one brick and one coin' principle of Maharaja Agrasen who played a significant role in the betterment of society. In the present time, corporate sectors are more connected with society. They contribute to the betterment and upliftment of society. Healthcare and Education sectors are the most attractive sectors in the form of CSR activities.

References

Gupta, A. K. (2017). अग्रवाल समाज और स्वाधीनता संग्राम.

Gupta, R. (2020). भारतीय स्वतंत्रता आंदोलन और हरियाणा का वैश्य समाज . alfa .

Kolli, S. K., & Srikanth, A. (2020). The Participation Of Indian Firms During Covid-19 Pandemic-A Corporate Social Responsibilty Perspective. *European Journal of Molecular & Clinical Medicine, 07*(08).

M, S. B., & S, U. P. (2021). CSR contribution towards the normalcy and upliftment of the society during COVID-19 pandemic. *PalArcg's Journal of Archaeology of Egypt/Egyptology, 18*(9).

Mishra, L. (2020). Corporate social responsibility and sustainable development goals: A study of Indian companies. *Wiley*. https://doi.org/10.1002/pa.2147

Mitra, N., & Chatterjee, B. (2020). India's Contribution to the Sustainable Development Goals (SDGs) With Respect to the CSR Mandate in the Companies Act, 2013. *The Future of the UN Sustainable Development Goals: Business Perspectives of Global Development in 2030*, 383-396. https://doi.org/10.1007/978-3-030-21154-7_19

Patil, V., Jauhari, S., & Maheshwari, D. (2017). CSR Activities and its Impact on Socioeconomic Upliftment: An Integrated Review. *Learning Community, 8*(2), 65-69. https://doi.org/10.5958/2231-458X.2017.00009.4

https://www.mca.gov.in/Ministry/pdf/CompaniesActNotification3_2014.pdf

https://www.un.org/development/desa/disabilities/envision2030.html

https://csr.gov.in

10

Maharaja Agrasen and Ratan Tata: Mission & Execution for Social and Economic Upliftment of Society

Mamta Aggarwal[1], Komal Jindal[2], Indu Bansal[2]

Abstract

This article describes the Great Leader Maharaja Agrasen mission and principles in ancient India and how his principles are still being followed in current era by the big personalities like Ratan Tata. His idols helped the society in overall social and economic development. Maharaja Agrasen believes in nationalism, socialism, equality and self-reliance and Ratan Tata is also a great philanthropist and administrator. Ratan Tata worked for his whole life by providing livelihood to the marginalised sections of the society. Hence we all can learn from the Maharaja Agrasen and implement his philosophies in practical world. Government can also take help form his administrative view of how to lead the economy to be higher than mountains.

Introduction

Maharaja Agrasen is regarded as a nonviolent icon, a peace messenger, the personification of Sacrifice, Compassion, and Prosperity, and a True Socialist. King Ballabh of Pratapnagar gave birth to Emperor Agrasen. He was the oldest of three sons. The age

1. Assistant Professor, Department of Commerce, IGU, Meerpur-Rewari, Haryana.
2. Research Scholar, Department of Commerce, IGU, Meerpur-Rewari, Haryana.

at the time, according to the Mahalakshmi Vrath, was the last stages of Dvaapar Yug. Maharaj Agrasen was born around 5185 years ago, according to the current calendar. Suryavamshi was King Ballabh (lineage from the Sun). Prince Agrasen was distinguished for his generosity even when he was very young. When Agrasen was a young man, he went to the Swayamvara of King Nagaraj's daughter, Princess Madhavi. Many kings from over the world gathered, including King of the Devas Indra. Princess Madhavi chose Prince Agrasen in the swayamvara by placing the garland on him. (Tantiya, 2015).

Maharaja Agrasen was the fabled Indian monarch of Agroha, a trading metropolis. He is a descendant of Kush, Lord Ram's son, and was born in the 35th generation after Lord Ram. He is credited with establishing Agroha, a trading kingdom in North India, and is famed for his kindness in refusing to slaughter animals in yajnas. On the advice of goddess Mahalakshmi, he abandoned Kshatriya tradition in favour of Vaishya tradition, and she also bestowed blessings on him and his successors. Every year on the birthday of the renowned Hindu king Agrasen Maharaja, also known as King of Agroha, Agrasen Jayanti is observed. Maharaja Agrasen Jayanti is a regional festival celebrated in the states of Haryana, Punjab, and Uttar Pradesh on the fourth day of the Hindu calendar's Ashwin month (the seventh month).

The Government of India also issued a postage stamp in honour of Maharaja Agrasen in 1976. There are many remarkable events which depicts that Agrasen was the true socialist, entrepreneur and self-independent. He laid the foundation of corporate social responsibility and self-reliant economy in ancient times. His idols are being followed in current era also. There are many big personalities who adopted the principles of Maharaja Agrasen and implement in their business like Ratan tata. Indian industrialist and philanthropist Naval Ratan Tata is a former chairman of Tata Sons. His ancestors Jamestji Tata also focus on creating livelihood for his countrymen. He has People-centric approach which is similar to Maharaja Agrasen principles of equality and employment (Mandal, 2018). Ratan Tata is also a supporter of education and rural development.

Hence this article associates the mission and execution of Maharaja Agrasen philosophies in social and economic Upliftment of the society. This article motivates the young researchers, entrepreneurs, government and society as a whole to follow his idols in real life based on which new business and societal developments shall be introduced in the economy.

Maharaja Agrasen: Mission and Execution

He always worked for the upliftment of society and economic development of his people. His main aim is to make his state prosperous and focus on administration (Patiyala University, 2019). He was a benevolent king. He has many principles based on which he leads the society which are as follows:

- Doing agricultural and business activities
- Not harming animals
- Always use profits from business in development of society
- Follower of Ahimsa
- Helping the marginalised section of the society
- Always save part of income for the future uncertainties
- Simple living, high thinking

These principles are being followed and executed by Maharaja Agrasen in that ancient India by introducing many policies (Gupta, 2019).

Maharaja Agrasen was a symbol of socialism, nonviolence, and a peace messenger. He was the epitome of self-sacrifice and a true socialist. (www.Snephost.com, 2021).

Pioneer of Socialism and Architect of Self-Reliance

His personality of social upliftment can be evident at his early stage of childhood. From a very young age, Prince Agrasen of Pratap Nagar was well-known for his compassion. His nature of equality was very much famous among people. He introduced the concept of socialism as early as 5200 years ago. He also followed the policy of "One Brick One rupee, a welfare activity. It was the notion that each and every local should provide a brick and a rupee to any foreigner wishing to establish there, so that they can start their new firm with a thousand bricks and a thousand rupees. He believed that every citizen of his state should be very self-dependent and be an entrepreneur (Gupt, 2017).

Establishment of Democracy and Welfare State

He believes that every person must divide his income into four parts that is:

- Family development
- Business development
- Public utilities and welfare
- Future and state development

He introduced the concept of social co-operation with decision making must be done by both the ruler and the one who is being ruled (Garg, 2021).

Believer of Ahimsa and ordered total ban of Animal Sacrifice

He was renowned for executing numerous yagnas for the welfare of the populace of his kingdom. He broke the custom of sacrificing horses for prosperity when, during one of these yagnas, one horse struggled to move far from the altar. Agrasen declared that his kingdom would no longer tolerate acts of cruelty, such as the death of mute creatures, while remaining strongly attached to Ahimsa's argument.

Corporate Social responsibility- Foundation laid by Maharaja Agrasen

Every year, on the first day of the moon in the month of Ashwin, Maharaja Agrasen's birth anniversary is commemorated. He was a big proponent of allocating 25 percent of revenue to the wellbeing of society's living creatures. He also urged people to set aside 25 percent of their salary as a reserve for unforeseen circumstances. He places a higher importance on humanities than caste, community, fortune, employment, or religion. In his realm, farming communities that produced food grains were honoured, and for him, the best service was to bring assistance to everyone. (Goel, 2014). His way of dealings with business problems was believed to be very great.

Ratan Tata: Mission and execution

Ratan Tata is a great philanthropist, connoisseur of art and former CEO of the TATA group. He is perceptive to the difficulties faced by normal citizens. His main aim is to use the all the wealth for the betterment of society. He focused on how to provide quality life to the public. Although Sir Ratan helped his older brother Dorabji handle the many Tata businesses, his true passions were social and charitable activities. He recognised the significance of Mahatma Gandhi's fight against racism in South Africa and gave it both spiritual and financial support by donating a total of ₹ 125,000 to the cause. Overwhelmed by the generosity of this support, Gandhi wrote, "That India has been roused is evident from the generous gift of Mr Ratanji Jamsetji Tata... He will probably be followed by other Indians. Parsis are known the world over for their generous gifts. Mr. Tata has been true to that spirit of generosity."

Gopal Krishna Gokhale, a significant Indian social reformer and liberation warrior, had a close friendship with Sir Ratan. Sir Ratan made a ten-year donation of ₹ 10,000 to Gokhale's Servants of India Society to assist its efforts to help the weaker segments of society after being moved by the organisation's activities. (Tata.com).

Also, in current time, Tata group is doing many things for the society and economy of India. Tata Steel went over and beyond to assist its employees during the second wave of Covid-19 and extended social security programmes to the relatives of the employees affected by Covid-19. The steel plant in Jamshedpur has stated that it will continue to provide monthly salaries to the families of all of its employees who passed away as a result of COVID-19 (Tripathi, 2021). The announcement further stated that the pay will be provided up until the deceased person's 60-year retirement age. The person's monthly wage would be equal to the last salary they received before passing away. The employer would offer housing options and medical perks in addition to the compensation.

Tata in the Community

We developed a group-level volunteering platform, Tata Engage, in 2014 to promote collaborative volunteering across group companies and to harness the combined force of over 700,000 Tata employees, their family members, and retirees around the world. The Tata Engage platform helps volunteers connect with the community by giving their time and abilities through three different formats: skill-based, weekend projects through Pro Engage, experience volunteering events through Tata Volunteering Weeks, and volunteering for Tata Disaster Responses. The Tata group has logged more than 1 million volunteer hours a year over the previous five years, ranking us among the top 15 corporate volunteering programmes worldwide. The organisation recorded 1.52 million volunteer hours in FY20, setting a record for the most hours above 1.5 million ever.

Empowerment

Through training and numerous literacy programmes, Ratan Tata empowers rural communities, farmers, and youth, enabling them to live independent lives. Tata companies help people gain more independence by providing them with the resources they need to prosper in a global economy. The organisation provides knowledge, technology, and the ability for communities to produce better results. They had taken many initiatives like:

- ***Okhai***

  It's similar to a brand created by the Tata Chemical Society for Rural Development to represent the empowerment of rural and semi-urban women and to support traditional handicraft methods. In the villages of Okhamandal, numerous self-help organisations are created.

- ***Tata Steel Samvaad- A Tribal Conclave***

  Samvaad is a four-day gathering that honours the indigenous people. Reviving, preserving, and promoting tribal culture is ingrained in Tata Steel's culture.

- ***Tata Strive***

  The primary area of concentration for national development is skill development. Building capacity to prepare kids for employment, entrepreneurship, and community enterprise is the main goal of this mission. This mission aids sections that are struggling financially and helps them adjust to the evolving workplace.

CSR Activities and Tata

Tata group has done many corporate social initiatives under the guidance of the Sir Ratan Tata like:

- **Building right capabilities:** They helped the marginalised sections of the society to acquire skill-based training and provide entrepreneurship opportunities.
- **Enables progress through education:** Tata group helped the underprivileged children through education. They launched the "**Titan Kanya Initiatives**" focuses on Girl child education and encourage the computer-based functional literacy.
- **Advancing holistic developments:** It encompasses a broad array of initiatives from providing critical healthcare facilities.
- **Creating livelihood opportunities:** They set up the Tata Motors Grihini Social Welfare Society in 1974 to give women the entrepreneurship opportunities. They are aiding Indian fishermen through Fish Friend through mobile app.
- **Achieving more together and reaching out at the time of crisis:** Tata group helped in various natural disasters like Cyclone Hudhud, Nepal Earthquake Relief and Covid-19. The organisation spent INR 1,095 crore on CSR expenses in the 2019 fiscal year, and it had a positive impact on 11.7 million lives. (Tatasustainibility.com).

Two personalities: One mission

As we can see from the above description that all big personalities actually followed the Maharaja Agrasen principles and implement them in current era in societal and economic development. It was Maharaja Agrasens idea to make the nation self-reliance and bring equality. Following his footsteps, Ratan Tata also helped the society by various initiatives and increasing Entrepreneurship. Maharaja Agrasen policy of "**One Brick, One coin**" laid the foundation of self-independent economy. Likewise, Agrasen ji laid the foundation of corporate social responsibility. Tata group has clearly executed CSR activities by helping the disadvantaged sections of the society.

Conclusion

Overall study reflects that Maharaja Agrasen has done a lot for the society as a whole and his principles helped in current business era. His socialistic view will motivate the government to form policies for the economic development. So, this article tells that how Ratan Tata has also done a lot for the society, for self-reliance economy. Actually, it is connected to the views of the Maharaja Agrasen that one must live for the society. Hence, we can conclude this article by saying:

"If you want to walk Fast, walk alone. But if you want to walk far, walk together"

References

Garg, J. K. (2021). Pioneer of socialism & nonviolence maharaja Agrasen - Ajmernama. https://ajmernama.com/vishesh/368274/

Goel, M. M. (2014). Learn Corporate Social Responsibility (CSR) Lessons from Maharaja Agrasen: The India Post. https://www.theindiapost.com/articles/learn- corporate-social-responsibility-csr-lessons-maharaja-agrasen/amp/

Gupt, C. (2017). *Shreshta Samaaj-Yasahasvi Bharat* (1st ed.). Agroha Vikas Trust, Agroha, Hissar.

Gupta, K. (2019). *Maharaja Agrasen: Agravansh ka Sanskipt Itihaas.* GenNext publication, New Delhi.

Mandal, S. (2018). JRD: A capitalist who practiced socialism - The Statesman. https://www.thestatesman.com/supplements/section/jrd-capitalist-practised-socialism- 1502717884.html

Patiyala University, Punjab. (2019). Maharaja Agrasen Chair. http://www.punjabiuniversity.ac.in/pages/Department.aspx?dsenc=171

Tantiya, H. (2015). *Agroha Darshan* (six). Agroha Vikas Trust, Agroha, Hissar.

Tata.com. Sir Ratan Tata | Tata Group. Retrieved February 11, 2022, from https://www.tata.com/about-us/tata-group-our-heritage/tata-titans/sir-ratan-tata

Tatasustainibility.com. CSR - TATA Sustainability Group. Retrieved February 11, 2022, from https://www.tatasustainability.com/SocialAndHumanCapital/CSR

Tripathi, S. (2021). Tata Steel Wins Heart For Extending Social Scheme Plans For Covid Affected Employees. https://www.indiatimes.com/trending/human-interest/tata-steel- extends-schemes-for-employees-541127.html

www.Snephost.com. (2021). Maharaja Agrasen: 21 Historical Life Events and Stories of Agroha King. https://www.snehpost.com/2019/09/agrasen.html

11

Role of Principles of Maharaja Agrasen in the Development of Society

Bharti[1], Durga Dutt Goyal[2]

Abstract

The principles of Maharaja Agrasen, a legendary king of the Agarwal community in India, have been regarded as a significant source of inspiration for the development of society. This paper aims to explore the role of Maharaja Agrasen's principles in the development of the society. The findings suggest that the principles of Maharaja Agrasen have played a crucial role in promoting social cohesion, economic development, and cultural preservation among the Agarwal community. The principles have also been instrumental in promoting ethical and moral values, which have contributed to the development of a just and equitable society. The study concludes that Maharaja Agrasen's principles continue to be relevant in the contemporary context, and can provide valuable insights for the development of a more sustainable and inclusive society. Agrasen was a Kshatriya king and a great personality. The idea of socialism was practiced by Maharaja Agrasen about 5000 years back and this concept is replicated in the modern era. The present study is conceptual and it aims to study the principles of King Maharaja Agrasen and connect these principles with societal development. The study finds that his philosophy is still carried out in the modern era and contributes to the development of society.

1. Student, Department of Commerce, Indira Gandhi University, Meerpur-Rewari, Haryana.
2. General Secretary, Haryana Pradesh Vaish Mahasamelan.

Introduction

Maharaja Agrasen was a legendary king who is believed to have lived in ancient India during the era of the Mahabharata. He is revered as a symbol of peace, prosperity, and community welfare. His contributions to society are many and have had a lasting impact on Indian culture and society. One of the major contributions of Maharaja Agrasen was the establishment of a social and economic system based on mutual cooperation and trust. He founded the Agrawal community, which was based on the principles of honesty, hard work, and self-reliance. Agrawal is a term used to refer to those who are "Children of Agrasen" or "the Agroha city's inhabitants." 18 Agarwal Gotras were established by him. He was the son of suryavanshi King Vallabh. He was a doer who desired prosperity for all. In the socialist system he founded, anyone who suffered a financial loss could borrow money from him. Maharaja Agrasen performed numerous yajnas for the sake of the people's peace, progress and prosperity. At that time, the yajna represented prosperity. Maharaja Agrasen is also credited with the establishment of the first cooperative society in India. This society was based on the principle of pooling resources and sharing profits. It helped the members of the community to access credit, purchase raw materials, and market their products. The cooperative society was a precursor to the modern-day cooperative movement, which has played a significant role in the development of India's rural economy. Furthermore, Maharaja Agrasen is also known for his philanthropic activities. He is said to have donated large sums of money for the welfare of the poor and the needy. Maharaja Agrasen is also known for his advocacy of non-violence and peace. He is said to have emphasised the importance of resolving conflicts through dialogue and negotiation, rather than through war and violence. His teachings have had a profound impact on Indian culture, and continue to inspire the principles of peace and non-violence today. Furthermore, Maharaja Agrasen's contributions to society have been recognised through various awards and honours. In 2002, the Indian government issued a postage stamp in his honour, recognising his contributions to society. There are also many temples dedicated to Maharaja Agrasen throughout India, where his followers continue to gather and celebrate his teachings. Corporate Social Responsibility is a contemporary version of the old idea of social responsibility therefore, it can be linked with the principles of Maharaja Agrasen. Maharaja Agrasen had a wonderful personality and contributed significantly to societal advancement.

Literature Review

Begum (2021) examined how CSR improved society during the COVID pandemic. They found that corporations bought technological equipment for children who couldn't afford it. Various countries received donations of medical supplies and coronavirus test kits from Jack Ma, who is one of the co-founders of Alibaba. Tata Sons donated ₹ 1000 cr. to COVID-19. Many businesses also offered assistance during the COVID-19 Pandemic.

Kolli & Srikanth (2020) the involvement of Indian businesses in COVID-19 was studied. Many Indian corporations made contributions during Covid, according to secondary data they collected. Companies and the nation both benefited from CSR practices. It supports businesses in fostering consumer loyalty.

Patil et al. (2017) explored the effect of corporate social responsibility on socio-economic development. They concluded in their analysis that the CSR idea contributes to economic growth and societal improvement to some extent. The corporate sector is still only minimally involved in CSR activities.

Objective of the study

The primary objective of the present study is to examine the role of the principles of Maharaja Agrasen in the societal development of the Indian economy.

Research Methodology

The present study is descriptive that is based on secondary data which is collected from National CSR Portal (https://csr.gov.in) and other websites.

Role of principles of Maharaja Agrasen in the development of society

- **One brick and one coin:** According to this rule, each

household in the city of "Agroha" shall donate one brick and one coin to each visitor who intends to live there permanently so they can start a home with bricks and a business. This philosophy assisted them in bringing equality. In the current scenario, the government brings equality through Fiscal policy. Income tax is a progressive tax, meaning that tax rates rise as taxable income rises. The government uses the money it collects in the form of income tax to assist the underprivileged. This is how the government tries to reduce the gap between rich and poor and brings equality.

- **Prohibition of animal killing:** Maharaja Agrasen's Ideals of "No to mute animal killing for sacrifice" and "support to peace and non-violence" are still carried out in the present time. As per the Prevention of Cruelty to Animals Act 1960, hurting any animal is illegal.
- **Contribution of 25 percent of the income on social welfare:** Maharaja Agrasen was a proponent of spending 25 percent of the income on social welfare. This idea is replicating in the form of Income Tax. The introduction of Income Tax in India dates back to 1860 when it was first introduced by Sir James Wilson. The Income Tax Act of India was passed in 1961 and came into effect from April 1, 1962, and it is applicable throughout India. As a direct tax, income tax is imposed on individuals and entities based on their income, and the tax rate increases progressively as the income increases. The income tax system has the potential to contribute to economic growth. The PM CARES Fund was established to provide assistance to those affected by the COVID-19 pandemic. The contribution made by individuals in this PM CARES Fund will be eligible for 100 percent exemption. This is an opportunity for taxpayers to help the nation as well as reduce tax liability. Taxes are used by the government for social welfare and economic development.
- **Replication of the traditional concept of social responsibility in the form of CSR:** Corporate social responsibility (CSR) is the modern manifestation of the traditional concept of social duty. According to Section 135 of the Companies Act 2013, companies with a turnover of

at least ₹ 1,000 crore, a net worth of ₹ 500 crore or more, or a net profit of ₹ 5 crore or more during the previous financial year must allocate at least two percent (2%) of their average net profits from the preceding three financial years to specific CSR initiatives. A total amount of ₹ 20,360 crores had been spent by 8,633 companies during FY 2020-21 in CSR activities for the betterment of society. CSR initiatives support the achievement of sustainable development goals. The Sustainable Development Goals were adopted by 193 UN members in 2015, and they went into force on January 1st, 2016. The 2030 Agenda for Sustainable Development, which has 169 targets and 17 Sustainable Development Goals, aims to create a more secure world by that year. It is also known as "Global Goals," The Millennium Development Goals, which were launched in 2000, were replaced by these goals. Eight Millennium Development Goals (MDGs) were intended to be accomplished by the year 2015, but due to inconsistent progress until that point, they were extended until 2030 under the new name Sustainable Development Goals, which comprises 17 Goals. SDG- I "No Poverty", SDG- II "Zero Hunger", SDG- III "Good Health and Well Being", SDG- IV "Quality Education", SDG- V "Gender Equality", SDG- VI "Clean Water and Sanitation", SDG- VII "Affordable and Clean Energy", SDG- VIII "Decent Work and Economic Growth", SDG- IX "Industry, Innovation and Infrastructure", SDG- X "Reduced Inequality within and among countries", SDG-XI "Sustainable Cities and Communities", SDG- XII "Responsible Consumption and Production", SDG- XIII "Climate Action", SDG- XIV "Life Below Water", SDG-XV "Life on Land", SDG-XVI "Peace and Justice Strong Institution", SDG- XVII "Partnership to Achieve the Goal". These goals can be met through corporate social responsibility (CSR) efforts. CSR initiatives include eradicating poverty, malnutrition, and hunger as well as advancing healthcare. It includes contributions to Swach Bharat Kosh, preventative healthcare, and sanitation. Promoting education by providing specialised instruction and job training to women, children, and disabled persons also includes contributions to publicly supported universities, Indian Institutes of Technology (IITs), and other research and development programmes that have received central government approval. It consists of promoting gender equality and women's empowerment. The establishment of old age homes, women's and orphan's homes, various facilities for the elderly, and measures to alleviate inequity experienced by economically disadvantaged communities are all included in this. It covers environmental sustainability, resource conservation, soil preservation, flora and wildlife preservation, animal welfare, air and water quality, and ecological balance. The Central Government established the Clean Ganga Fund to revitalise the Ganges River. Contributions to the Clean Ganga Fund are also included. It includes several measures for the benefit of veterans of the armed forces, war widows and their dependents, veterans of the Central Paramilitary Forces (CPMF), and veterans of the Central Armed Police Forces (CAPF) and their dependents to "promote rural sports, nationally recognised sports, paralympic sports, and Olympic sports" (including widows training), Rural development projects and Slum area development. These are the specified CSR activities that are related to SDGs and these activities help in achieving Sustainable Development Goals. CSR refers to the moral conduct of the corporate sector for the advancement and improvement of society.

Conclusion

The principles of Maharaja Agrasen are as relevant today as they were about 5000 years back. He established good governance by taking the initiative to eliminate social evils. His principles are replicating in the modern era for the betterment and upliftment of society. Socialism is not a new concept. About 5000 years ago, Maharaja Agrasen used this method, and it is still used today under the name "Corporate Social Responsibility." Corporate sectors are more integrated with society today. The contributions of Maharaja Agrasen to society have been immense. Maharaja Agrasen's contributions to society have been vast and far-reaching. His teachings of non-violence, cooperation, and community welfare have had a lasting impact on Indian culture and society.

References

Begum, S. (2021). CSR contribution towards the normalcy and upliftment of the society during COVID-19 pandemic. *PalArch's Journal of Archaeology of Egypt/Egyptology,* 18(09), 16–27.

India Code: Income-tax Act, 1961. (n.d.). Retrieved 15 January 2023, from https://www.indiacode.nic.in/handle/123456789/2435?sam_handle=123456789/1362

Kolli, S. K., & Srikanth, D. A. (2020). The Participation Of Indian Firms During Covid-19 Pandemic-A Corporate Social Responsibilty Perspective. *Clinical Medicine,* 07(08).

National CSR Portal. (n.d.). Retrieved 15 January 2023, from https://csr.gov.in/content/csr/global/master/home/home.html

Patil, V., Jauhari, S., & Maheshwari, D. (2017). CSR Activities and its Impact on Socioeconomic Upliftment: An Integrated Review. Learning Community-*An International Journal of Educational and Social Development,* 8(2), 65. https://doi.org/10.5958/2231-458X.2017.00009.4

People still carry out Maharaja Agrasen's ideals. (2017). https://www.dailypioneer.com/2017/state-editions/people-still-carry-out-maharaja-agrasens-ideals.html

Prevention of Cruelty to Animals Act, 1960. (n.d.). http://indiacode.nic.in/handle/123456789/1547

Sneha. (2021). Maharaja Agrasen: 21 Historical Life Events and Stories of Agroha King. Snehpost. https://www.snehpost.com/2019/09/agrasen.html

Sustainable Development. (n.d.). Retrieved 15 January 2023, from https://sdgs.un.org/

12

महाराजा अग्रसेन द्वारा प्रवर्तित समाजवाद की वर्तमान प्रासंगिकता

आर. डी. अग्रवाल[1]

समाजवाद एक व्यापक सिद्धांत है, जो राज्य में समस्त नागरिकों को सभी प्रकार की नागरिक सुविधाएं एवं जीवन–यापन संबंधी सभी आवश्यकताएं पूर्ण रूप से, सुख–सुविधा के साथ उपलब्ध कराता है। इतिहास के झरोखे से ज्ञात होता है कि महाराजा अग्रसेन के समाजवाद की शुरुआत एक अत्यंत सुंदर ढंग से की गई, जहां प्रत्येक नागरिक समानता, समरसता, समन्वय, सहयोग एव समाजवादी तौर पर एक साथ रह सके। उनके राज्य के एक लाख परिवारों में यदि बाहर से कोई नया परिवार आकर बसता, तो प्रत्येक परिवार एक रुपया, एक ईंट से उसका स्वागत करता तथा उसे अपने समकक्ष बना देता। उस एक रुपया एक ईंट से आगुंतक परिवार अपना मकान एवं आजीविका सुचारू रूप से चला सकता था। इतना ही नहीं, उसके बिरादरी एवं भाईचारे के बिना किसी भेदभाव व द्वेष के पारिवारिक संबंध स्थापित हो जाते। कैसा सुंदर वातावरण था इस छोटी सी सुंदर पहल से। इस भाईचारे के चलने पर समन्वय एवं समरसता की अमृतधारा बहती थी।

महाराजा अग्रसेन ने अपने राज्य को सुचारू रूप से चलाने के लिए उसे 18 गणराज्यों में विभक्त किया और राज्य में हिंसा पर पूर्ण रूप से प्रतिबंध लगा दिया एवं यज्ञ में पशु बलि का निषेध कर दिया। उन्होंने अपने राज्य में बहुत से धार्मिक, सामाजिक एवं शैक्षणिक कार्य प्रजा की भलाई के लिए किए। वे सदैव न्याय प्रिय शासक रहे।

---

1. नई अनाज मंडी, रेवाड़ी–हरियाणा।

भारत की द्वितीय पंचवर्षीय योजना में समाजवादी ढंग की स्थापना की योजना थी, लेकिन अब हम देख रहे हैं कि समाजवादी व्यवस्था को लागू करने में हमारा देश पूर्ण रूप से असफल रहा क्योंकि राजनीतिज्ञों ने परिवारवाद, जातिवाद व मसल–पावरवाद के रहते उस व्यवस्था पर करारी चोट की। विश्व के अन्य अविकसित देशों जैसे पाकिस्तान, बांग्लादेश, श्रीलंका एवं अरब देशों में व्याप्त भ्रष्टाचार, परिवारवाद, कट्टरवाद एवं आतंकवाद के चलते समाजवाद की जड़ें खोखली होती चली गईं। इसके अतिरिक्त विश्व के अन्य विकसित देशों में भी, जैसे फ्रेंच–क्रांति 1864, बर्लिन जैसे देशों में भी समाजवाद और सफल हो गया। कार्ल मार्क्स की थ्योरी के अनुसार नारा दिया गया था 'दुनिया के मजदूरों, एक हो जाओ। तुम्हारे पास गंवाने के लिए कुछ नहीं है, लेकिन पाने के लिए पूरा जहां है'। परिणामस्वरूप दिल दहलाने वाली हिंसात्मक क्रांति रूस में 1848–49 में लेनिन के समय में हुई।

अग्रवाल समाज की प्राचीन काल में ही यह परंपरा थी कि एक लाख आबादी वाले अग्रोहा नगर में जो भी नया परिवार बसता था उसे प्रति घर से एक रुपया तथा एक ईंट दिया जाता था ताकि मकान एवं आजीविका चला सकें। इसी संदर्भ में सभी को विदित है सन् 1992 के बाद अयोध्या में भगवान राम का मंदिर बनाने हेतु देश के सभी गांवों से एक ईंट/शिला तथा धनराशि का पूजन करके अयोध्या भेजी गई। यह महाराजा अग्रसेन द्वारा अपनाई गई परंपरा का ही पालन है।

'रामचरित मानस' में जब भगवान राम एवं लक्ष्मण सीता जी के वियोग में घूमते हुए किष्किंधा कांड में वर्षा काल का वर्णन करते हुए लक्ष्मण से कहते हैं कि:

दामिनी दमक रह न घनमायी।
खल कि प्रीति जरा थिर नाही।।
क्षुद्र नदी भरी चली तोराई।
जस थोरेहु धन खल इतराई।।

लेकिन अग्रवाल समाज भरपूर साधन संपन्न होते हुए भी अहंकार नहीं करता तथा अपने संपर्क एवं संबंधों को बनाए रखता है।

महाराजा अग्रसेन एक अहिंसावादी सम्राट थे। एक बार की घटना उल्लेखनीय है कि उन्होंने एक शेरनी का शिकार किया लेकिन बाद में देखा कि शेरनी के पेट में बच्चा तड़प रहा है। इस दुखद स्थिति को देखते हुए उन्होंने

भविष्य में हिंसा ना करने का प्रण लिया तथा अपने वंशजों के लिए भी यह संदेश दिया कि उनके वंशज भी राजपूतों से वैश्य में परिवर्तित होने के बाद भी हिंसा नहीं करेंगे। इसके परिणामस्वरूप अग्रवाल समाज हिंसा में तभी से विश्वास नहीं करता। इसके अतिरिक्त अग्रवाल समाज के घटक जैन मत अपनाने के बाद कट्टर अहिंसा वादी जीवन व्यतीत कर रहे हैं। इसके साथ ही अग्रवाल समाज तथा जैन समाज में गोत्रों के हिसाब से वैवाहिक संबंध बन रहे हैं।

आज देश में लगभग 90 प्रतिशत धार्मिक स्थल, मंदिर, धर्मशालाएं, कुएं, बावड़ी एवं पाठशालाएं समाज द्वारा पोषित एवं संचालित हैं जो अनाथ बच्चों के लाभार्थ एवं हितार्थ कार्यरत हैं एवं असहाय कन्याओं की शादियां भी कराते हैं।

महाराज अग्रसेन एक सूर्यवंशी राजा थे एवं भगवान राम भी सूर्यवंशी सम्राट थे। इससे प्रतीत होता है कि समाजवाद एवं रामराज्य का दृष्टिकोण महाराजा अग्रसेन ने अपनाया था तथा इससे यह भी प्रतीत होता है कि महाराजा अग्रसेन राम के वंशज ही हैं।

स्पष्ट है, अगर विश्व में सच्चा समाजवाद लाना है, तो महाराजा अग्रसेन द्वारा दर्शाए गए रास्ते पर ही चलकर संभव हो सकता है। यह पूर्ण रूप से प्रासंगिक है क्योंकि यह समन्वय, समरसता, सहयोग, एकता, समाजवाद व भाईचारे के पुट से ओतप्रोत है। इससे सारे विश्व में एक मनोवैज्ञानिक संदेश जाता है, जिससे भ्रष्टाचार, आतंकवाद, परिवारवाद, जातिवाद जैसे भ्रष्ट आचरण पर अंकुश लगेगा तथा 'वसुधैव कुटुंबकम' का वातावरण तैयार हो सकेगा।

13

A Study of History and Principles of Maharaja Agrasen

Aditi Sharma[1], Manorama[2]

Abstract

Maharaja Agrasen was the founder of Agrawal community. This legendary king belongs to the lineage of Lord Rama. He was born in the era of Dwapar Yug during last stage in Mahabharat epic era. Maharaja Agrasen was the heir of king Kush, son of Lord Rama and the son of King Vallabh, ruler of Partapnagar. Since childhood, Agrasen was admired for humble nature and supporting equality among people. Later, on the advice of Goddess Mahalakshmi, he adopted Vaishya tradition of trade for the prosperity of his subjects and established a city of traders, known as Agroha, in North India. His principles of socialism, nationalism, non-violence, and equality were the pillar of his kingship. The duties he performed towards his subjects and the concept of his kingdom made him centurial man. The aim of this research article is to gain understanding about life history and principles of Maharaja Agrasen. This research article is about only Maharaja Agrasen's life history and principles. A thorough academic investigation is required to fully understand the Maharaja Agrasen's diverse contribution.

Keywords: Maharaja Agrasen, Life, Socialism, Principles.

1. Associate Professor, Department of Commerce, Indira Gandhi University, Meerpur, Rewari.
2. Research Scholar, Department of Commerce, Indira Gandhi University, Meerpur, Rewari.

Introduction

"In order to live in heaven after death, we shall have to live in heaven before death" -**Maharaja Agrasen**

Maharaja Agrasen is recognised as a model of non-violence and peace-maker, a messenger of non-violence, an example of selflessness, a great socialist and an advocate of empathy. Indian government issued postage stamp in the honour of iconic personality Maharaja Agrasen. The Aggarwal family has significant contribution throughout the history. In both pre-modern and modern eras, Aggarwals are grown as prominent mercantile and commercial group and also, contributed in development of Indian economy. In addition to this, they took part in India's war for independence with Lala Lajpat Rai who deserves special consideration in this context.

Life History of Maharaja Agrasen

Maharaja Agrasen was legendary Kshatriya ruler of Pratapnagar. He was born around 5000 years ago in the last stage of Dwapar Yuga in the epic era of Mahabharat. Maharaja Agrasen was the eldest son of king Vallabh and successor of Kush, son of Lord Rama. He belongs to the divine lineage of Sun. It is believed that Maharaja Agrasen was contemporary to Lord Krishna. It is further claimed that he was the senior grandparent of Krishna Vrishni and Balarama, the senior sibling of Shoorsen Vrishni, and a lineal descendant of Maharaja Yayati, ruler of Khandavprastha.

The young prince Agrasen was revered for his empathy, a symbol of non-violence, and a bringer of peace. His followers were satisfied and happy because he never preached discrimination. At a young age, Agrasen married Princess Madhavi, daughter of King Nagaraj Kumud. Princess Madhavi was a Naagvanshi (from the family of the Naaga) and King Agrasen was a Suryavanshi (from the Surya family), hence their marriage was a mingling of distinct cultures. Till now Aggrawals worship snakes as they believed that snakes are from their maternal background. Hindu mythology states that Indra, king of Devas, also wanted to marry the princess. As the princess chose King Agrasen, Indra got annoyed of him and decided to took revenge. He made sure that Agrasen's state wouldn't get any rainfall. When the situation got worst in Pratapnagar, Agrasen wage a war against King Indra. Agrasen's strength and bravery can be gauged by the fact that Indra approached Sage Narada to mediate peace between them. As per the suggestion of Maharishi (sometimes called Maharshi) Garg, he also wed Sudaravati for prosperous and health. According to some people, he was married to 17 Naga Kanyas.

Birth of Agroha City

The misery of his compatriots during the battle touched Agrasen. Maharaja Agrasen initiated a severe penance in Kashi to appease Lord Shiva after becoming aware of the state of his kingdom. When Lord Shiva saw strong devotion of Agrasen, he was pleased and advised him that he should worship the goddess Mahalaxmi in order to regain the wealth of his realm. For the blessings of Maa Mahalaxmi, Maharaja Agrasen once more started penance. Pleased with penance of Agrasen, Mahalaxmi appeared to blessed him and advised him that in order to ensure the prosperity of his subjects, he should abandon his Kshatriya tradition and adopt the Vaishya tradition of trade. She persuaded him to establish a new empire and made a prosperity-bestowing vow to him and his lineage. Maharaja Agrasen followed Mahalaxmi's word and opted Vaishya tradition. With the blessings of Goddess Mahalaxmi, in order to choose a location for a new empire, Agrasen wandered throughout India with his queen. At one point during this wondering, they found a few tiger cubs and wolf cubs playing together. They found it an auspicious indication that area was Veer Bhoomi i.e., a land of braves and decided to choose that area for their new kingdom. They named that location as 'Agreya'. Later the name Agreya got famous as Agroha. Under the kingship of Agrasen, Agroha became very prosperous as agriculture and trade flourished with the blessing of Mahalaxmi. Agroha were the habitat of hundred thousand of businessmen and traders in its heydays. The evidences, like bricks having human heads design, Yudheya and coins, sculptures, terracotta seals, found by archaeological at the place of Agroha proved that this city is older than third century BC. Many hearts that ignited into jealousy were drawn to the Agroha empire and prosperity of its population.

Principles of Maharaja Agrasen

Maharaja Agrasen was a doer (a Karm yogi) who conjured

prosperity for all. He was an effective leader who founded his kingdom on the ideals of nonviolence, socialism, equality, and nationalism. He was a supporter of socialism and came up with a novel law to guarantee an equitable society system. Each city resident was required to provide "One Rupee and One Brick" to either a community man who was insolvent or an immigrant who wanted to live in the city. This would leave him with 100,000 rupees to establish a new business and 100,000 bricks to construct a home for himself. As a result, nobody was jobless under his tenure, and each individual had their own home. This is the best possible illustration of the socialism of humanity practical idea. These ideas were put into practise in his realm where everyone lived on the give-and-take philosophy. Neither the receiver felt ashamed nor the donator felt proud. The core of the idea was a sense of brotherhood and social welfare. In the kingdom, there was no room for dishonesty or self-interest. The foundation of the prosperity of the empire and people's live entirely depend on dairy, agriculture, and trade.

Maharaja Agrasen used to execute numerous Yagnas for the well-being of the populace of his kingdom. In those days, the Yagna performance was viewed as a sign of prosperity. He adopted the nonviolent ideal while participating in the 18th Yagna and came to understand the pointlessness of animal sacrifices. In his words,

"Instead of targeting a crane with an arrow,
I wish to see it flying;
Instead of eating away a nightingale,
I wish to hear it singing"

He then declared that all animal sacrifices were forbidden. The result was that Maharaja Agrasen had only accomplished seventeen and a half yagnas and the eighteenth yagna was never completed. He got seventeen and a half gotras from the Sage Garga. He named the 18 Gotras after the respective Gurus of his children. These 18 Gotras and the eighteen chapters of Bhagavad Gita are analogous. Despite their differences, they are nevertheless interconnected and contribute to the formation of the whole. His commitment to nonviolence did not entail a lack of resistance to injustice; rather, he advocated for self-defence. He believed that every citizen had a responsibility to defend and preserve their country, and that it was not just the Kshatriyas, the warrior caste, who were responsible for these tasks.

Agroha was established as republic country by Maharaja Agrasen. Maharaja Agrasen split his empire into 18 segments and distributed them among his 18 children. That Gotra became a means of identification for all the citizens of that specific state unit. Maharaja Agrasen upheld the belief that a nuptial union could not occur inside the same Gotra and forbade persons within the same Gotra from intermarrying, a tradition that is still practised today. This rule enacted by Maharaja Agrasen fostered unity and fraternity among all 18 Gotras symbolised by state divisions. This assisted the state units' efforts to promote patriotism and cooperation. Maharaja Agrasen started a new governing system instead of old system of governance. To reorganise his kingdom, he again implemented the beliefs of Vedic Sanatan Arya culture, along with the development of agriculture-trade, industry, cow-rearing, re-establishment of moral values.

Maharaj Agrasen ruled for 108 years. The life values he imbibed shows a balanced harmony of tradition and experiment. On the one hand, he accepted the field of work directed for the Kshatriya varna in the Hindu scriptures and on the other hand he established new ideals in the context of the country. On the suggestion of Mahalakshmi, after reaching a certain age, appointed his eldest son Vibhu to the crown and went to Vanaprastha ashram. Agroha city gradually decayed until being completely destroyed by a massive fire. The Aggrawals, who were Agroha's residents, dispersed across different regions of India.

Honours given to Maharaja Agrasen

- On 24 September 1976, a 25 paise postage stamp was issued by the Government of India in the name of Maharaja Agrasen.
- In 1995, the Government of India purchased a special oil carrier (ship) from South Korea which was named "Maharaja Agrasen".
- The official name of National Highway-10 is at Maharaja Agrasen.

- In Delhi's Hailey Road, close to Connaught Place, is Agrasen ki Baoli. It is a 60 meter long and 25 meter wide stepwell, which is under the supervision of Archaeological Survey of India under the Archaeological Sites and Remains Act 1958.
- In 2012, a postage stamp on India Post Agrasen ki Baoli was issued.

Conclusion

Maharaja Agrasen has become the cultural icon and a representative of Aggarwal heritage. The term "Agrawal" refers to the "Son of Agrasen" since it is made up of the words "Agra," which means "Agrasen," and "wal," which means "balak." Therefore, for his descendants, Agrasen Jayanti is a day of immense significance and they celebrated with enthusiasm and gaiety. The values of Maharaja Agrasen are still followed by his descendants. The current Indian Constitution is based on socialism, non-violence, and equality ideals that Maharaj Agrasen articulated 5000 years ago. Despite the fact that the renowned King Agrasen is no longer physically present, his actions and those of his followers continue to promote harmony, altruism, community service, compassion and devotion.

Bibliography

Agrawal, O. (2016, september). Agradhara. 5 to 7. Shri Agrawal Sabha.

Bansal, K. K. (1992). Virta Ki Virasat, वीरता की विरासत. Hisar: Agroha Vikas Trust.

Gupta, S. K. (2019). *Maharaja Agrasen: A Brief History of Agradescent.* Gyan Book Pvt Ltd.

http://agarwalglobalfoundation.com/History-maharaj-agrase.aspx

http://agrohasheelamatamandir.com/introduction&agroha&maharaja-agrasen.html

https://en.wikipedia.org/wiki/Agrasen

https://mamc.edu.in/about-maharaja-agrasen/

https://www.amarujala.com/columns/blog/maharaja-agrasen-jayanti-2020-date-biography-in-hindi?pageId=1

https://www.dailypioneer.com/2017/state-editions/people-still-carry-out-maharaja-agrasens-ideals.html

https://www.snehpost.com/2019/09/agrasen.html

Mittal, J.P. (2006), *History of Ancient India (4250 BC to 637 AD)* page 675, ISBN 978-81-269-0616-1

SECTION-B

14

Start-Up Movements in India

Sarika Walia[1], Taruna Sharma[2], Shivani Arora[3], C.S.Yadav[4]

Abstract

The millennial generation is entering the third decade of the new millennium and moving into their most productive time of life. We have seen a number of outstanding millennial business leaders, such Mark Zuckerberg, the creator and CEO of Facebook. The global economy is rapidly changing and offering unique business chances to millennial everywhere. India has the second-highest population density in the world, with 1.2 billion people. So, there is a great opportunity for industry to support this massive population. But as per Asia Pacific Human Development Report, our country is experiencing scarcity of venture capital markets as well as a rise in youth unemployment. As a result, indian government initiated the "Start Up India" programme to assist those who want to start their own business. The government will help these people because they have ideas and the capacity to carry them out and develop. "Start up India Initiative", initiated on January 16, 2016, has introduced many programmes in order to assist entrepreneurs, creating a robust start up environment and transforming India into a nation that values job creation over job seeking. Over

1. Assistant Professor, Department of Management Studies, Gurugram University, Gurugram.
2. Research Scholar, University of Engineering and Technology Roorkee, Haridwar, Uttarakhand.
3. Assistant Professor, PDP Department, Graphic Era Hill University, Dehradun, Uttarakhand.
4. Professor, Shivalik Institute of Professional Studies, Dehradun, Uttarakhand.

80,000 start-ups have been created in the nation as a result of the start-up movement, which were about 350 before 2014. This chapter focuses on the numerous government initiatives and policies for start-ups and how they have affected India's development. It also comprehends, many challenges that start-ups face. It has also the mention of the opportunities given to start-ups through the Start-up India programme along with the current scenario of start-ups in India.

Introduction

Maharaja Agrasen, the renowned ruler of Agroha, was a recognised and esteemed emperor who was highly regarded by the residents of his empire. Maharaja Agrasen invoked prosperity for all. He created a novel law as a supporter of socialism to guarantee a democratic society. He issued a proclamation mandating that every Agroha resident contribute one rupee and one brick, to anyone moving to the city with the intention of making a permanent home there. With the bricks, he could construct a home for himself, and with the money he had accumulated, he could launch his own enterprise. A person could achieve equality in the community in this manner. We continue to uphold these beliefs that Agrasen Maharaj preached. The term "Agrawal" refers to the "Son of Agrasen" since it is made up of the words "Agra," which means "Agrasen," and "wal," which means "balak," or "son." As a result, his descendants attach enormous importance to Agrasen Jayanti. According to a tradition, Lord Shiva urged Maharaja Agrasen to perform Tapasya (austerities) in honour of Goddess Lakshmi. Goddess Lakshmi arrived in response to Maharaja Agrasen's devotion and advised him to setup a business in order to bring fortune to his people. Since then, the people who make up the Agrahari and Agrawal groups have been conducting business while praying to the goddess Lakshmi and the king who is thought to be the community's founder.

Therefore, Maharaja Agrasen had paved a path to be followed by entrepreneurs and start up organisations. A start-up is basically a small, recently founded business that takes the form of a partnership, small venture, or small organisation with the goal of rapidly expanding a new model of business. In other words, a startup is a fresh, young company that aims to take a proactive approach to develop a revenue-generating business model. Building a prototype known as a Minimum Viable Product (MVP) is typically the first step in developing a new endeavour. Startup has played a vital part in the expansion, modernisation, and industrialisation of many economies throughout the world and will likely continue to do so. The Indian government wants to foster innovation by building a strong environment for it. It will encourage long-term economic growth, generate employment opportunities, and decrease unemployment.

Start-ups concentrate on developing new items or new procedures for the entire market or a particular market sector. They must not be mistaken with small businesses because innovation marks their primary distinction. Prime Minister Narendra Modi introduced "Stand up India" on August 15, 2015, an initiative to aid start-ups and encourage entrepreneurship in India in order to create job possibilities throughout the nation. India ranks third among the world's start-up ecosystems in a report released in October 2015 by the National Association of Software and Services Companies (NASSCOM), just after the United States and the United Kingdom. In order to assist aspiring entrepreneurs, Nirmala Sitharaman, the head of the Commerce and Industry Ministry, has requested that Start-up hubs and incubators will be established in all of the states and Union Territories. In order to promote the start-up drive, the DIPP also suggests asking leading corporations to establish brand-new incubators or expand already existing incubators in partnership with educational institutions. The initiatives have been welcomed across the nation with open arms, and as a result, several state governments have begun making comparable efforts. The outcomes are highly satisfying. The fundamental essence of start-ups in India is technology-based, and young IIT graduates are the main drivers of these businesses. These businesses are launched in quite unusual industries like the medical sector etc. India is fortunate to have a young population, which is crucial for starting up businesses. The increased propensity for "having something of my own" mindset, is also assisting in the successful implementation of new concepts. Some of the top start-ups in the world, serving as a beacon for the others, had their origins in India.

Research Methodology

This study focuses solely on secondary material that was obtained from a variety of sources, including official websites, Google Scholar, online databases, books and journals.

Significance of Start-ups

- To explore eco-system of the start-ups and the drivers.
- To understand the benefits that the Indian government offers to new start-ups.
- To know the opportunities provided to start ups through "The Start-up India initiative".
- To assess the challenges that new businesses encounter.
- To comprehend the current state of start-ups in India.

Review of Literature

Sujata Chincholkar, M.D. (2021). Many start-ups have significant obstacles during the scaling up stage, according to research published in a study titled "Bottleneck to success: scaling up issues of start-ups." Her qualitative research explores the difficulties that the start-up businesses face as they grow. The findings indicate that some of the biggest obstacles faced by start-ups when building a model for scaling up are lack of financial resources, finding the proper talent and product approval.

Indian start-ups - difficulties, challenges, and prospects is the title of a study about start ups written by Dr. Walter D'souza in 2021. The article explored some of the difficulties and opportunities that an Indian start-ups confront in the current economic climate.

Arana Kausar and Md. Aziz Ahmed (2020) discussed financial deficiencies, the lack of market demand for goods or services and came to the conclusion that there is a significant need for financial literacy among business owners in their article titled "Case studies of failure of start-ups in India due to financial illiteracy." Lack of financial knowledge will deter inventors and increase the risk of business failure. The potential returns of any investment must be evaluated because having this understanding of financial management is crucial. Sustainable start-ups are essential for the development of better products and new jobs necessary for economic growth.

Deepashree Chatterjee (2020) discussed in his "Launch India" document about the several operational strategies and activities that the administration has launched through the Start-up India scheme. The study assesses the effectiveness of India's Start-up programme in promoting entrepreneurship and boosting the nation's GDP.

Institute for Business Value (2018) states that India is experiencing a surge of young entrepreneurs and start-ups, yet more than 90 percent of these businesses fail. The primary causes of this high failure rate include a lack of creativity, a shortage of competent labour and inadequate capital.

Theoretical Concept of Start-ups

Start-up is defined- According to Investopedia, "A start-up is a company that is in the first stage of its operations. These companies are often initially bankrolled by their entrepreneurial founders as they attempt to capitalise on developing a product or service for which they believe there is a demand. Due to limited revenue or high costs, most of these small-scale operations are not sustainable in the long term without additional funding from venture capitalists."According to Merriam-Webster, Start-up means "The act or an instance of setting in operation or motion" or "a fledgling business enterprise." The American Heritage Dictionary suggests "A business or undertaking that has recently begun operations."

The Ministry of Commerce and Industries' Department of Industrial Policy and Promotion (DIPP) has developed the following standards for what qualifies as a start-up:

- A company that has been registered as a limited liability partnership, a partnership firm, or a private limited company.
- In any of the previous financial years, turnover should have been below INR 100 crores.
- The start-up should be attempting to develop unique ideas or enhance currently available goods, services, and procedures, and it should have the potential to generate income or jobs.

- For a tenure of 10 years after the date of its establishment, an entity is regarded as a start-up. An organisation created through the division or reconstruction of an existing company is not regarded as a "Start-up."

Characteristics of Start-Ups

Start-ups differ from other pre-existing business enterprises in terms of their qualities and characteristics. They have very little room for organisational formalities or customs because these are very dynamic and peculiarly organised enterprises. The following is a further analysis to determine the distinctiveness of start-ups:

- **Innovation** - The fundamental characteristic of start-ups is that they are the most creative in terms of how they serve the market and their clients. The amount of innovation supported by start-ups is higher than that of any other entity, which causes disruption.
- **Company/entity/enterprise sizes:** Start-ups are often tiny, employing no more than 30–50 individuals. Their operations are similarly quite small in scope, though they have potential expand depending on demand and other considerations.
- **Structure of the organisation** - With highly flat, non-hierarchy based organisation, founders collaborate closely with the team members and treat them more like collaborators than as workers. Workers also feel associated with the company and contribute their best to the organisation.
- **Fast Expansion** - Due to the highly innovative and novel products and services being supplied to customers and the market, start-ups tend to develop quickly in terms of revenue and market share.
- **Alternative sources of funding** - By their very nature, start-ups are supported by alternative sources rather than traditional sources like financial organisations and banks. They are mostly supported by private investors, venture capitalists, angel investors, and business finance organisations (Softbank etc.).
- **Risk and uncertainty**- Start-ups deal with the unique products and services and are typically quite innovative.

More innovation brings with it more dangers and ambiguities. The most crucial characteristic of start-ups is that they are extremely unpredictable due to the market offerings, which are presented in a unique manner.

- **Initial focus on a single product or service** - New businesses initially concentrate on a single product or set of services for the target market. They are intensely focused on their product offers. They initially just promote a single product or service but may eventually add different variations.
- **Availability of resources**- Contrary to popular opinion, start-ups do not have a lot of reverse resources available to them. They frequently struggle and fail in their efforts to recruit funding. When people become aware of their presence or product, only then do they receive crucial resources. It is extremely rare for businesses and other commercial entities.
- **Overall environment**- The culture and environment in start-ups are quite distinctive and alive. Typically, the average age of employees in start-ups is very less. It contributes to a less bureaucratic and more productive workplace, which encourages people to be their best selves.
- **Flexibility**- One of the most crucial traits of start-ups is their high degree of flexibility and responsiveness to market developments. It is simple to implement the needed adjustments to combat changes that arise as a result of specific occurrences owing to their size of organisation and product line.

Drivers and Eco System for Start-Ups

The development and survival of start-ups in a country or region will be substantially hampered if that country/region fails to supply the usual eco system setup. Start-ups need government backing for policies and idea protection more than they do cash and infrastructure. Bill Gross, founder of Idealab, specifically listed five elements that are essential for any start-up's success: Ideas, Team, Business Model, Funding, and Timing.

- **Idea** - The most important factor in creating a successful start-up is an idea. Idea generation is a creative process where intangible thoughts gets converted into tangible business ideas.

- **Team** - Ideas are the most important aspect of building a successful start-up. Ideas come into existence only after the team of people chosen to execute it. So no one can achieve success individually. Collaborative efforts lead to better outcomes.
- **Business Model** - A successful business model can't generates millions of dollars in revenue until the theory is proven. The choice of a start-up's business model determines whether it will succeed or fail.
- **Funding** - Funding is an important aspect for the success of any start-up. A start-up needs enough funds to keep can grow your business organically. A company may experience fake growth if too much money is invested in it too soon. However, the best approach towards progress is through organic growth, which requires investing the amount of money necessary in the circumstances.
- **Timing** - We are all aware of how important it is to be at the right place at the right time. That holds true in technology even more so. The success of new technologies as they integrate into the innovation landscape depends on their capacity to be understood by a large audience, to be required for the expansion of other firms, and to be prepared for adoption.

Financial Life-Cycle of A Start –Up

Depending upon the stage and purpose of a start-up, broadly three kinds of funding are available to them.

- Angel and seed funding
- Venture capital
- Public markets
    - **Seed or Angel funding** - Early-stage businesses depend on seed money and angel investors. Such funding is only available to the entrepreneurs with great ideas. It doesn't really impose any corporate governance requirements on the entrepreneur.

- **Investment Capital** - It is used to scale the business model of the company. It is funded by larger institutional sources. Building the sales team and having a global presence are the main priorities.
- **Public Markets** - Start-ups may feel the need to actively reinvent their products or expand more aggressively at their later stage. They receive a lot of liquidity from private equity investors and public marketplaces.

Start-Up India Scheme

An innovative programme called Start-up India was established to support those who desire to launch their own businesses. These people are capable and have ideas. Therefore, the government will encourage them so that they can implement and develop their vision. On January 16th, 2016 in New Delhi, the "Start-up India" programme was initiated by the government of India.

Advantages of the Start-up India Plan

The following advantages are available to firms selected by DPIIT through the Start-up India Initiative.

- Self-Certification
- Start-up Patent Application and IPR
- Tax Exemption under 80IAC
- Section 56 Exemption
- Easy winding up of Company
- Easier Public Procurement Norms

Self-Certification

Its goal is to minimize start-ups' regulatory load so they may concentrate on their core businesses and keep compliance expenses down.

Benefits

- Start-ups are allowed to use a simple online approach to self-certify compliance with three environmental regulations and six labour rules.

- There won't be any assessments in the area of labour legislation for a period of five years. Start-ups can only be reviewed if a credible, verified allegation of a violation is received in writing and is approved by one level above person to the inspecting officer.
- For environmental regulations, businesses that fit into the "white category" (as the Central Pollution Control Board (CPCB) defines it) would be permitted to self-certify their compliance.

Registration Process

- Visit the Ministry of Labour and Employment's Shram Suvidha Portal and select the Startup Scheme tab.
- Sign up for a Shram Suvidha Portal account before logging in.
- Select the link "Is Any of your Establishment a Start-up?" after successfully logging in and then, adhere to the guidelines.

Intellectual Property Rights and New Patent Applications (IPR)

For their survival, startups rely on innovation. It makes sense that patenting your invention will increase the value of both your company and your goods. Patents are a tool to protect original concepts that give your company a competitive edge. But historically, getting a patent has been a costly and time-consuming process that many start-ups may find difficult. The objective is to reduce the cost and time necessary for a start-up to secure a patent in order to make it financially possible for them to protect their inventions and to encourage them to continue to innovate.

Benefits

- The speedy tracking of start-up patent applications.
- A panel of "organisers" must be elected by the Controller General of Patents, Designs, and Trademarks (CGPDTM), who will also supervise their work. The coordinators are responsible for providing general guidance on different types

of intellectual property and for protecting and marketing intellectual property in other countries.

- The Central Government will pay organiser fees for all the patents, trademarks, or designs and the start-up companies are only responsible for covering the appropriate legal costs.
- Start-ups will get 80 percent of their patent filing fees back.

Eligibility: The start-up must be recognised by DPIIT.

Registration Procedure: For the most recent information regarding the procedure and paperwork needed for a patent or trademark application, you should get in contact with an appropriate helper, based on your preferred industry and the jurisdiction of the facilitator.

Benefits of Tax Exemption under 80IAC:-

Eligible start-ups are free from paying income tax for three consecutive financial years out of the first ten years following their incorporation.

Eligibility

The start up must be a DPIIT-accepted business and must have been founded after April 1, 2016. Under Section 80IAC, only private limited businesses or limited liability partnerships are qualified for a tax break.

Registration

After registering on the Start-up India portal by clicking the "Register" tab, apply for DPIIT (Department for Industrial Policy and Promotion) recognition.

Documents Required for Registration:

- Memorandum of Association for Pvt. Ltd./LLP Deed
- The start-up's annual statement of accounts for the past three financial years
- Board resolutions
- Income tax returns (ITR) for the last three financial years.

Benefits of Section 56 Exemption

According to Section 56(2)(VIIB) of the Income Tax Act, investments made into qualified start-ups by listed organisations with a net worth greater than INR 100 crore or a revenue greater than INR 250 crore are exempt. This clause also exempts accredited investors, non-residents, AIFs (Category I), and listed organisations with a net worth or income of more than INR 250 crore from paying taxes on investments made into qualifying start-ups.

Eligibility

- A start-up must be recognised by DPIIT and be a private limited entity.
- You can obtain DPIIT recognition by clicking "Get Recognised" on the website startupindia.gov.in.
- Start up company must avoid investments in certain asset classes except in the regular course of business. They should refrain from investing in real estate, motor vehicles costing more than INR 10 lakh.

Registration Process:

- Get DPIIT Recognition by registering your start-up profile on the Start-up India Portal.
- Fill out the Section 56 Exemption Application Form.
- Within three days of submitting the declaration, CBDT should send you an email.

Easy Company Winding Up

Its objective is to make it easier for start-ups to shut down their operations, enabling owners to quickly allocate capital and resources to a variety of lucrative avenues. It will further encourage the owners to test out innovative and creative ideas without having to deal with challenging and drawn-out exit procedures where their capital would get stuck indefinitely in the event of a company failure.

Benefits

- According to the Insolvency and Bankruptcy Code of 2016,

start-ups with straightforward debt arrangements or those meeting particular income requirements must be shut down ninety days after filing an application for insolvency.

- A start-up must select an insolvency expert who will thereafter be in charge of operating the business (promoters and management are no longer in charge), as well as liquidating its assets and paying its creditors within six months of the appointment.
- After the insolvency the liquidator is appointed, closing the company quickly, selling off assets and paying creditors in accordance with the IBC's distribution waterfall.

Simpler Criteria for Public Procurement

The process by which the federal, state, local, and state-owned firms purchase products and services from the private sector is known as public procurement. Government organisations may provide a sizable market for start-ups due to their higher disposable income. The objective is to make it easier for enterprises to take part in public procurement processes and get access to a new market for their products and services.

Opportunities Made Available to Startups Through the Startup India Programme

The Start-up India programme offers a variety of possibilities to start-ups, including:-

- **Self-Certification for Entrepreneurs:** Start-up India's major goal is to empower start ups to concentrate on their core businesses by lessening their regulatory load and minimizing compliance costs. It can take a lot of time and effort to complete certain regulatory procedures that must be followed in order to comply with a variety of labour and environmental laws. Therefore, start ups will be able to self-certify compliance with nine labour and environmental laws using the start-up mobile app, simplifying the inspection process.
- **Tax Exemption on Investments Above Fair Market Value:** In the case of new businesses, while the concept is still in its infancy, determining the Fair Market Value of such

shares may be difficult. The Income Tax Act of 1961 states that any excess payment made to a startup company for issuing shares over the Fair Market Value (FMV) of those shares is taxable income. Currently, incubator investments are tax-exempt, and this exemption will also apply to venture capital investments made in start-ups.

- Organisation of Start-up Fests: To encourage the growth of start-ups in India, the government plans to create Start-up Fests on a national and worldwide scale. Such events would provide Indian start-ups the chance to showcase their creative thinking and hard work to a wide audience, which would include prospective investors, mentors, and other start-ups.

Exemption from Capital Gains Tax: Using capital gains from the sale of capital assets, the government hopes to promote investments in start-ups. To do this, anyone who make capital gains during the year are exempt if they put those gains in the Fund of Funds that the government has recognised.

Tax Exemption for three Years: The earnings of start-up initiatives shall be exempt from income tax for a period of three years in order to promote the expansion of start-ups in India. A similar exemption will encourage company growth across a range of industries and help business owners get the working capital they need.

New Research Parks being Set up: The government is constructing seven new research parks at the following institutions: IIT Hyderabad, IIT Guwahati, IIT Kanpur, IIT Bangalore, IIT Gandhinagar, IIT Kharagpur and IIT Delhi, each with an initial expenditure of INR 100 crore. These research parks will be built on the model of the research park already created by IIT Madras.

- **Promotion of Start-ups in the Biotechnology Sector:** Along with its Public Sector Undertaking, the Department of Biotechnology will put policies in place to promote start-ups in the industry, such as the creation of the Biotechnology Research Assistance Council (BIRAC), Bio-incubators, Seed Fund, Equity Funding, and other similar initiatives.
- **Atal Innovation Mission:** In order to encourage start-ups to develop creative ideas, the Atal Innovation Mission (AIM),

which is a component of the Start-up India programme, will have two main objectives. These objectives include promoting entrepreneurship through Self- Employment and Talent Utilisation (SETU) and innovation.

- **Establishment of Innovation Centres at National Institutes:** To boost the country's efforts in research and development, the government wants to construct 31 centres of innovation and entrepreneurship at national institutes, including 13 start-up centres and 18 technological company incubators.
- **Innovation centric programmes for students:** The government will put into effect programmes like the Innovation Core Programme, which is intended for schoolchildren, the National Initiative for Developing and Harnessing Innovations, which will grant INR 10 lakhs to 20 student innovations, and the Uchhattar Avishkar Yojana, which will support IIT students conducting extremely high-quality research.
- **World Class Incubators:** To invest in the development of world-class incubators, the government will identify and choose 10 incubators that have the ability to accomplish so. These incubators will act as the industry standard for others that are created with the goal of offering best-in-class services.

Indian Government's Initiatives for Start-Ups

The Indian government is currently making many efforts to foster the growth of start-ups. It has introduced some programmes that are overseen by distinct departments and different ministries.

Table 1: Government Schemes under the start up India initiative

Name of the Scheme	Headed By	Industry Applicable	Fiscal Incentive
Support for International Patent Protection in Electronics & Information Technology (SIP-EIT)	Department of Electronics and Information Technology (DEITY)	IT services, analytics, business software, tech gear, the Internet of Things, and artificial intelligence	For each creation, up to INR 15 Lakhs or half of the total costs associated with handling and recording the patent application whichever is lower.

MSME Market Development Assistance	Office of the Development Commissioner (MSME)	All Sectors	The programme provides funding up to 90% of the cost of round-trip air travel for MSME entrepreneurs attending international trade missions or fairs. It also offers money for MSMEs and associations to produce publicity materials (up to 25% of costs), conduct sector-specific studies (up to ₹ 2 lakhs), and contest anti-dumping cases(50% up to ₹ 1 lakh).
Coir Udyami Yojana	Coir Board	Agriculture	This credit-linked subsidy programme isfor the construction of coir units with a maximum project cost of ₹ 10 lakhs plus one cycle of working capital, which cannot be more than 25% of the project cost.
Raw Material Assistance	National Small Industries Corporation (NSIC)	All Sectors	In order to assist MSMEs, this Scheme finances the acquisition of raw materials (both indigenous & imported) so that MSMEs can concentrate more on producing high-quality goods.
Bank Credit Facilitation Scheme	National Small Industries Corporation (NSIC)	All Sectors	This scheme assists MSMEs in filling outloan applications, gathering necessary documentation, and submitting those to banks. It assists MSMEs in obtaining competitive interest rates from banks.
Software Technology Park (STP) Scheme	Software Technology Parks of India (STPI)	IT services, fintech, enterprise software, analytics, AI	Foreign equity may be held at 100%. Hardware and software importsinto STP units are totally duty-free and import of second hand capital goods is also permitted. Capital products may also be re-exported .

Pradhan Mantri Mudra Yojana (PMMY)	Micro Units Development and Refinance AgencyLtd. (MUDRA)	All Sectors	Loans in the PMMY are offered in one of three categories: Up to ₹ 50,000 Shishu Between ₹ 50,000 and ₹ 5,00,000 Kishor Between ₹ 5 lakhs and 10 lakhs forTarun
Credit Guarantee Trust Fund	Small Industries Development Bankof India (SIDBI) and Ministry of Micro, Small and Medium Enterprises	Retailers, self-help groups, educational institutes, SMEs, and farmers.	It primarily caters to manufacturing and service-related enterprises. Both working capital or term loans may be claimed under this programme upto 1crore.
Venture Capital Assistance Scheme	Ministry of agriculture and farmers welfare	Agriculturalsector	Entrepreneurs in the agriculture sector are eligible for interest-free debt and overdrafts to cover up their working capital needs under this programme.

Source: Start-up India website.

Major Challenges Faced By Entrepreneurs

- **Striking a Work-Life Balance:** Finding enough time and energy for your personal life is one of the main problems of running a startup. While it is true that there is a direct link between the number of hours worked and income development, taking care of your physical and mental health will benefit you in the long term on both a personal and professional level.
- **Obtaining finance without losing focus on your product:** Typically, identifying a genuine issue and developing a workable solution could be accomplished within a budget. However, as you begin developing your product and growing your firm, you'll discover that you need money because most projects are too labour-intensive for you to manage alone and you'll need money to pay employees.

- **Intense competition:** The business world is quite competitive. One of the major obstacles to the survival of new firms is competition. And the competition becomes more difficult if you are just starting an online business. Since there is no room for error, the competitive atmosphere keeps start-ups on their toes. Businesses engaged in both B2B and B2C transactions frequently experience the heat of intense competition. Start-ups need to play aggressively and punch above their weight to obtain the much-needed prominence among the groups of ever-challenging and developing firms if they want to thrive in this cut throat business environment, which includes both traditional and online businesses.
- **Financial Management:** Financial management is one of the greatest problems that start ups nowadays have to deal with. Small businesses, especially start ups, can struggle to properly manage their finances during periods of surges of cash. They have to rely on investors. In order to manage financial difficulties, consulting with a reputable financial consultation organisation can be quite helpful.
- **Social Pressure:** As an entrepreneur you won't have many people with whom to share ideas or get advice. People would make fun of you, which is very depressing.
- **Human Talent:** It is exceedingly challenging to hire somebody to work for a company during the early stages of business setup. Due to their financial situation and lack of access to appropriate funding sources, they are unable to pay the employees they have hired to work for them. As a result, people either try to do it themselves or discover a solution.
- **The Poor Educational System and the Conservative Style of Living:** Indian education is structured in a way that gives students greater theoretical knowledge but little practical experience. This ultimately serves as a barrier to any student who wishes to launch their business. Additionally, they do not acquire understanding of every aspect of the organisation, including management, finance, accounting, technology, sales, and marketing.
- **Decelerators:** One of the biggest obstacles is the influence of outside organisations that want to manage, control, or

profit from their occasions, audiences, or brands under the cover of mentorship. The majority of cutting-edge, quickly expanding businesses that began turning a profit at a young age were independent and were never nurtured or mentored. Although the growth might have started off more slowly, it gives better consistency and long-term financial benefits. In order for the start up to grow faster, influence from outside organisations and entities must be reduced.

- **Risk Management:** Risk can arise everywhere for a start-up. Be it client or customer preferences, market orientation, competition, economic changes and so on. In order to face this, we should just confront these risks, reduce their effects on the business, prioritize them and adjust to the changing environment. There is no sugar coating on the start up even after they overcome these challenges. Start ups face challenges on a daily basis. The biggest challenge with start ups in the twenty-first century is the fear of embracing failure. It is important to dream, have the ambition and vision to set the bars high to enter a whole new world of startups that will drive strengths, diversity and intensify the economy of the country.
- **Cyber Security:** Small companies, particularly those operating online, must be extremely quick to combat the so-called dangers to online security if they are to survive the rigours of this period. Hackers are omnipresent, and they will exploit any security flaw in a new company's computer systems.

List of India's Top Start-Ups Till 2022

Table 2: India's Top 25 start –ups listed by LinkedIn

Sr. No.	Name of the company	Headquarters	Year	Deals in
1.	CRED Financial Company	Bengluru	2018	It is a credit card rewards app for members that has become well-known for its amusing advertisements.
2.	UP Grad	Mumbai	2015	It offers professionals and college students the chance to advance their skills while they are employed.

3.	Groww	Bengluru	2016	This online investment platform offersan accurate evaluation of numerous stock and mutual fund investment options.
4.	Zepto	Mumbai	2021	With a wide selection of groceries, dairy products and more, Zepto delivers orders within 10 minutes.
5.	Skyroot Aerospace	Hyderabad	2018	It develops technologies for quick, dependable, and affordable access to space.
6.	MBA chai wala	Ahmedabad	2016	Due to the unusual beginnings of its creator, this network of tea-serving cafes became well-known.
7.	Spinny	Gurugram	2015	It is a pre-owned vehicle marketplace that promises to make the buying and selling of vehicles transparent and easy.
8.	The Good Glamm Group	Pune	2017	This content-to-commerce platform promotes and helps with the sales of numerous sustainable cosmetic and personal care businesses through the use of social media.
9.	GrowthSchool	Bengluru	2021	This online learning environment strives to advance users' personal and professional development.
10.	BluSmart	Gurugram	2019	With a fleet of more than 2,000 electric vehicles, this all-electric taxi service provides consumers with a cleaner, more sustainable means of transportation.
11.	ShareChat	Bengluru	2015	It is a social media startup with Share Chat App and Moj having more than 400 million active users each month.
12.	ditto	Bengluru	2018	It offers information and guidance to people who wishes to buy insurance.
13.	simpl	Bengluru	2015	With its mobile-first platform, this purchase now, pay later software seeks to give customers and merchants more control over their online shopping experience.
14.	Rapido	Bengluru	2015	It is a doorstep pickup bike- taxi service.
15.	classplus	Noida	2018	It offers private coaching organisations, a centralised platform to coordinate and connect with students, and monetize courses through their very own super applications.

16.	Park+	Gurugram	2019	This programme provides for the daily requirements of automobile owners, including parking, Fastag management, auto insurance, and more
17.	Blissclub	Bengluru	2020	With technical clothing made to fit the needs of various body types, this firm specialises in active wear for women in India.
18.	Dealshare	Bengluru	2018	It is an e-commerce platform that supplies home groceries to your doorstep
19.	Ultrahuman	Bengluru	2019	With the use of glucose biomarkers and experts, it is a fitness platform that assists users in monitoring and improving their food and physical activities.
20.	Livingfood	Bengluru	2018	It offers a variety of freshly created locally sourced organic products in packaging that is recyclable or compostable.
21.	Fampay	Bengluru	2019	It promises to make the generation's switch from cash to digital payments secure and seamless by enabling teens to make online and offline payments without a bank account.
22.	AgnikulCosmos	Chennai	2017	It creates, produces, tests, and launches rockets with sufficient thrust to send nano- and microsatellites into Earth's orbit.
23.	Stanza Living	Gurugram	2017	With amenities like internet, laundry, housekeeping, and even meals, it provides people with co-living services in fully equipped flats.
24.	Pocket FM	Bengluru	2018	With this audio streaming app, you may listen to podcasts and tales from a variety of genres.
25.	Zypp Electric	Gurugram	2017	With their fleet of electric scooters, this distribution approach to multiple e- commerce enterprises is sustainable.

Sector-Specific Distribution of New Businesses in India

Through 2022, the corporate technology industry had the highest start-up percentage (15%). About 50 percent of India's new start-ups come from the top five categories, which include retail, educational, financial, and health technologies. The edtech sector acquired six percent, logistics got five percent, and real estate, travel, and healthtech as a whole obtained eight percent of the total Indian start ups.

Current Scenario of Startups in India

Over the past six years, start-ups have experienced a spectacular growth in India. Over 14,000 new recognised companies will exist by 2021–2022, up from just 733 in 2016–17. According to the study, India currently has the third-largest start-up environment in the world, behind the US and China. India is also experiencing a higher CAGR (compound annual growth rate) in venture capital inflow than China. From 2014 to 2021, investments in Indian start-ups grew at a CAGR of 49 percent, compared to a 12 percent CAGR in China. Strong government backing and coordinated efforts from all ecosystem actors helped the Indian start-up ecosystem to emerge. India would become the nation with the second- largest start ups by 2025 due to this synergy.

- According to a report, the value of artificial intelligence start-ups climbed from $ 20 million in printing market will increase by a compound annual growth rate of 23.2 percent to $34.8 billion by 2024. With a constant annual growth rate (CAGR) of 14.41 percent from 2020 to 2025, the size of the industrial robots market in India is projected to rise from 5,000 units in 2019 to 11,760 units by 2025. In the next five decades, it is anticipated that IOT will account for up to 20 percent of the global IOT market.
- The NASSCOM Enterprise CXO Survey 2022 finds that 60 percent of CXOs anticipate spending six percent more on technology in 2022 than in 2021, with an emphasis on customer service, supply chain, and sales and marketing. With around 30 percent of respondents planning to extend their technology team by over 15 percent, end-user businesses are emerging as job creators in the technology industry.
- India had 107 unicorn start-ups, or companies valued at $1 billion or more, as of September 7, 2022, with a combined worth of $340.79 billion. Even though there were many “soonicorns” (future unicorns) waiting in line, a record 44 players joined the privileged unicorn club in 2021.

However, the promising Indian start up environment is also facing tremendous hurdles, in part because of the current global socioeconomic reality.

- With only $885 million in funding received in August 2022, Indian entrepreneurs appear to be facing an early winter in contrast to the $4.6 billion in capital they received in January 2022. The third quarter of 2021 saw a $14.8 billion peak in the quarterly funding of Indian start-ups, which has since been progressively dropping. Global macroeconomic developments, particularly the shifting interest rate regimes between 2020 and 2022, are to blame for such a "funding winter". As the epidemic broke out, several central banks, especially the US Federal Reserve, adopted easy monetary policies to maintain the flow of credit in the economy in an effort to curb the worst consequences of the pandemic. In addition to reduce its quantitative easing programme and other measures taken to deal with the pandemic and the ensuing liquidity crunch, the US Fed hiked interest rates four times already in 2022. Foreign investors have pulled $26 billion from domestic markets (particularly equity markets) as a result of this since January 2022, which has caused the rupee to depreciate by roughly seven percent between January and September 2022. To combat inflation, the Reserve Bank of India (RBI) has also increased interest rates three times this year.

Conclusion

Technical entrepreneurs have had the opportunity to showcase their full potential to the world during India's industrial and commercial history. Together, the government and those who develop policy have formed a remarkable intersection. For potential investors and new technical start-ups, it makes the entryway more flexible. Young start-up technopreneurs from India are well-equipped to rule the entire commercial globe. The time is now to change Indian job seekers into Indian job creators. Finally, the story of India's triumph will undoubtedly be reflected in the world economy. We are currently expecting the adversaries' reactions. Even while the potential for start-ups to transform the world is oftentimes overestimated, successful entrepreneurs can have a significant positive impact on the world. Even failing firms continue to have an effect, particularly through the lessons learned for the founders, workers, investors, and other stakeholders. As a result, Indian entrepreneurs and innovators can play a crucial role in fostering national independence. In 2023, more emphasis will be placed on income and growth, with potential layoffs during the funding winter in mind. In India, the number of new start-ups would be limitless in 2023. This will result in an extremely harsh process of elimination for investors when choosing their investments. Although start- ups can enter the fiercely competitive corporate software sector and compete against the established players. In India and other countries, the quick service restaurant (QSR) industry is expanding quickly. By 2026, the size of India's e-commerce market is predicted to be $200 billion, thanks to rising internet usage and the spread of smartphones. Direct-to-consumer firms have a big chance to connect with and do business with customers online. The market for start-up electric vehicles (EVs) is expanding. Technology start-ups are developing new battery systems, charging stations, EV parts, and self-driving systems, among other things. By 2030, it is anticipated that the Indian EV market will generate 50 million indirect jobs in addition to 10 million new direct jobs. India's market for digital health is expanding as a result of the adoption of digital technologies in the healthcare industry. The emergence of telemedicine, the application of AI and ML, personalised medicine, the widespread adoption of wearable and remote monitoring devices, the integration of digital health technology into traditional healthcare systems, and the role of governments are some of the developments that will take place in the future.

References

Anitha, M. (2022). Challenges Faced by Start up Entrepreneurs-A Review Study. *EPRA International Journal of Multidisciplinary Research (IJMR),* 8(4), 188-190.

Ayyappan, P., Jha, B. K., & Rekha, B. J. (2022). *A Descriptive Study on Start-Up India– Progress towards Development and Harnessing Innovation.* Weser Books, 114.

Baporikar, N. (2015). Framework for social change through start ups in India. *International Journal of Civic Engagement and Social Change* (IJCESC), 2(1), 30-42.

Chandiok, S. (2016). India the world's fastest growing startup ecosystem: A Study. *Amity Research Journal of Tourism, Aviation and Hospitality,* 1(2), 84-93.

Chincholkar, S. (2021). Bottleneck to Success: Scaling up Issues of Start-Ups. Sujata Chincholkar (2021), Bottleneck to Success: Scaling up Issues of Start-Ups, *The Journal of Oriental Research Madras,* 2021.

Dwivedi, R. (2019). Indian Startups: Analyzing Their Vulnerabilities &Prevailing Challenges. *SMS Journal of Entrepreneurship & Innovation,* 6(1), 61-79.

Kausar, A.& Ahmad, M. A. (2020, December). A Study on Financial Literacy Creating Sustainable Startups in the Indian Context. In e-journal-First Pan IIT *International Management Conference*–2018.

Malviya, P., & Maurya, N. (2022). Industry 4.0 Opportunity for a Start up (With Special Reference To India). *EPRA International Journal of Economics, Business and Management Studies* (EBMS), 9(3), 16-19.

Paramasivan, C., & Muthusamy, S. (2016). Emerging trends in new start-up technopreneurs. *Journal of Business Management,* 2(7).

Sarkar, A. (2016). Startup India-A New Paradigm for Young Entrepreneurs (A Conceptual Study). Available at SSRN 2835322.

Study. *Amity Research Journal of Tourism, Aviation and Hospitality,* 1(02).

Suresh, B., & Sridevi, K. (2019). A study on issues and challenges of start-ups in India. *Int. J. Finance.* Manag. Econ, 2, 44-48.

Suresh, B., & Sridevi, K. (2019). A study on issues and challenges of startups in India. Int. J. 10. Bindal, M., Gupta, B., & Dubey, S. (2018). Role of startups on Indian economy. *International Journal of Engineering and Management Research* (IJEMR), 8(5), 14211.

Vahoniya, D. R., Halpati, J., Baruri, S., & *Garval, A.* (2022). Start-up India: Eligibility, benefits and current scenario.

https://community.nasscom.in/communities/it-services/growth-indian-tech-startups-fy2022- nasscom-strategic-review-report-2022

https://dpiit.gov.in/

https://economictimes.indiatimes.com/tech/startups/layoffs-to-make-india-startups-more-cash- conservative-growth-focused-in-2023-report

https://inc42.com/reports/the-state-of-indian-startup-ecosystem-report-2022

https://www.cnbc.com/2022/10/03/linkedin-here-are-the-top-25-start-ups-to-work-for-in- india.html

https://www.dailypioneer.com

https://www.india-briefing.com/news/indias-unicorn-startups-sector-distribution-funding- ecosystem-global-comparison-25104.html/

https://www.indiafilings.com/start-up-india?matchtype=p&device=c&campaign

https://www.livemint.com/

https://www.startupindia.gov.in

15

Impact of CSR Activities on Socio-Economic Development

Sonal Gupta[1], Sarla[2]

Abstract

The concept of CSR is implanted with physical and psychological frontiers of the organisation by building ethics, regulations, philanthropy and economy. Every business unit has a natural phenomenon of earning huge profits. The significant goal of an organisation is maximizing returns with minimum investment. A business organisation also has to fulfill social obligations towards the society as they are using the resources from the society only. In India, the concept of CSR emerged from the Vedic period. The corporates should feel motivated by a strong protagonist, Maharaja Agrasen who was spending 25% of his income on the welfare of human beings in society. CSR should be linked with strategic planning, mission and vision of the organisation. Nowadays, government is also taking initiatives for controlling the business activities having a harmful impact on society. The organisations are suggested timely for enacting a structure concerning corporate social responsibility including its activities, areas etc. This study is critically analyzing several reviews based on papers related to activities of CSR and their impact on societal upliftment. Secondary data is used for this study. Today, the investors and customers expect the businesses to act responsible and sustainable which leads to the promotion of CSR

1. Research scholar (JRF), Faculty of Management & Commerce, Baba Mastnath University, Rohtak.
2. Research scholar, Faculty of Management & Commerce, Baba Mastnath University, Rohtak.

strategies by the businesses in an increasing number over the past few years. The implementation of CSR initiatives will positively impact society at large.

Keywords: Corporate social responsibility, Societal upliftment, Sustainable, Philanthropy, Strategic planning, Socio-economic Development.

Introduction

The term CSR is used to describe the efforts of a company for the improvement of society in some way. These efforts range from monetary donations to non profit organisations for the implementation of eco-friendly practices in the workplace. CSR creates valuable contributions to the reduction of poverty, directly impacts the organisation's reputation and also improves the brand image, the CSR concept is much more than that also (Mitra and Rene, 2017). Researchers mainly focus on the benefits of societal obligation to the organisations and the need for proper implementation, only a few researchers mention the benefits of CSR to society. The development of society through CSR is seen as a model for the reduction of poverty and reducing the gap of inequality in the country (Bhuiyan et al., 2021). Maharaja Agrasen started the tradition of giving one brick and coin to the newcomer to help them to earn their living and promotes peace, progress and prosperity of people. Maharaja Agrasen was an icon of peace, who embodies prosperity, progress, compassion, sacrifice and a true socialist. Now, Corporate social responsibility is a trending catchphrase of new millenniums worldwide and the government along with the corporates should also focus on this. It means voluntary self-regulation adopted by the organisations for improving the aspects related to the environment, human rights and labour of the organisation. CSR is a way for businesses to show their human face. Corporations deal with society or the public that's why the need arises to connect businesses through human languages by expressing humanity (Kamal, 2013). Businesses use CSR to indulge in the progression of society by their activities and initiatives towards the community. The activities performed by organisations in society affect the community and economy at large. The initiatives and practices of CSR help in portraying the human aspect of the organisation. Organisations, by their use of CSR actions, help the affected groups, which affects due to their business activities society also uses the socio-economic lens to scale the effect of organisation's practices of CSR (Rjiba et al., 2020).

Objectives of the Study

- To examine whether CSR is an important tool in socio-economic development.
- To evaluate the impact of CSR on socio-economic development.
- To evaluate the benefits and limitations of CSR activities.

Significance of the Study

- CSR is a way of connecting with customers and keeping them engage with the organisation as the campaigns of CSR benefits everyone. The initiatives of CSR help in contributing towards society. A business can contribute to society through national or local charitable contributions.
- The involvement of businesses in society helps in progressing them through social initiatives such funding for homeless care initiatives and educational programmes for underprivileged and street youngsters.
- The organisations can promote material recyclability, development of better functionality and durability of the product and use renewable resources at less cost for keeping a clean environment and contributing towards the ecology of the nation (Shahzad et al., 2020).
- The initiatives of CSR have a positive impact on society along with its benefits to the company. The businesses get the benefit of increased sales, low operating costs, increased productivity, customer loyalty and the ability to keep and attract skilled employees, getting more capital through investors (Singh et al., 2013).
- The contribution towards social value is the most important prerequisite for starting a successful business. To add value to their organisations, businesses need to adopt social responsibility and good corporate practises.

Review of Literature

Jiang et al. (2021) explored the role of corporate social responsibility in the financial performance of firm. They use regression analysis to know the moderating role of corporate social responsibility in the financial performance of firm. For the purpose of the study data were collected from Chinese listed companies. The study's findings indicate that CSR considerably improves a company's financial success, and that having more female directors on a board is favourably associated to that performance.

Bhuiyan et al. (2021) examined the impact of corporate social responsibility activities of banks in sustainable development. For the purpose of the study 200 beneficiaries were selected from Islamic banks of Bangladesh. The results of this survey showed that respondents strongly agreed with almost all of the activities and that they were very satisfied with the ongoing CSR efforts of Islamic banks, suggesting that the beneficiaries of CSR activities had positive opinions. The study's findings also support how respondents felt about Islamic banks' CSR efforts in the areas of contemporary art and culture, education and health, socioeconomic well-being, and societal improvement.

Meza et al. (2021) in their paper titled "the economic consequences of the loan guarantees firms' performance: A moderate role of corporate social responsibility" evaluated the connection between a loan guarantee and a company's performance using a moderate amount of CSR. For the objective of the study, information was gathered from 350 Chinese non-financial companies. The study's findings indicate a strong favourable correlation between the performance of the firm and the loan guarantee. Also, a little amount of CSR contributes to the improvement of the link between the success of the company and the loan guarantee.

Huan et al. (2021) in their paper titled "Role of Corporate Social Responsibility in Sustainable Energy Development in Emerging Economy" explored how corporate social responsibility affects the creation of renewable energy sources. Least squares method was used to analyze the data. The findings of this study revealed that Corporate Social Responsibility significantly affects the sustainable energy development.

Shahzad et al. (2020) in their paper titled "Impact of knowledge absorptive capacity on corporate sustainability with mediating role of CSR: analysis from the Asian context" analyzed the impact of employees' knowledge absorptive capacity on firms' corporate social responsibility. Data were collected from 587 ISO certified multinational manufacturing corporations through convenience sampling. The findings of the study revealed that KAC has positive impact on CSR activities.

Rjiba et al. (2020) in their paper titled "corporate social responsibility and firm value: guiding through economic policy uncertainty" analyzed the impact of uncertainty of policy on the relationship between corporate social responsibility and corporate financial performance. The study's findings showed that the social capital created over time through CSR investments balances out the detrimental effects of uncertain economic policies on business financial performance.

Karaman et al. (2021) researched the connections between the four facets of corporate social responsibility. Data was gathered from 2244 establishments. The study's findings confirm the predicted connections, bolster the signaling theory, and debunk the recent energy industry tendency of "greenwashing."

Kamal and Mona (2013) in their paper titled "The Role of Corporate Social Responsibility (CSR) in the Egyptian Banking Sector" examined how the banking industry in Egypt's financial performance relates to corporate social responsibility. The findings of the study show a negative and statically significant relationship between CSR dimensions and banks' profitability.

Research Methodology

The Fundamental and Exploratory research design has been used in this research article. This method of research design is adopted by keeping in mind the set objectives and to obtain in-depth analysis and greater accuracy of the research study.

The data used for this research study is Secondary. The data that has previously been composed and is now readily available for research purposes to the researchers is known as secondary data.

The sources of secondary data that has been used in the research are Journals, Websites, Books and Different news articles.

Discussion

The responsibility of business is not only to the stakeholders but also towards the environment, society and a sustainable planet at large. According to World Business Council, Corporate Social Responsibility is the ongoing efforts made by businesses to behave morally, promote social and economic progress, improve the quality of life for their employees, and benefit the community and society at large. The concept of CSR is a management concept in which organisations take part in the environmental and social concerns of their business actions (Brejning, 2016). CSR is a way for the organisation to achieve stability between the environmental, social and economic imperatives; we also know this as the "Triple Bottom line approach". The expectations of stakeholders and shareholders are also addressed in the triple bottom line approach. The approach of the triple bottom line is used as the basis for the reporting and measurement of the performance of corporates against social, environmental and economic performance. TBL is an attempt for the alignment of corporations towards the goal of global and sustainable development by providing wide-range purposes of working rather than just profit. The perspective behind CSR is that the organisation can only be sustainable in cases, where there is financial security, the negative impacts on the environment reduce and also meet up societal expectations (Bhuiyan et al., 2021). The organisations should learn from Maharaja Agrasen, a strong protagonist who spends 25 percent of their income on the welfare of society. He saves them for future for coping with the financial crisis when the quality of life is expensive due to uncontrollable inflation. CSR affects nonprofits, employees and companies. The practice of CSR is not mandatory, it is something more than the companies do for the improvement of the global as well as the local community (Huan et al., 2021). According to Section 135 of Companies Act 2013, the BOD ensures that the company contributes a minimum of two percent of the average net profit of immediately preceding three financial years in the cases where the net worth is more than 500 crores, turnover more than 1000 crore and net profit more than five crores. If in any case company fails with the provisions of CSR spending, the company punish with a fine of a minimum of ₹ 50,000 which can be increased to ₹ 5 lakh. The general public can also be benefited from the practices of CSR. The main objective of CSR is giving back to society, involvement in philanthropic causes and also providing positive societal value (Kamal, 2013). The key issues involved in corporate social responsibility are the engagement of stakeholders, relations between employees and community, working conditions and labour standards, gender equity, proper governance, human rights and environmental management (Jiang et al., 2021).

Socio-Economic Development

The proper implementation of the concept of CSR brings a competitive edge, like enhancement in the access of market and capital, increased profits and sales (Huan et al., 2021). Savings of operational cost, improvement in the quality and productivity, enhanced reputation and brand image, improved customer loyalty, the better process of decision making and the process of risk management (Kinderman, 2014). CSR not only provide benefits of a wide range to the organisation but also contributes towards the betterment and wellbeing of society. Providing benefits to society as a whole should be a crucial factor for the organisations to initiate and continue the involvement of CSR (Levermore, 2010). The participation of organisations in the societal and local community problems assists in the creation of better surroundings and ambience. Those who get assistance from organisations activities feels happy and enhance their living standards (Shahzad et al., 2020). By seeing the care from the corporations towards the community, the society feels safer and decreases the chances of corruption in society. The proper adoption of CSR rules by organisations helps in reducing the defects at the initial stage of production itself, it diminishes the level of the complaint and enlarges the satisfaction of customers (Brejning, 2016). Therefore, the changes in CSR by a company leads to cost deduction which directly benefits the customers because of price fall. The responsible behaviour of organisations also inspires the general public to do something like that for societal benefits. From this we can say, CSR is not only money donation or saving trees but something more than that which contributes towards and welfare of society. Economic responsibility is included in the practice of CSR, in which the organisation supports all its economic choices with the thinking to perform better in the environmental, ethical and philanthropic areas (Saleh et al., 2021). The main goal is not only the maximisation of profit but to have a valuable impact on society, people and the environment.

Limitations of CSR Activities

The investment in CSR activities leads to increased expenses and costs, businesses have to reorganise finances for accommodating the changes in their budget. The customers, clients or shareholders may have to experience the financial burden of the CSR activities of the organisation (Karaman et al., 2021). The investment of an organisation in CSR has to be more responsible and accountable for their activities as the operations of your business have a negative impact on the environment than there is the need to do damage control and assess the operations before making the investment in the CSR measures (Midttun et al., 2006). The organisations operate in a socially and ethically responsible manner and they are bound to show their shortcomings in their CSR report which is available for the public and this negatively impacts the brand image of the organisation in the market (Singh et al., 2013).

Conclusion

The significant goal of an organisation is maximising returns with minimum investment. A business organisation also has to fulfill social obligations towards the society as they are using the resources from the society only. Corporate social responsibility is a trending catchphrase of new millenniums worldwide and the government along with the corporate should also focus on this. This study is critically analyzing several reviews based on papers related to activities of CSR and their impact on societal upliftment. Secondary data is used for this study. Today, the investors and customers expect the businesses to act responsible and sustainable which leads to the promotion of CSR strategies by the businesses in an increasing number over the past few years. The implementation of CSR initiatives will positively impact society at large.

References

Bhuiyan, Md Anowar Hossain, Md Abud Darda, and Md Belal Hossain. "Corporate social responsibility (CSR) practices in Islamic banks of Bangladesh." *Social Responsibility Journal* (2021).

Brejning, Jeanette. *Corporate social responsibility and the welfare state: the historical and contemporary role of CSR in the mixed economy of welfare.* Routledge, 2016.

Huan, Ngo Quang, and Tran Thi Thuy Hong. "Role of corporate social responsibility in sustainable energy development in emerging economy." *International Journal of Energy Economics and Policy* 11.2 (2021): 172.

Jiang, Lisha, et al. "The moderating role of CSR in board gender diversity and firm financial performance: Empirical evidence from an emerging economy." *Economic Research-Ekonomska Istraživanja* 34.1 (2021): 2354-2373.

Kamal, Mona. "The role of corporate social responsibility (CSR) in the Egyptian Banking Sector." *Available at SSRN 2227621* (2013).

Karaman, Abdullah S., et al. "CSR achievement, reporting, and assurance in the energy sector: Does economic development matter?." *Energy Policy* 149 (2021): 112007.

Kinderman, Daniel. "Corporate Social Responsibility and the Welfare State: The Historical and Contemporary Role of CSR in the Mixed Economy of Welfare." (2014): 70-72.

Levermore, Roger. "CSR for development through sport: Examining its potential and limitations." *Third world quarterly* 31.2 (2010): 223-241.

Midttun, Atle, Kristian Gautesen, and Maria Gjølberg. "The political economy of CSR in Western Europe." *Corporate Governance: The international journal of business in society* (2006).

Mitra, Nayan, and René Schmidpeter. "The why, what and how of the CSR mandate: The India story." *Corporate Social Responsibility in India.* Springer, Cham, 2017. 1-8.

Ramos Meza, Carlos Samuel, et al. "The Economic Consequences of the Loan Guarantees and Firm's Performance: A Moderate Role of Corporate Social Responsibility." *Global Business Review* (2021): 09721509211039674.

Rjiba, Hatem, Abderrahman Jahmane, and Ilyes Abid. "Corporate social responsibility and firm value: Guiding through economic policy uncertainty." *Finance Research Letters* 35 (2020): 101553.

Rodnyansky, Dmitry, Ruslan Sadyrtdinov, and Elena Zagladina. "Corporative social responsibility and its role in strategy of social-economic development of the region." *Mediterranean Journal of Social Sciences* 5.12 (2014): 135.

Saleh, Mohammed WA, et al. "Does board gender enhance Palestinian firm performance? The moderating role of corporate social responsibility." *Corporate Governance: The International Journal of Business in Society* (2021).

Shahzad, Mohsin, et al. "Impact of knowledge absorptive capacity on corporate sustainability with mediating role of CSR: Analysis from the Asian context." *Journal of Environmental Planning and Management* 63.2 (2020): 148-174.

Singh, Namrata, Rajlaxmi Srivastava, and Rajni Rastogi. "CSR practices & CSR reporting in Indian Banking Sector." *International Journal of Scientific and Research Publications* 3.12 (2013): 1-8.

Sisaye, Seleshi. "The influence of non-governmental organisations (NGOs) on the development of voluntary sustainability accounting reporting rules." *Journal of Business and Socio-economic Development* (2021).

Tapasvi, S. K. "Book Review: Jeanette Brejning, Corporate Social Responsibility and the Welfare State: The Historical and Contemporary Role of CSR in the Mixed Economy of Welfare." (2012): 353-355.

Uduji, Joseph Ikechukwu, Elda Nduka Okolo-Obasi, and Simplice A. Asongu. "Oil extraction in Nigeria's Ogoniland: The role of corporate social responsibility in averting a resurgence of violence." *Resources Policy* 70 (2021): 101927.

16

Managerial Skills to Handle Risk and Uncertainty in Trade

Jyoti[1], Samridhi Tanwar[2]

Abstract

The focus of this paper is on managerial decision-making in the face of risk and uncertainty. Like other management disciplines, risk management has experienced substantial changes in order to adapt to the shifting demands of stakeholders and the environment of corporate operations. Management professionals must now perform a new management function called risk management out of need rather than choice. The goal of this essay is to define a manager's role in making decisions under risk and ambiguity. The development of managerial functions in the field of risk management is offered in order to accomplish the desired goal.

Key words: Risk taking, uncertainty, decision making.

Introduction

Uncertainty and its influence in decision-making is a significant phenomenon that has gotten a lot of attention in international business studies. The international business environment is influenced by the global economy's paradoxical evolution, as well as the phenomena of instability that define most national economies. As a result of the intricacy of today's worldwide economic interactions, one may

1. Research Scholar, IMSAR, Maharshi Dayanand University, Rohtak.
2. Associate Professor, Indira Gandhi University, Meerpur, Rewari.

claim that international business is performed in the face of multiple hazards. Traders often have little assurance that the business end will provide them the desired results, therefore decision-making in this sector is fraught with risk and uncertainty.

The connection between normative, descriptive, and prescriptive decision-making frameworks has garnered more attention recently. It's critical to understand the similarities and distinctions between the three theories in order to construct decision aids. Furthermore, because decision-making and risk-taking are context-dependent, The context of decision-making needs to be thoroughly researched. The manner decisions are made and the type of decision analysis are both influenced by the situation in numerous ways. Organisational structure and culture must both be studied, as they have a significant impact on decision-making processes. Managers' perceptions of risk and risk taking have received little attention in research.

Background

Defining Risk

Risk is described in the context of finance as the variation of an investment (Markowitz, 1952). Risk is defined in the context of business by the (unfavourable) volatility in performance indicators like revenue and cost (March and Shapira, 1987). Wherever there is a concern for public safety, risk is defined as the frequency and seriousness of important events (CSChE, 2004). Risk is defined by the international standard for risk management as the effect of uncertainty on objectives (International Standards Organisation, 2018).

Process risk has been a problem for risk analysis as a field. The renowned risk analysis researcher spoke at the Society for Risk Analysis's Annual Conference in 1996. Stan Kaplan said, "The words of risk analysis are, and still be a haul. several of you here remember that once our Society for Risk Analysis was different, one in every of the primary things it did was to ascertain a committee to outline the word 'risk'. This committee laboured for four years and then gave up, language in its final report, that perhaps it's higher to not outline risk. Let every author define it in his own method, solely please every ought to justify clearly what method that is" (S. Kaplan, 1997).

Risk Management

Risk management is a series of operations within an organisation that are organised with the goal of reducing risk (International Standards Organisation, 2018). It is an ongoing process.

Risk is recognised, examined, and evaluated as part of the risk management process. Management of risks also entails decision-making in terms of risk treatment implementation (Rausand, 2011). The first stage in doing a risk assessment is to identify the potentially harmful occurrences that can cause a negative effect on a part or the overall system. This is commonly referred to as a danger or hazard identification. The next phase in risk assessment is to identify unfavourable events.

Finding the likelihood and potential consequences of these events is the next step in the risk assessment process after identifying undesirable events. Finding the frequency (let's say, annually) of an undesirable occurrence occuring is the aim of a likelihood analysis. A consequence analysis's objective is to estimate the potential loss that could arise from an unfavourable situation (Rausand, 2011).

The risk measure is then compared to risk tolerance criteria in the final step of the risk assessment (Rausand, 2011). A risk matrix is a standard tool for assessing risk in a given situation way. A risk matrix is a tool that is used to assess the risk of a specific event.

Decisions for risk treatment are influenced by the findings of a risk assessment. Treatment alternatives are not always mutually exclusive, and they can take many different forms. Treatment may include lowering the likelihood of the unfavourable outcome preventing an event (prevention), limiting the consequences (mitigation), or sharing the risk (mitigation) insuring (transfer). Treatments at the extreme end of the spectrum could include completely removing the source of danger (International Standards Organisation, 2018).

Uncertainty

Uncertainty must be understood in a way that is fundamentally distinct from the accepted notion of risk, from which it has never been adequately distinguished. The crucial fact is that "risk" might refer to a number that can be quantified in some situations but not in others, and depending on which of the two is actually there and operating, there are significant differences in the consequences of the phenomenon. A quantifiable uncertainty, or "risk proper," as we'll refer to it, looks to be so different from an unquantifiable uncertainty that it hardly qualifies as an uncertainty at all.

Uncertainty might result from a lack of knowledge about available facts. That is, there may be some doubt about whether a new endeavour will succeed, but this doubt can be dispelled through additional research and experimentation.

Research methodology

The methodological approach was a complete study of the literature, led by bibliometric and content analytic approaches. To get varied information, national and International articles are been used. Apart from journal articles, books, and reports, websites have also been accessed.

Discussion

In general, risk denotes a state of uncertainty. Every organisation is exposed to some level of risk. These dangers are linked to their odds of succeeding. As a result, a greater awareness of hazards and good risk management can improve the chances of success. You can take full advantage of these opportunities if you have good risk management skills. To clarify, responding well to these situations can lead to long-term success for your organisation.

Risk must be managed at all levels of the organisation, and if a leader is unable to manage risk, their upward mobility will be limited. Because they mitigate or prevent risk, the finest risk managers are frequently undiscovered. People are more likely to notice when things go wrong than when they go right.

To be an effective risk manager, you must have the awareness and knowledge to identify potential hazards and deliver them to the individuals who can best fix the situation. A risk manager does not have to make the fix; all they have to do is bring it to the attention of the person who can. The majority of individuals link risks with negative outcomes. However, this perspective is incomplete. This is a trade off between a chance and the uncertainty that comes with it. Things go wrong all the time, and they always do. But then then, so do good things. There is an opportunity in every uncertainty. It could be construed as either a positive or negative event. Managers must identify risks and keep track of the potential for negative things to happen. Focus on the positive consequences and use excellent management skills to achieve the greatest results. Corporations must work hard to achieve positive results. At the same time, they must keep an eye out for undesirable consequences.

Companies must contend with a variety of external and internal issues in order to function. As a result, it's unclear whether the corporation will meet its objectives. In a nutshell, risks are these occurrences and circumstances. We've had the preconceived notion that a risk is something bad since the beginning. To be honest, risk does not necessarily have a negative outcome. Risks are unpredictably occurring events. They might have both beneficial and bad consequences.

Possibilities are connected with positive risks. Risk managers are constantly looking for methods to maximise these possibilities. As a result, a company develops value by exerting control over something that has the potential to inflict harm.

Risk management requires being conscious of potential dangers and potential negative outcomes, both anticipated and unforeseen. Risk managers are knowledgeable about every sort of risk within their purview and, if practical, beyond. They comprehend how such risks would affect the business, what actions, if any, should be performed, and what backup plans should be in place in case of emergency.

Risk management is a difficult and all-encompassing skill. It isn't a soft skill at all. Compliance, security, operational, and financial risks are just a few examples. Compliance is crucial since there are few dangers more dangerous than running afoul of government regulatory authorities. They are significantly more powerful than a hacker or out-of-date software in terms of causing damage.

The risk management framework follows a set of steps. This is a strategy for reducing and controlling hazards within a company. An enterprise risk management framework has five major steps, which are as follows:

Describe the situation

This entails assessing the risks that a company faces from both external and internal sources. Managers have to think about it from the outside such as the current economic situation, the future economic climate. Other external influences include: A competitive environment, political turbulence, Changes in the regulatory environment.

Risk Exposures Must Be Recognised

Organisational risks are mostly derived from the organisation's borrowing and investments. These kinds of dangers require careful attention. Because the vulnerability of risks varies with changes in interest rates and the market, this is the case.

Similarly, for organisations with limited resources, time management is an important element to consider when assessing these risks. Return on investment timing that is off can cause future investments to be unbalanced. As a result, loan payments may be stretched too far.

Analysis of risk

This step entails comprehending the risk's nature. It is accomplished by identifying the most likely actual exposures. The likelihood of occurrence of a risk is multiplied by the risk's potential losses to calculate risk.

Line managers, middle managers, and all other staff follow procedures to minimise the risk of loss. Their major goal is to reduce losses and increase profits. Protecting the investment of their shareholders is one strategy that organisations prioritise. Managers safeguard the investment as if it were a business asset. This process is repeated until the return begins to flow in.

Risk managers use the risk register to calculate the likelihood of certain events occurring. This is an essential component of qualitative risk analysis.

These are some skills of smart manager:

- **Analytical skills:** Risk managers need to be analytically strong in order to gather data and base important choices on it. They need to look for problems and gaps in systems, infrastructure, and other areas that others might have overlooked.
- **Problem solving skills:** Risk managers must be able to address problems as well. While some dangers may necessitate informing someone above their pay grade, others will be solved by the management. As a result, they must enjoy getting their hands dirty.
- **People management and leadership skills:** If managers can't stir the soldiers, all their problem-solving skills are meaningless. Risk managers need good people and leadership abilities to inspire and encourage staff. Managers must preserve their team's respect in the midst of difficulty since risk management may require upsetting the apple cart.
- **Relationship building skills:** This skill complements the preceding one. Risk managers must be able to form bonds with others, not just their immediate subordinates. The ability to collaborate well with co-workers and managers from various departments is a requirement.
- **Financial knowledge:** Risk managers need to know how much network failures and security breaches cost on average. The possibility of losing money will catch everyone's attention. Managers need to be aware of the potential financial penalties, which can be disastrous, as well as the repercussions of wasted opportunities for output and income.
- **Regulation knowledge:** If there's one thing the government excels at, it's regulating things. Regulation is ever-changing and continual. Risk managers must devote work hard to staying informed about and comprehending all changes.
- **Ability to quantify risk:** Risk managers must be able to evaluate the likelihood and severity of each risk on a scale of their choosing after generating a list of probable hazards. A thorough list that rates the dangers from most likely to

least likely and from most severe to least severe should be provided.

- **Ability to choose mitigation strategy:** According to the website Skills You Need: Mitigation, there are four basic forms of mitigation action or plan.
    (a) **Acceptance:** This suggests that you ignore risk mitigation efforts and accept the risk. Threats that won't make much of an impact or are unlikely to materialise fall into this category.
    (b) **Avoidance:** This requires making all possible efforts to stay away from the threat. This is for really serious risks that are almost certainly to happen.
    (c) **Limitation:** This is the most prevalent risk mitigation method, which seeks to reduce the risk's likelihood or impact.
- **Transference:** Transferring risk to someone else who is willing to accept it is what this is. This is used in situations where a risk manager's primary competency is not necessary.
- **Strategic thinking:** No sports team has ever won solely by playing defence, and the same is true here. If a risk manager considers how various factors affect the business as a whole, they may be able to devise a more effective strategy. They have a responsibility to consider the big picture, and they can notice something that others miss.
- **Adaptability:** Risk management necessitates ongoing education and knowledge of current events. No one had heard of ransomware ten years ago. It is quickly rising to the top of the list of major hazards to companies. Regular reading of news websites and industry publications is advised.

Conclusion

A company's goal cannot be defined without effective risk management outlines. The goal of risk management is to ensure that the organisation can withstand any problems that arise while it is in operation. As a result, anticipating future events and being prepared for them will assist organisations in overcoming unexpected problems at a low cost.

A risk manager's job is a rewarding one. In the entire organisational function, the risk manager performs a critical role. As a result, he must work with all other departments. Managers have to cope with a lot of obstacles as a risk manager because to be dealing with tumultuous financial situations. It is, without a doubt, one of the most prestigious jobs in a company.

As new legislation emerge, risk managers must study, understand, adapt, and execute them as quickly as possible. Risk management is all about being proactive. Dealing with a problem after it has become one is what is meant by a reactionary strategy. Risk managers must constantly stay one step ahead of the curve. Furthermore, while analysing managerial performance, a big stumbling block the elicitation methods and the actual challenges are the decision problems. Both probability and utilities are used. As a result, Increased use of computer-based decision-making tools is essential. Last but not least, there is a prescriptive computer-based method that tries to help managers make better decisions by identifying discrepancies between actual (descriptive) and interpreted (prescriptive) data.

Bibliography

Armstrong, M. (2011). *How to be an even better manager: A complete AZ of proven techniques and essential skills*. Kogan Page Publishers.

Beranova, M., & Martinovičová, D. (2010). Application of the theory of decision making under risk and uncertainty at modelling of costs. *Agricultural Economics, 56*(5), 201-208..

Carter, T. (2010). Risk and uncertainty. *Journal of Hospital Marketing & Public Relations, 20*(1), 66-86.

Douson, M. L., Felter, S. P., & Robinson, D. (1996). Evolution of science-based uncertainty factors in noncancer risk assessment. *Regulatory Toxicology and Pharmacology, 24*(2), 108-120.

Fisher, E. (2011). What practitioners consider to be the skills and behaviours of an effective people project manager. *International journal of project management, 29*(8), 994-1002.

Gough, J. D. (1988). *Risk and uncertainty*. Lincoln College and University of Canterbury. Centre for Resource Management..

Harrison, E. F., & Pelletier, M. A. (2000). The essence of management decision. *Management decision*.

Iessandri, T. M., Ford, D. N., Lander, D. M., Leggio, K. B., & Taylor, M. (2004). Managing risk and uncertainty in complex capital projects. *The Quarterly review of economics and finance, 44*(5), 751-767.

Kaplan, S. (1997). The words of risk analysis. Risk analysis, 17(4), 407-417.

Lindley, D. V. (2013). *Understanding uncertainty*. John Wiley & Sons.

Liu, Y., & Rausand, M. (2011). Reliability assessment of safety instrumented systems subject to different demand modes. Journal of Loss Prevention in the Process Industries, 24(1), 49-56.

March, J. G., & Shapira, Z. (1987). Managerial Perspectives on Risk and Risk Taking. Management Science, 33, 1404-1418.

Markowitz, H. (1952). The utility of wealth. Journal of political Economy, 60(2), 151-158.

Molinsky, A. L., Davenport, T. H., Iyer, B., & Davidson, C. (2012). Three skills every 21st-century manager needs. *Harvard Business Review*, *90*(1/2), 139-143.

Moore, D. S. (1990). Uncertainty. *On the shoulders of giants: New approaches to numeracy*, 95-137.

Pleskac, T. J., Diederich, A., & Wallsten, T. S. (2015). Models of decision making under risk and uncertainty. *The Oxford handbook of computational and mathematical psychology*, 209-231.

Raheem, M. N., & Adrees, M. (2021). The Effect of Risk and Uncertainty Factors on Managerial Decision Making. *Journal of Education and Vocational Research*, *12*(1): 30-37.

Riabacke, A. (2006). Managerial Decision Making Under Risk and Uncertainty. *IAENG International Journal of Computer Science*, *32*(4).

Rowe, A. J., Boulgarides, J. D., & McGrath, M. R. (1984). *Managerial decision making*. Chicago: Science Research Associates.

Syed, Z., & Lawryshyn, Y. (2020). Multi-criteria decision-making considering risk and uncertainty in physical asset management. *Journal of Loss Prevention in the Process Industries*, *65*, 104064.

Vroom, V. H. (1973). A new look at managerial decision making. *Organizational dynamics*.

17

The Role of SHGs in Women and Rural Development

Parul Mittal[1], Sonal Gupta[2]

Abstract

Women empowerment means the ability of women to enjoy their human rights and avail benefit from resources, income, assets, time and many more. It can be achieved with the help of education, self-help groups, income and employment. SHGs focuses on the empowerment of women with economic and social aspects. These groups not only micro-credit to women and rural people but also provides opportunities for employment, enhance leadership qualities, awareness programmes, and training regarding self-employment and also provide a better and more confidential life to the members. The role of women and rural people is indispensable in society. This paper covers women's empowerment in the context of economic empowerment, social empowerment, psychological empowerment, political empowerment and managerial empowerment aspect. The concept of SHGs is just like a ray of hope in the dark for the government of India to empower women and for the development of the rural section of society. This study is purely based on secondary data that is available on websites, various research papers and government reports. Here, we also discussed the role and importance of SHGs in the development of rural areas and rural people. The role of Self-help Groups is admirable for the development of women and rural people.

Keywords: Self-Help Groups, Rural development, women empowerment, SHGs.

---

1. Assistant Professor, Department of Commerce, KLP college, Rewari.
2. Research Scholar (JRF), Faculty of Management & Commerce, Baba Mastnath University, Rohtak.

Introduction

Rural development means the improvement in the economic well-being and quality of life of people residing in isolated areas (Robert et al., 2021). In the country like India, it is essential to study the concept of rural development. Here, most of the population living in rural areas. In a developing country like India, development is possible in the true sense from the rural section (Dahiya et al., 2014). Self-help groups are small voluntary groups of the informal nature of individuals who meet for addressing common issues. The socio-economic background of these individuals is mostly similar. The major focus of these groups is the mutual support idea means individuals help one another (Swain and Das, 2021). SHGs serve various purposes but it all depends on the need and situation. For example, in the sector of development, SHGs use as the strategy for the alleviation of poverty, social empowerment and human development. The focus of Self-Help groups is on activities of income generation and micro-credit programmes.

The members of SHGs are united by the common condition like addiction or sickness. A single person from a family can be a member of SHG (Agrawal, 2017). These members are either generally women or men only. A single Self-Help Group has 15-20 members and have not been registered under any law or act. The first motto of every SHG is to save first and spend later. SHGs work on the concept of cooperation rather than competition. Microfinance means providing entire financial services to the needy section and covers entrepreneurial development, and up-gradation of skills that helps in overcoming poverty (Puhazhendi and Satyasi, 2002).

Review of Related Literature

SHGs are created for the purpose of addressing the common issues faced by people in society. These groups created the habit of savings and use these savings for the benefit of their family members. They prioritise their needs and set some standards for keeping the track of savings and their expenditure. Banks also start providing loans to these people on the basis of their savings and without any collateral. This study is based on secondary data and found that SHGs are a powerful tool for the eradication of poverty and the empowerment of women (Ramakrishna et al., 2013). The author tried to evaluate the economic empowerment level of women with the help of SHGs. Here, the savings, income and expenditure levels of the participants were evaluated. The study found that there is a positive relationship between women's economic empowerment and the income of the members of SHGs. The family expenditure of the group members also increased in both blocks after joining the SHG as there was a change in the member income of the Self-Help Group (Dahiya et al., 2014). The operating system of the Self-Help Group was analysed by the author. SHGs works for the needy section and provide functions like saving mobilisation, managing group funds, providing credit to the poor people, loan repayment, leadership building, setting links with the banks and analysing the social benefits to its members. The study revealed that there is a need to maintain uniformity in the extension and formulation of financial assistance by the banks to the women in all blocks. The procedure of sanctioning loan by the bank to the members of SHGs should be quick, convenient and simple (Tyagi and Kathpalia, 2021). There is an impact on the level of income, employment, and expenditure of the members of SHGs. The facility of training provided should be improved for the SHGs and banks procedures should also be minimised for the SHG members. The study found that the success of SHGs depends on the factors like education level, family planning, collective strategy, social customs and hard work. Further, the facility of micro-credit also empowers women as it increases the chance to share their outcomes. The political space and social culture are vital components for the empowerment of women (Agrawal, 2017).

The author conducted a study to find that whether microfinance helps in the socio-economic empowerment of the members of the group. Further, if it encourages entrepreneurial activities so, at what extent the groups and members mobilize the thrifts. It is concluded that micro-financing with the help of women SHGs had brought a positive change in the life of SHG members (Swain and Das, 2021). SHGs play a drastic role in enabling financial inclusion for people living in rural areas. They also empowered women living in rural areas financially and socially. There is a need for financial and social capital to expediting the economic growth of India. SHGs were formed for the purpose of alleviation of poverty and rural development. The socio-economic status of rural people improved after the formation of SHGs. The participation of women in local community also increases with the help of SHG. The problems faced by rural people are like illiteracy, lack of skills, unemployment, basic infrastructure, sanitation and health and these problems somehow solved with the help of Self-Help Groups. The savings are made by a group member with the bank but the major decisions regarding the loan activities and savings are taken by the members of a group (Robert et al., 2021).

Objectives of the Study

- To study the role of Self-Help Groups in rural development
- To study the role of Self-Help Groups in women's empowerment.

Research Methodology

The present study is content analysis and conceptual in nature as here we discuss the available content on Self Help Groups and its role in rural development and women empowerment. The data were collected from secondary sources with the help of websites, journals, thesis, newspapers, etc.

Discussion

Self-Help Groups played a crucial role in empowering financial inclusion in rural areas. These groups empowered the women living in rural areas financially. Self-help Groups have the potential to expediate the growth of India financially, socially and economically. SHGs help in addressing the problems at the grass root level. India has diverse traditions, historical antecedents and culture, that's why it is hard for the government to handle the socioeconomic issues on its own (Robert et al., 2021). For catering the requirements like bringing together people of similar interests, the need for SHGs arises.

Credit Availability: The credit provided by the bank is not accessible easily to the poor section, but after the formation of the Self-Help Group, there are better prospects for bank credit availability (Ramakrishna et al., 2013). Under the programme of SHG-Bank linkage, many Self-Help Groups are now the institutions of Micro-Credit.

Entrepreneurship: It creates opportunities in people for self-employment with the help of setting micro-enterprises. They support the entrepreneurship at the micro level which lowers the dependence of people on single income source and widens the horizons of income for the members (Agrawal, 2017).

Skill Development: The program of skill development undertaken by the Self-Help Groups enhances the level of employment of the involved members.

Rural poverty: These groups become a vehicle for the under privileged people and lift these people from the poverty line and also create awareness about the government schemes, and also monitor their implementation. The schemes are for the backward and marginalised section of society

Improves the living standard: As it creates job there is also an increase in income which boosts access to health services, food, clothing and it overall raise the standard of living (Ramakrishna et al., 2013). It enhances the standard of living, birth control, literacy rate and healthcare of the weaker section of society.

Women empowerment: It helps in providing opportunities for employment, social security and financial assistance to women which improves the status of women and also creates awareness regarding their responsibilities and rights. They try to make women independent intellectually and financially.

Financial Discipline: The members of Self-Help Groups are encouraged to open accounts in banks which promotes the habit of savings and improves the condition of living by spending more money on health and education (Swain and Das, 2021).

Examples

- In Kerala, Kudumbashree has provided assistance in poverty eradication and the skill development of women.
- They work as a pressure group for the formulation of policies as perceived in the legislation making for the prohibition in

Bihar which resulted from the pressure of several women Self Help Groups in Bihar (Swain and Das, 2021).

- Tamil Nadu used Self Help Groups for the inculcation of habits of sanitation among the people living in the community under the concept of Swachh Bharat Abhiyan.
- The Government of Haryana uses Self Help Groups for increasing the sex ratio and making Beti Bachao Beti Padao.
- Various Self-Help Groups like Lizzat papad and SEWA promotes the culture of entrepreneurship among women.
- The programme for the alleviation of poverty by the Government of Andhra Pradesh was successfully integrated by the women of Self-Help Groups.

Women's participation in Self-Help Groups has a vital impact on the empowerment of women. SHGs help women in understanding and realising their potential and develop the courage to think independently. Now, women have their own future goals and also have the self-belief to attain future goals (UmaShankar, 2006). The sub-divisions of women empowerment are discussed below:

Economic Empowerment: The following changes are observed in the women after the formation of Self-Help Groups.

- They are now able to purchase items of small and large nature
- Take ownership of useful assets like houses, savings of cash, land etc.
- Increase their investment in health, marriage, housing and education
- Lowers the level of poverty and now less dependent on men for economic resources (Tyagi and Kathpalia, 2021).
- Able to meet the expenditures that are necessary for running their life.

Social Empowerment: The value of women increased in society and family after the Psychological and Economic empowerment. The social empowerment of women has been observed in the following ways:

- Involvement in the decision-making power like the purchase of land or any other livestock (Ramakrishna et al., 2013).
- The attitude of family, household and society changes
- The gender-based violence reduced
- The bargaining power increased with the other members of the family
- Develop the network and interact more with family and other societal members (Tyagi and Kathpalia, 2021).

Psychological Empowerment: The psychological empowerment of women has been shown in the following outcomes.

- Confidence and Self-esteem
- Increased knowledge, awareness and the literacy rate (Robert et al., 2021).
- Increased awareness regarding health, sanitation, education, food and nutrition
- Creation of positive self-image
- The strengths, feelings and perception of women changes
- Recognise their skills and abilities because of the confidence and self-esteem

Political Empowerment: "The one who didn't get the chance to rule, will perish soon". Women are also like the above quote. They have no knowledge about their basis rights, if they are not empowered politically. SHGs ensures women to be prospective future leader. Women also start participating in the local government processes. Further, political awareness increased like the knowledge of key political and national figures, and the law of participation (Robert et al., 2021).

Managerial Empowerment: The Managerial empowerment of women has been shown in the following outcomes.

- Able to establish micro enterprises
- Group work and Management
- Development of skills to achieve future aspirations
- Communicate freely

- Develop the skills of planning, co-ordinating, financial and decision-making (Agrawal, 2017).
- Formulate collective interest and organisation of groups.

Findings and Conclusion

Self-Help Groups are a way to empower women living in rural areas and alleviate poverty. The aim of women's empowerment is that women should realise their strengths and weaknesses, and their potential and power in all aspects of life. But in real women's empowerment is possible in all aspects like political, psychological, managerial, financial, economic and social. Women should be confident, self-motivated, recognised and speak well in their family and community matters and increase their participation wherever they are present. This process is continuous and consistent but women and people in the rural area should make extra efforts willingly for their overall growth and development. Self-Help groups work on all the above matters in a recognised manner. They have the potential to make a significant impact in the lives of women and rural people. The concept of SHGs mooted along the semi-urban and rural areas to improve their condition of living. It helps in the reduction of poverty by providing opportunities to the rural section like wage employment opportunities and self-employment that further results in sustainable improvement in their livelihood. Nowadays, the main motive of most of employment schemes is to create grass root institutions like SHGs. Thus, we can say Self-Help Groups show the way ahead to reduce poverty with the rural and women development.

References

Agrawal, M. (2017). Role of Self Help Groups in Empowering Rural Women in India. In *Int'l Conf. on Law, Education, Business and Corporate Social Responsibilities (LEBCSR-17)* (pp. 75-77).

Beevi, S., & Devi, V. G. (2011). The Role of Self Help Groups in Empowering Rural Women in India. *International Journal of Interdisciplinary Social Sciences*, *5*(9).

Das, T., & Guha, P. (2019). Measuring Women's Self-help Group Sustainability: A Study of Rural Assam. *International Journal of Rural Management*, *15*(1), 116-136.

Manjunatha, S. (2013). The Role of Women Self–Help Groups in Rural Development of Karnataka State, India. *International Research Journal of Social Sciences*, *2*(9), 23-25.

Namboodiri, N. V., & Shiyani, R. L. (2001). Potential Role of Self-Help Groups in Rural Financing Deepening. *Indian Journal of Agricultural Economics*, *56*(3), 401-409.

Poddar, K. K. (2013). Role of self help groups in economic empowerment of women in India. *Anusandhanika*, *5*(1/2), 237.

Robert, F. C., Frey, L. M., & Sisodia, G. S. (2021). Village development framework through self-help-group entrepreneurship, microcredit, and anchor customers in solar microgrids for cooperative sustainable rural societies. *Journal of Rural Studies,* 88, 432-440.

Sharma, A., Dua, S., & Hatwal, V. (2012). Micro enterprise development and rural women entrepreneurship: way for economic empowerment. *Arth Prabhand: A Journal of Economics and Management*, *1*(6), 114-127.

Shireesha, E. (2019). Empowerment of Women through Self-Help Groups. *International Journal of Scientific Development and Research (IJSDR)*, *4*(12), 13-16.

Sihag, R. (2018). Reasons to join self-help groups with reference to Haryana state. *Indian Journal of Health & Wellbeing*, *9*(3).

Swain, S. K., & Das, R. (2021). An Analysis of the Role of Self Help Groups in the Socio-Economic Development of Rural Poor. *International Journal of Recent Advances in Multidisciplinary Topics*, 2(7), 173-177.

Terdal, M. S. (2018). Rural Development in India: A Role of Self-help Group. *International Journal of Advanced Research in Education & Technology*, *5*(3), 32-34.

Tyagi, R., & Kathpalia, J. (2021). Role of self-help groups in women empowerment rural communities of Haryana. *The Pharma Innovation Journal,* 10(4S), 416-426.

Vinodhini, R. L., & Vaijayanthi, P. (2016). Self-help group and socio-economic empowerment of women in rural India. *Indian Journal of Science and Technology*, *9*(27), 67-89.

Vishnuvarthini, R., & Ayyothi, A. M. (2016). The role of SHG in women empowerment-A critical review. *IOSR Journal of Economics and Finance*, *7*(3), 33-39.

18

Start-Up India: An Initiative of the Indian Government

Garima Dalal[1], Priya Rani[2]

Abstract

Any nation's economic development is greatly influenced by entrepreneurship. As it results in the creation of jobs, a contribution to national income, rural development, industrialisation, technological progress, export promotion, etc., entrepreneurship serves as a pillar for a country's economic growth. India is home to numerous great legends who achieved global fame as a result of their labour, intellectual prowess, and high level of talent. Indian youth are extremely gifted, highly skilful, and full of original ideas. However, they are denied the chance because of a lack of reliable support and appropriate direction. Thus, on January 16, 2016, the BJP government unveiled the "START-UP INDIA STAND UP INDIA" programme to support Indian youth in leveraging their fresh and creative ideas to move the country in the correct direction. Collectively, the article aims to understand the start-up ecosystem in India along with the initiatives taken by the government for providing a supporting ecosystem.

Introduction

Munshi (2019) told that the core motive behind start-ups

1. Associate Professor, Institute of Management Studies and Research, Maharshi Dayanand University, Rohtak, Haryana.
2. Research Scholar, Institute of Management Studies and Research, Maharshi Dayanand University, Rohtak, Haryana.

is to "transform India from a nation of job searchers to a nation of job providers." The kind of business that qualifies as a start-up is not limited by any set criteria. The policymaker and the entrepreneurs define the term "start-up" as a mindset and culture of innovating on current concepts to deliver answers instead of a state of mind. Since it is often considered that these enterprises would not exist without the crucial component of "technology," the word is usually used to describe high-technology firms which are using the latest automation to resolve pressing issues. Technology has a designated role to play in the establishment of start-ups. The Indian government has launched an initiative called "Start-up India". On the 15th of August 2015, Narendra Modi, the Prime Minister of India made the very first announcement of the campaign while giving his speech.

Start-up India programme

Start-up India is all about defying expectations and inspiring a revolution of distinctive and compelling business models created by young people. It serves as a prelude to India assuming a central role in the new global order. This initiative facilitating easier patent application, providing research and development credits, and facilitating admission for the Indians are expected to prosper as a result of massive mentality and cognitive shifts. It is adding feathers to the Indian's fragile wings. To avoid a second global crisis, the world is struggling. Start-up India is all about defying expectations and inspiring a revolution of distinctive and compelling business models created by young people. It serves as a prelude to India assuming a central role in the new global order.

Start-up India offers an enthralling opportunity for the future. The complexity and brutal reality of modern businesses are recognised by the Indian government and thus, the central government made an effort to solve the issues faced by ambitious Indian entrepreneurs whose capacity for taking risks and new projects is unmatchable all over the world. Some of the obstacles which are encountered by entrepreneurs include policy stagnation, a lack of openness, etc.

This initiative's action plan focuses on three areas:

- Simplifying and supporting.

- Financial Aid, Support, and Rewards.
- Incubation and business collaboration.

Definition of start-ups

According to "The Department of Industrial Policy and Promotion" (DIPP) under "The Ministry of Commerce and Industry", a "START-UP FIRM" is defined as an organisation registered or originated in India and satisfies the following conditions:

- An entity is considered a start-up until seven years have elapsed after the date of incorporation and for the start-ups in the field of biotechnology the tenure limit is ten years;
- The turnover of the entity should not exceed twenty-five crores in any prior fiscal year annually;
- If it is trying to develop, launch, and commercialise new goods, services, or procedures that are based on technology or intellectual property.

As a result, if a partnership firm under the Partnership Act of 1932 as well as a private limited enterprise under the "Companies Act, 2013" or a limited liability partnership under the "Limited Liability Partnership Act, 2008" is sevens years old, they all will be considered as a start-up by the "Start-Up India" programme. Instead, it will lose its status as a start-up entity when seven years have passed since the date of its incorporation or registration or if the annual turnover of the entity exceeded twenty-five crores in any prior fiscal year.

Journey of a Start-up

The journey of a Start-up initiates with an idea in the mind of an entrepreneur and at this stage, there are neither revenues nor operating losses. After this, the idea is converted into a start-up most probably with low revenues and relatively high operating losses and further on these start-ups are converted into well-established companies.

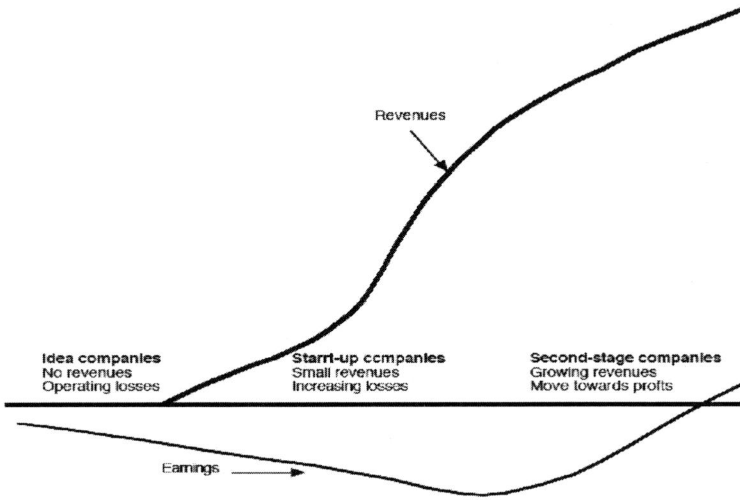

Source: Sarkar (2016).

Figure 1: Journey of Start-ups.

Benefits of the 'Start-up India programme'

Chakraborty (2017) mentioned that this project promises some advantages like easier registration of intellectual property rights and streamlined exit norms. In this regard, the Ministry of Corporate Affairs has been informed in writing by the "Department of Industrial Policy and Promotion", the prime organisation for this programme to declare these firms as "Fast-Track Firms", allowing firms to dissolve themselves within ninety days after submitting their application for the winding up. The Bharat Navodaya additionally advised the above in their report on "Start-up India Reform".

The compendium of good practices for motivating such firms in the nation, the union territory and state start-up rating scheme and the start-up India kit are three new tools that the "Ministry of Commerce and Industry" recently unveiled to rank union territories and states on "start-ups" across the nation. The motive behind this thought is to promote the growth of a better ecosystem for start-ups at the ground level (Munshi, 2019).

Discarding restrictive State Government regulations in this sector, like Foreign Investment Proposals, Licence Raj, Environmental Clearances and Land Permissions is another area related to this endeavour. The (DPI & IT) "Department for promotion of industry and internal trade" organised it. An organisation with Indian headquarters, that was founded less than ten years ago, and that generates less than a hundred crores as an annual turnover is referred to as a start-up.

A selected group of business leaders that support Start-up India call for increased bandwidth, tax benefits on low-cost cell phones that support indigenous languages, streamlined "Know Your Customer" procedures and better accession to financing. They are collaborating with decision-makers to eliminate regulations that inhibit investment. For the youthful, tech-savvy, and clever entrepreneur, crisp paperwork is a pipe dream. The industrialised nations have made great efforts to simplify business procedures. This setting offers the administration of the day a tough and engaging environment for policymaking. A 19-point plan was launched by the prime minister to advance the culture of start-ups. The plan featured tax breaks, management facilitation, and modernisation to help businessmen in initiating and expand their enterprises (Start-up India Is Work-in-Progress - Forbes India, n.d.).

Financing of start-ups

The I-MADE programme, which aims to assist Indian entrepreneurs in creating the "MUDRA Bank's scheme (Pradhan Mantri Mudra Yojana)" and (one million) ten lakh smartphone app start-ups, which aims to provide microloans at a relatively low rate of interest to business owners from poor socioeconomic backgrounds, have already been introduced by the government under this initiative. For this project, an initial capital of 20,000 crores has been allotted to the scheme, which is equivalent to 240 billion rupees in 2020.

The government has pledged to provide Start-up India with basic funding of ten thousand crores over a period of four years. By 2022, the initial outlay might attract 10 times as much funding. A credit guarantee scheme is another motivator for start-up financing. On January 16, 2016, a start-up strategy was revealed in front of domestic and foreign business owners. Internet-based enterprises, including those in the fields of food, fashion, health, education, travel, and payment systems, have recently assumed a prominent role ("PM Modi Announces ₹ 1,000-Crore," n.d.).

The Prime Minister of India has declared that the country would observe 16 January as "National Start-up Day". On the occasion of the first National Start-up Day, the Honourable PM recognised 48 businesses out of which four businesses from Pune, Maharashtra, won this time. The former Indian finance minister Arun Jaitley gave the event its official opening on January 16, 2016. CEOs, founders of start-ups, and venture capitalists attended the event. The entrepreneur is elevated in the above positions like the organised and policy pillar, the capital opportunity, and the entrepreneurial civilisation. By replicating the start-up ecosystem in the enlarged states, the government should supervise entrepreneurship in a developing society like India and promote the commercialisation of innovative and bright ideas.

The RBI announced that it would take action to enhance the "ease of doing business" in the nation and support the development of an environment that is favourable to the expansion of start-up companies. The country's prosperity and the culture of entrepreneurship are being promoted by vigorous actions of the state and federal governments via the policies proposed by them. A favourable environment for entrepreneurs is being created by government initiatives and legislation that enable the creation of the framework, incubators, and cooperative-working areas, as well as in some cases, accession to marketing and capital financing.

Significance of the Study

As we all know in terms of the population of India is increasing day by day and government enterprises are not enough to employ the increasing population. Thus, there is an emerging need to convert the country from job-seekers to job providers and start-ups play a pivotal role in this conversion and in creating jobs. This study plays a major role in defining the firms which fall under the category of start-ups as per administration and also throws light on the ecosystem for start-ups in India which is very important for studying the entrepreneurial environment and its scope in the nation. This study has also brought the start-up programme into the limelight which was introduced by the government to inspire and encourage newcomers to engage in business, advance their careers, and strengthen the national economy.

Review of Literature

Behl (2022) conducted a study to discover how technology start-ups can boost their company performance and acquire a comparative edge by utilising big data analytics. China and India are the two nations for whom the study is conducted and 233 and 269 responses were gathered from these countries respectively. "Warp PLS 6.0" was used for analysis. The findings of the study revealed that big data analytics skills have a significant and positive effect on the comparative edge and the performance of the firm. While innovation, the age of the enterprise didn't have any significant effect and the origin of the country was found to have a major role in making the firm successful.

Mukul & Saini (2021) discovered how small business owners use social capital to overcome the problems faced by them in the acquisition of talent and to examine the methods of recruitment used by them. Six case studies were used to analyse the practices of acquisition of talent in newly opened enterprises in Karnataka. The findings revealed that low-quality talent, not being able to provide a justified and competitive wage and lack of trademark and other negative points of destination were some challenges faced by the firms. Entrepreneurs take advantage of human support by carefully selecting talent based on an acquaintance or reliable connections and referrals. According to this report, trustworthiness and worker culture match are key factors in attracting top talent to businesses.

Chaudhari & Sinha (2021) investigated the trends that are fuelling the expansion of the ecosystem for start-ups in India. To determine the key trends, the 200 start-ups which were on top as per valuation were chosen as a sample. This study surveyed the sample companies regarding the adoption of the latest developments like crowdsourcing, the participative economy and large data within their organisations, as well as the concrete and intangible effects on their enterprises. The findings revealed 10 leading developing themes that fuel the expansion of the ecosystem for start-ups in India were found, and the sectors in which they can be tapped into were determined.

Singh et al. (2020) analysed the Indian start-up environment using Twitter statistics. The study analysed approximately 50,000 tweets representing Fifteen Indian companies across a wide range of sectors using content and descriptive analytics. To offer insights into the Indian start-up environment, the study also used methods like the "Naive Bayes Algorithm" for analysing emotions and the "Latent Dirichlet Allocation Algorithm" for subject-designing Twitter posts. The start-up environment of the nation leans toward digitization, cares about people, the earth, and money, and views knowledge and information accessibility as the foundation for prosperity. According to the research, tweets' emotions were classified into good, moderate, or bad. Findings suggested that were more good than bad opinions towards the start-up environment of the nation. The survey also offered an observation that "Digital India" will be the destiny of the start-up environment of the nation.

Prashantham & Kumar (2019) via discussions and conceptual study expanded the notion of the "distribution of innovative work" to thoroughly examine the viewpoint of international companies about collaborating with start-up companies. The study found three aspects in this field. The first capacity aspect shows that the complementary competencies of businesses and start-ups have the ability to generate value. The second aspect of connection focuses on the realisation of the above-mentioned potential. It emphasized the growth of systematic corporate activities and third party experts.

The final aspect of contextuality draws attention to the geographic distinctions while highlighting the special opportunities and difficulties MNCs face when cooperating with start-ups in developing economies.

Conclusion

When COVID was spreading in the world and even in the post-covid period many people lost their jobs and start-ups came into the limelight. And in modern days, the government is also focusing to follow the latest concept of start-ups, especially in rural areas.

However, it is also true that a thriving economy has a great number of young ideas and businesses vying for a place in the market. Entrepreneurs supply the energy for the economy's growth. Start-ups require assistance and motivation from a variety of sources during their initial stages as well as during their growth phase and establishment on solid ground. In India, technology-based start-ups are quite important. Overall, it can be concluded that Start-up India is a cooperative strategy for the empowerment of young entrepreneurs. This study has the drawback of being a thorough conceptual study of start-up India utilising secondary data only. Other studies in this field can be done by utilising primary information and other statistical approaches.

References

Behl, A. (2022). Antecedents to firm performance and competitiveness using the lens of big data analytics: a cross-cultural study. *Management Decision, 60*(2), 368–398. https://doi.org/10.1108/MD-01-2020-0121

Chakraborty, S. (2017). *DIPP in touch with Corporate Affairs Ministry to update start-up rules | Business Standard News*. March 17. https://www.business-standard.com/article/companies/dipp-in-touch-with-corporate-affairs-ministry-to-update-start-up-rules-117031700762_1.html

Chaudhari, S. L., & Sinha, M. (2021). A study on emerging trends in Indian startup ecosystem: big data, crowd funding, shared economy. *International Journal of Innovation Science, 13*(1), 1–16. https://doi.org/10.1108/IJIS-09-2020-0156

Mukul, K., & Saini, G. K. (2021). Talent acquisition in startups in India: the role of social capital. *Journal of Entrepreneurship in Emerging Economies, 13*(5), 1235–1261. https://doi.org/10.1108/JEEE-04-2020-0086

Munshi, A. (2019). Assessment of Competitiveness of Food-tech Start-ups in India. *Indian Journal of Public Administration, 65*(1), 201–224. https://doi.org/10.1177/0019556118821268

PM Modi Announces Rs 1,000-crore. (n.d.). *Moneycontrol*. Retrieved January 15, 2023, from https://www.moneycontrol.com/news/business/startup/pm-modi-announces-rs-1000-crore-startup-india-seed-fund-6355761.html

Prashantham, S., & Kumar, K. (2019). Engaging with startups: MNC perspectives. *IIMB Management Review, 31*(4), 407–417. https://doi.org/10.1016/j.iimb.2019.01.003

Sarkar, A. (2016). *Startup India-A New Paradigm For Young Entrepreneurs (A Conceptual Study)*. http://ssrn.com/abstract=2835322https://ssrn.com/abstract=2835322Electroniccopyavailableat:http://ssrn.com/abstract=2835322

Singh, S., Chauhan, A., & Dhir, S. (2020). Analyzing the startup ecosystem of India: a Twitter analytics perspective. *Journal of Advances in Management Research*, *17*(2), 262–281. https://doi.org/10.1108/JAMR-08-2019-0164

Start-up India Is Work-in-Progress - Forbes India. (n.d.). Retrieved January 15, 2023, from https://www.forbesindia.com/article/startup-india-2016/startup-india-is-workinprogress/41945/1

19

Investing in mutual funds in India: A study on factors affecting investor's sentiments

Sanjay Kumar Hooda[1]

Abstract

The study has concluded on the mutual funds in the nation to examine the attitudes of additional investors on the path shown by Maharaja Agrasen five thousand years ago, considered the era of the mutual fund. For millions of investors, mutual funds have opened up new possibilities. Most individuals rely on data that neither offers an inflation hedge nor produces positive absolute returns. Mutual funds have proven to be a beneficial resource for these investors. The markets had a challenging year in 2022 due to rising inflation, tightening liquidity by international central banks, increases in interest rates, and significant geopolitical concerns. Despite these challenges, the mutual fund sector in India experienced consistent growth. India's mutual fund market will expand at a CAGR of 21.5 percent by 2027. A study of 100 knowledgeable investors from Delhi/NCR was done. The results showed that the main elements influencing mutual fund investors' purchasing decisions are creditworthiness, vantage, and supportive analysis. Academicians, AMCs, brokers, distributors, and other potential investors will all greatly benefit from this study.

Key words: Mutual Funds, investor, creditability, brokers and Maharaja Agrasen.

---

1. Associate Professor, Department of Commerce, Indira Gandhi University Meerpur-Rewari, Haryana.

Introduction

Maharaja Agrasen, the founder of the Agrahari and Agrawal families, was born almost 5,000 years ago. However, his ideas of socialism and economic equality in society are being upheld by his descendants. The Vaishya community honours Agrasen Jayanti, which falls on September 21 and coincides with the first Navratri, by hosting numerous cultural and charitable events throughout the city. This day is seen as lucky for starting a new business. Maharaja Agrasen, the fabled ruler of Agroha, was a renowned and esteemed monarch who was highly regarded by the populace of his realm. Members of the Agrawal and Agrahari communities worship Maharaja Agrasen with devotion on the day of Agrasen Jayanti and also give prayers to Goddess Lakshmi to obtain her blessings for peace, harmony, and success in their personal and professional lives. Harendra Garg of the SIDCUl Manufacturers Association told The Pioneer that King Agrasen, a Kshatriya by caste, joined the Vaishya dharma due to his works. Formerly, the "Varnashram system" (which divided society into the four factions of Brahmin, Kshatriya, Vaishya, and Shudra) was based on one's karmas rather than their place of birth (actions). The founder of Agarwal Samaj introduced the idea of economic equality. He invited each community member to donate one brick and one rupee for the economically weaker brother to empower those who lived below the poverty line, reasoning that if one lakh people did so, it would enable the underprivileged to construct a home for them. Continuing to uphold these beliefs that Agrasen Maharaj espoused, the Government of India started a mutual fund scheme in 1963 only through the path shown by Maharaja Agrasen. Based on duration, the mutual funds have been divided into the following five phases: The first phase started from 1964 to 1987, the second phase was from 1987 to1993, the third phase was from 1993 to 2003, the fourth phase started from Feb. 2003 to April 2014 and fifth means current phase started from May 2014 to till date (Association of Mutual Fund in India).

Mutual funds in India have a promising future. Formerly, about 200 different plans were spread among numerous universities, but now there are 1000, a five-fold increase. There will be a phase in the development of mutual funds in India that will draw many more investors. Because of the fintech sector's tremendous growth, even those living in rural locations may now access financial markets very quickly. The availability of various schemes is advantageous since it accommodates a wide range of investors with various risk tolerances. The markets had a challenging year in 2022 due to rising inflation, tightening liquidity by international central banks, increases in interest rates, and significant geopolitical concerns. Despite these challenges, the mutual fund sector in India experienced consistent growth. According to market researchers, India's mutual fund market will expand at a CAGR of 21.5 percent by 2027.

This report briefly overviews the mutual fund sector and its investment plans. Additionally aids in comprehending the significance of investor perception and investment trends in mutual fund investing. The primary goal of this research study is to comprehend the factors that influence investors' investing behaviour towards mutual funds, investigate the causes of mutual funds' lack of widespread acceptance, and analyse investors' perceptions of various characteristics offered by mutual fund businesses. Therefore, it is crucial to understand the elements influencing mutual fund investment decisions and how behavioural aspects affect investors. This research also tries to identify the barriers stopping people from investing in mutual funds. Most elements, such as investment goals, fund kinds, and the stock market, encourage investing in mutual funds. This study focuses on numerous driving forces that entice potential investors to invest in mutual funds so that mutual fund service providers can develop effective market-attracting strategies and examine investor awareness and perception of mutual funds investment. This research will outline the various elements influencing the decisions of stakeholders and investors in mutual funds. In this age of globalisation and competitiveness, an industry's success can be linked to the performance of its equities on the stock market.

Additionally, investors like to invest in the stocks of only those businesses they may earn the most. Investors needed more options for investing in the early years of the mutual fund industry's inception. However, as the contemporary stock market has developed, investors now have many options for where to put their money based on their needs. Mutual fund investment is one of these methods.

Need of the study

The study aims to investigate the idea that investors use mutual funds as a source of investing opportunities. Since specialists manage mutual funds, they better understand market trends. Additionally, they contribute some competence to their work. Additionally, they optimise profits through wise investment choices and timing. Investors are afforded a reasonable level of protection by the mutual fund system. Currently, all mutual fund schemes offer tax benefits under Section 80 and Section 88 of the Income Tax Act, which has increased the value of mutual funds in the eyes of investors.

Scope of the study

The study aims to ascertain how investors view mutual funds as a form of investing. Due to COVID, information was gathered online from 100 investors in the Delhi/NCR region exclusively.

Review of Literature

According to Kankhal Pradeep Chaudhary, a former president of the Vaishya Samaj Sabha, "Maharaja Agrasen was the epitome of what socialist beliefs are. Prof Gauri Prabhu & Dr N.M. Vechalekar (2014) concluded in their research that the numerous elements influence how investors see investing in mutual funds. The research will enable mutual fund companies to pinpoint the areas that need development to raise investor knowledge of mutual fund investments. Jiang, J., Liao, L., Wang, Z., & Xiang, H. (2020) found that Investment decisions have increased dramatically due to financial literacy. The relationship between financial literacy and investing choices is mediated mainly by risk perception. Notwithstanding the notion that demographics like gender and age have an adverse impact on decisions in mutual funds investment.

A literature survey demonstrates that despite the number of behavioural finance research publications, more information on investor preferences, opinions, attitudes, and behaviour still needs to be collected. The relative weights of the many impacting factors are rarely indicated. A summary of certain pertinent pieces of evidence, such as investor opinions and impressions, was provided by the researcher. The type of mutual fund scheme, the goal of investing, the function of financial consultants and brokers, the sources of pertinent information, and difficulties in the services offered by mutual fund managers have also been demonstrated.

Second, the investigation was made into why mutual funds were not considered a vital investment choice. In order to secure their long-term affiliation by encouraging investor loyalty, this research also examined fund characteristics, sponsor qualities, and financial advantages. Studies have also been done to understand mutual fund investors' preferences, knowledge, and mindsets.

Objectives of the study

- To evaluate the investor's perception and awareness regarding investment in mutual funds.
- To investigate the variables affecting investor's perception of mutual funds.

Research methodology

The method considers sample size, analytical framework, and data sources and data. The primary data were gathered online from 100 respondents using a standardised questionnaire that included various investor groups according to geography, demographics, etc., in Delhi/NCR.

Findings of the study

Hundred respondent's worth of data has been gathered. Table 1 displays the categorisation on numerous grounds. According to age, 45 respondents belong to the age of 20 and 30, 40 respondents belong to the age of forty and sixty, and fifteen respondents belong to over the age of 60. There were 51 males and 49 females, respectively, according to gender. According to the classification of respondents' educational backgrounds, there were 23 professionals, while 37 and 40 respondents were graduates and postgraduates. According to the occupation, 12 individuals own their businesses, 19 professionals, 43 people work in the private sector, and the government employs 21 people. Regarding the concern for monthly-wise income,

32 respondents' incomes were below $20,000, 50 respondents were between $20,000 and $40,000, and 18 had $40,000 or more revenues. According to investment type, 63 respondents were from the new generation, whereas 37 were hereditary investors. According to classification based on investor category, 11 and 19 respondents fell into the day trader and both categories, whereas 70 respondents fell into the long-term investor category. Twenty-three respondents had less than three years of investing experience, 52 had between three and five years, and the remaining 25 had five years or more of investing experience. Based on the estimated magnitude of the investment, 30 respondents invested less than ₹ 1 lakh, 45 respondents between ₹ 1 lakh and ₹ 2 lahks, and 25 respondents between ₹ 2 lakhs and ₹ 25 lakhs. Eighty-nine respondents had invested their resources, six had invested borrowed money, and five had done both, according to the source of their investments. Seventy-three respondents have made investments, according to the classification based on the sum of money invested in mutual fund schemes. The 27 respondents, in contrast, have not made any mutual fund investments. Seventy-three respondents indicated they would, while 27 said they would not suggest others invest in mutual funds.

All of the included methodologies have been used to analyse the data for this research project. Kaiser-Meyer-Olkin (KMO) Test has been used primarily. Based on sample data, it is a test to see if the factor analysis technique is appropriate. Kaiser-Meyer-Olkin (KMO) Test values are found below 0.693 which are indicating inappropriate/insufficient sampling and corrective action must be taken in this regard.

Table 1: Detail of respondents of demographic analysis:

No. of Respondents							
Age			Gender		Educational Background		
20 to 40	40 to 60	Above 60	Male	Female	Graduation	Post Graduation	Professionals
45	40	15	51	49	37	40	23
No. of Respondents							
Occupation				Monthly Income			
Private Employees	Govt. Employees	Business	Professionals	Up to 20,000	20,000 to 40,000	Above 40,000	
43	21	12	19	32	50	18	
No. of Respondents							
Investors types		Investor Category			Investment Experience		
Continuous/ hereditary	New Investor	Long duration	Daily trading	Both	Below 03 years	From 3 to 5 years	Above 05 Years
37	63	70	11	19	23	52	25
No. of Respondents							
Recommendation for Investments				Yes	73	No	27

Source: Compiled by author.

Table 2: Showing the results by the Kaiser-Meyer-Olkin and Bartlett's test:

Analysis of sampling Adequacy by Kaiser-Meyer-Olkin.	0.693
Value of Chi-Square (Approximately)	736.121
(Bartlett's Test of Sphericity) df	378
Sig	0.00

Table 2 demonstrates that the sample is adequate using the factor analysis technique by showing the 0.693 value of the Kaiser-Meyer-Olkin test's analysis of sampling adequacy. The data showed multicollinearity between the values and the independent variable, as shown by a chi-squared statistic value of 736.121 and a significance value of 0.00. Any communality value is more significant than 0.5. In the 0.0 to 0.4, a variable has problems significantly loading on any component. Due to the position, all of the study's variables are only somewhat loaded when all circumstances are considered.

The study reveals out the undermentioned important points:

- As mutual funds are viewed as a profitable investment, 83 percent of respondents advised their peer group to participate in them.
- For the 40 percent of respondents, in accordance with investments found comparatively worth less than ₹ 2 lakh, mutual funds are preferably invested by investors.
- The primary outcome of this study is that those investors' perceptions of unconventional investment routes have altered in a favourable and forward-looking way.
- The qualities of the funds invested and its worthiness, the ease of the process, and varying success rates are important considerations for investors while investing in mutual funds.
- The first found component is fund characteristics, which explains 37.410 percent of the variance. This component considers low initial investment, strong returns, price, and capital appreciation.
- Credibility is the second discovered factor, with an 18.736 percent variation explained. This element considers brand perception, preferred information sources, prior results, and transparency.

- Convenience is the third factor discovered and has a variance explained of 12.902 percent. This aspect considers switching options, prompt grievance procedures, and prompt service.
- Success factors, the fourth identified factor, with a variance explained of 6.544 percent. This aspect considers research, document simplicity, and service excellence.
- A fund family is the fifth identified factor, with a variance of 6.379 percent. This aspect considers elements like outsourcing, significant funds, and organisational structure.

Conclusion

A study on factors affecting investor's sentiments shows that while the mutual fund investment industry is still in its childhood transition phase, the study's findings show it has much potential to grow. Success is based on measurable returns and the expertise of fund management. Buying and selling mutual funds directly on the market or through a broker should be straight forwarded. Mutual funds have grown to be a substantial part of the financial markets and, until recently, have given investors reliable and long-lasting profits. The study found that various demographic factors, including gender, influence investors' impressions. The demographic makeup demonstrates the necessity for greater utilisation of the female market and the importance of paying more attention to those with higher incomes. To increase mutual fund investment levels, fund managers should assess the possibility of investments relating to the female and higher income categories. The study's findings also included details on the factors affecting investors' perceptions. It reveals how fund features, creditability, convenience, success factors, and fund family highly influence investors' perceptions of funds. They receive the boost they need from these elements during the investment process. Fund managers must enhance these asset aspects to entice additional investors. Just 100 participants in the most recent study examined investing behaviours. With a bigger sample size and additional factors that might be seen as pertinent in the Indian mutual fund business, this research could be broadened. Delhi-NCR is the core data-gathering area for studying investors' attitudes and perceptions regarding mutual funds as an investment choice. Still, the study might be expanded to other regions of the nation to examine the attitudes of additional investors on the path shown by Maharaja Agrasen five thousand years ago.

References

Goel, A., & Khatik, R. (2017). A study on investors' awareness and preference towards mutual funds as an investment option. *International Journal of Commerce and Management Research,* 3(3), 61–65.

Goel, S., Sharma, R., & Mani, M. (2012). A Review of performance indicators of mutual funds. *Asian Journal of Management Research,* 3(1), 116–124.

Jiang, J., Liao, L., Wang, Z., & Xiang, H. (2020). Financial literacy and retail investors' financial welfare: Evidence from mutual fund investment outcomes in China. *Pacific-Basin Finance Journal, 59,* 101242.

Kaur, S., Batra, G. S., &Anjum, B. (2013). Investor's perception towards selection of mutual funds rather than stock market. *International Research Journal of Business and Management,* 5(2), 53–63.

Kumar, R., &Goel, N. (2014). An empirical study on investors' perception towards Mutual Funds. *International Journal of Research in Management & Business Studies,* 1(4), 83–91.

Mane, P. (2016). A Study of Investors Perception towards Mutual Funds in the city of Aurangabad. *Financial & Business Management (IFBM),* 4(2), 38–44.

Pandey, P., & Kishore, R. (2013). Investor's preferences towards mutual funds and future investments: A case study of India. *International Journal of Scientific and Research Publications,* 3(11), 1–3.

Prabhu, G., & Vachalekar, N. M. (2014). Perception of Indian investors towards investment in mutual funds with special reference to MIP funds. In the 7th *International Business Research Conference, India.*

Radhamani, V. (2013). Investor's preferences towards the mutual fund industry in Trichy. *IOSR Journal of Business and Management,* 1(1), 14–29.

Reddy, R., &Sudhakar, D. (2016). The perception of individual investors towards the performance of mutual funds. *IOSR Journal of Business and Management,* 18(9), 9–14.

Saha, S., & Dey, M. (2011). Analysis of Factors Affecting Investors' Perception of Mutual Fund Investment. *IUP Journal of Management Research, 10*(2).

Saini, S., Anjum, B., & Saini, R. (2011). Investor's awareness and perception about mutual funds. *International Journal of Multidisciplinary Management Studies,* 1(1), 14–29.

Sharma, A., & Agrawal, D. (2015). Investor's perception and attitude towards mutual funds as an investment option. *Business Management & Social Science Research,* 4(3), 51–59.

Walia, N., & Kiran, R. (2009). An analysis of investor's risk perception towards mutual funds services. *International Journal of Business and Management, 4*(5), 106-120.

20

The Skill Development and Entrepreneurship

Pooja Vyas[1], Kanwar Singh[2]

Abstract

This paper discusses a comprehensive view on establishing the relation been the skill development and the socio-economic development in the changing development scenario. Even after the 75 years of independence of India, there is only 2.3 percent of the total work force, are skilled workers in comparison with the developed countries. It was expected that the government of India, that over 50 million of the people will be trained through their skill development programme for the self-employment in the various areas in the rural and the urban areas by the end of the year 2022. This skill development area was aimed at developing the youth, women and the disadvantageous people to improve them and to provide an opportunity to live an esteemed life. Further, the paper discusses the challenges, faced by this programme in the country, and its vital role in empowering the women in the society with their consistent efforts to overcome the barriers.

Keywords: Entrepreneurship, Skill Development, socio-economic development, Self-Employment, empowering the women.

Introduction

The National Entrepreneurship Policy formulate and submitted by the Entrepreneurship Development Institute (EDI) of India to the

1. Assistant Professor Department of Management IGU, Meerpur, Rewari.
2. Research Scholar, Department of Management IGU, Meerpur, Rewari.

Government is expected to pave the way to implement the development agenda throughout country with the help of entrepreneurs and the business houses of the country. The multiplier effect of the potential expending of the businesses will be conducive to generate the additional sources of the revenue and the taxes for the government. It is because of adding the additional employment opportunities; provided by different these entrepreneurs in the forms of the goods and services will ensue to promote the multiple economic activities in their respective areas. Also, the process of entrepreneurship is expected to help in transforming ideas to innovations thereby creating new economic opportunities and thus entrepreneurship plays a crucial role in the growth of any nation. In order to develop a favourable entrepreneurial and innovative and friendly environment in the country, Skill and knowledge are of Utmost importance. Thus, Entrepreneurship, Skills and Knowledge are crucial for economic growth and social development of any country. The Indian economy is currently valued at around 3.5 trillion USD and the government aims to be a Five Trillion USD by the year 2025. This aim can be achieved only if we are increasing economic activities and promote new business, ideas and provide industrial opportunities.

That forms a basis for development. Apart from this, it will require the factors such as the entrepreneurship, Skill development through skilled human resource, innovative modern technologies, knowledge, and innovation etc. It is because of the demonstration effects, by the ongoing business and industrial environment which acts as a catalyst for promoting us towards the progressive path. The notion of the 'Unity in Diversity', as on the India's composite culture will hold good at the concept of the entrepreneurship and skill development which always approve conducive to achieve the targets of this "National Integration" through "Economic Development". In order to achieve this target, it becomes imperative to acquire a effective and skilled work force, belonged to different business streams; depend upon them for its uninterrupted operations and make available goods and services in accordance with the requirement of the prospective customers.

The Skill Development is an essential element for a **successful entrepreneurial culture** in a country and both are complement to each other. According to the Economic Survey of India, 2018-19; which had highlighted the importance of entrepreneurship and expected to call for making the MSME sector of India; more productive and competitive at the International Level. With this view, there are various factors related to entrepreneurship and the skill development which are enlisted as follows:

- Why Entrepreneurship and Skill development are important in boosting the economy of a country.
- Review of the Policy and Institutional efforts taken by the government in promoting entrepreneurship and the skill development and its relating challenges.
- Role of Entrepreneurship and Skill development in the women's empowerment and for the youth.
- Potential efforts for the promoting the entrepreneurship and Skill development.
- Role of Entrepreneurship and Skill development in attainment of SDGs in the coming decade (2020-30).

The **entrepreneurship** refers to those business and industries that undertake different economic activities by utilisation and effective management of available resources to provide for and fulfill the needs of people and organisations by producing and distributing required goods and services. This is also marked by the risks of market Demand. Skills can be defined as the capability acquired by a person to works in any of the particular area. Thus, the Skill development can be defined as honing up of one's skills that will help him in becoming an efficient and able Human Resource. As per the reports of National Skill Development and Entrepreneurship Policy-2015, India is having largest young working population between the age group of 15-59 i.e. nearly 62 percent of our total population. Also, 54 percent of our population is below 25 years of Age. So, this energetic and dynamic demographic dividend can be transformed a power house of human resource which is expected to play a vital role in the nation building and eradication of the poverty, unemployment situation and other the social evils if they are provided with better skill training. The country-wise distribution of formally trained work force percentage is tabulated in the Table 1 which is as shown as follows:

Table 1: Country-wise Distribution of formally trained workforce percentage of workforce

S. No.	Country	Formally Trained Workforce out of total Workforce (%)
1.	India	2.3
2.	United Kingdom	68
3.	Germany	75
4.	USA	52
5.	Japan	80
6.	South Korea	96

Source: International Labour Organisation, 2020.

The vicious circle of the entrepreneurship; shown in a diagram as follows:

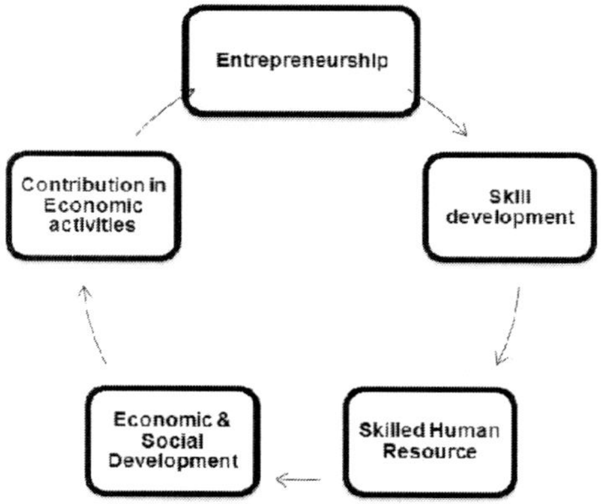

Diagram 1: Entrepreneurship, Skills and Human Resource Development.

The Government of India has aimed at imparting the Skill Education to 50 crores of the people in the different areas by this year in the rural and the urban areas. All the programmes have paved the way to find a sustainable livelihood to the youth, women and the people, belonged to other backward class and transfer these people in to rich human resources.

Role of Entrepreneurship and Skill Development in Economy of a Country

- To assist in elimination of social problems like Poverty, Hunger, Unemployment etc. in both urban and rural settings.
- Changes in the lifestyle of common man and participation in Nation Building through economic activities.
- Providing opportunity for young entrepreneurs to showcase their talent through various creative activities.
- Important contribution in providing skilled work force in various fields.
- To ensure social integration by providing better livelihood activities to all including women, Specially-abled people, Transgender etc.
- To promote Innovation and help in raising living standards of the people.
- Encouraging Industrial and commercial activities in rural and urban areas that will help our youth in becoming self-reliant.
- Development of MSMEs especially in rural sectors and encourage them to take risks and ensure growth.
- Important role in eradication of various social evils.

Policy Efforts undertaken to promote Entrepreneurship and Skill Development

It is evident that Industries, Businesses and other commercial activities are always possible due to high quality skills and workmanship. The reason India was called as **'Golden Bird'** was its abundant resources, entrepreneurial environment and market opportunities. And hence, various efforts have been undertaken to promote Entrepreneurship and Skill Development in our country since Independence.

Also, after the New Economic Policy of 1991-92 that initiated liberalisation, Privatisation and Globalisation, the Government, private Sector and people in general were drawn towards realising their goals of better living standards and economic growth.

The decade from 2011-2019 has been quite important with respect to **Entrepreneurship and Skill Development** in rural and urban areas alike as it was pushed greatly due to e-commerce and Information and communication technology. The Central and various state Governments have played an important role in providing conducive environment for growth of Entrepreneurship and Skill Development.

National Skill Development Policy-2009: Salient Features

- Focus on providing wholesome employment to people depending upon their skills and knowledge.
- Special emphasis on Institution based Skill Development.
- Unified Cooperation of various interest holders in the process of Skill Development.
- Empowering the backward communities, Minorities, specially Abled people, women, and BPL population for Inclusive skill development.
- Formation of National Skills Qualification Framework.
- Policy Initiative for enhancing skills of people working in the unorganised sector.

National Skill Development and Entrepreneurship Policy-2015: Salient Features

- Promoting innovation-based entrepreneurship for providing sustainable employment and livelihood opportunities to people.
- Swift promotion of Skill Development on Large Scale.
- Ensuring focus and coordination among factors responsible for increasing entrepreneurship.
- To integrate skill development with formal education.
- The policy aims at providing equal skill development and entrepreneurial opportunities for people who are socially/ geographically backward, deprived and for women.

Start-Up Policy by All India Council for Technical Education (AICTE): Salient Features

- Developing an ecological system for promoting

entrepreneurship in all Indian Educational Institutions of Higher Education.

- Strengthen the Inter-Institutional partnership among leading Educational Institutions of India to promote Entrepreneurship and Skill development.
- The policy aims at providing 10 lakh employment opportunities by 2025 and also incubates one lakh Tec based student Start-Ups.
- To promote the idea of entrepreneurship among the students of Science and Technology.
- To provide self-employment opportunities amongst students of rural India by identifying various commercial activities at the regional/local level.
- To link entrepreneurship, skill development and human resource development to promote latest industrial opportunities.

Important Programmes for promotion of Entrepreneurship and Skill Development in India.

Numerous programmes for entrepreneurship and skill development etc. have been taken up by various ministries of the Union Government as well as different State Governments. Some of these are discussed below in Table 2.

Table 2

S. No.	Programme/ Scheme	Description
1.	**Start-Up India**	Launched on 16th January, 2016. It aims at developing the Start- Up ecosystem, providing assistance to entrepreneurs, and to create Job-Givers rather than Job-Seekers. It helps in providing easy compliance, dissolution of firms and other legal assistance, grants etc.
2.	**Stand-Up India**	This scheme is aimed at helping Women and people belonging to SC/ ST category by providing those loans ranging from 10 lacs to One Crore in sectors related to Manufacturing, Services and other trades.
3.	**PM MUDRA Scheme**	Launched on 8th April, 2015. This scheme provides loans under three categories: **Shishu** (Upto 50,000), **Tarun** (Upto 5 lacs) and **Kishore** (Upto Ten Lacs) for Non-Corporate and non-agricultural MSMEs. These loans will be provided by Commercial Banks, Regional Rural Banks, Small MFIs and NBFGs.

4.	**Atal Innovation Mission Incubation Centers (AIC)**	It aims at developing Tech and Innovation based enterprises/ Start-Ups by providing assistance related to commercial planning, market entry and financial Advises etc.
5.	**PMKVY (2.0)**	Launched in 2015-16. It was the first step in the direction to provide skill training to youth and create opportunities for employment. The Second edition 2.0 (2016-20) aims at providing skill training to 1 Crore individuals by training them in skill development courses of 2-6-month duration.
6.	**SANKALP**	This programme is being carried out with the help of World Bank and aims at promoting Skill development and entrepreneurship by strengthening national and state level institutions; providing skills, training, and education to the deprived sections of the society and helping in making 'Make in India' programme a success by providing skilled human resource.
7.	**Deendayal Upadhyay Gramin Kaushal Yojna**	This scheme is related to various social and economic initiatives of the government like Make in India, Digital India, Smart Cities, Stand-Up India etc. and is dedicated to youth between the age group of 15-35 years. It is an empowerment scheme to provide the employment-oriented skill development scheme and creating a Market oriented skilled workforce.

These programmes aim at developing a positive outlook regarding entrepreneurship amongst the middle class and common people, initiate calculated risk-taking capacity amongst them and a chain of first Generation Entrepreneurs. As per the Annual Report of Ministry of Skill Development and Entrepreneurship, GoI, the primary challenges for promoting entrepreneurship and skill development are:

- Attitude of people towards skill development activities is negative believing that it is for the deprived and uneducated community.
- Need for enhancing capabilities of the coordination and surveillance system for skill development programmes of Government of India.
- Plurality in certification and evaluation of skill development programmes that result in different outcomes for the employers which causes misconception for them.
- Lack of the skilled trainers and inability to attract best professional talent for this purpose from the industry.

- Decrease in participation of women in total labour force.
- Lack of integration of entrepreneurship in formal education system.
- Lack of financial resources and technical expertise for new ventures.
- Insufficient push to innovation-based entrepreneurship.
- Inability of Higher education and Skill development in promoting Employment, Self-employment and entrepreneurship.

Ministry of Skill Development and Entrepreneurship MoS Sh. R.K. Singh told the Indian Parliament that around 60 lakh people had enrolled under the Pradhan Mantri Kaushal Vikas Yojna (PMKVY) and some 52 lakhs of them were provided with Skill Training. i.e. 90 percent of the enrolled candidates were provided with the benefits of this scheme and only some 9.75 percent people left midway of training. The main reasons for such leave were lack of interest among candidates, imbalance between expectations and aspirations, absence during the course, failure and lack of awareness etc.

The Ministry is trying hard to overcome all the aforesaid hindrances and skill development ecosystem is being developed by ensuring better human resource training and effective partnership and involvement of the industrial sector. For this purpose, three Indian Skill Development Institutes are proposed to come up at Kanpur, Ahmedabad and Mumbai by the Union Cabinet. These upcoming centres will focus on fulfilling international level skill development requirements; quiet differently than the existing Industrial Training Institutes (ITI's), Poly-Technic and other training centres. The Government of India is providing short term and long term loans as well as training facilities via different schemes to promote employment, self-employment and entrepreneurship opportunities to Indian Youth. Training programmes are prepared as per the industry needs after having close conversation with industrial honchos by various institutes like Rural Self-employment Training Institutes, PM Entrepreneurship Development Programme, National Career Service etc.

The Table 3 indicates all those businesses that are skill based and tech based and which are important in creating employment, self-employment and entrepreneurship opportunities.

Table 3

S.No.	Area
1.	Tech-based e-Commerce, Online Retail Business.
2.	Travel, Transportation and Delivery of Goods.
3.	Hotel and Lodging
4.	Processing and Marketing of food and other perishable goods.
5.	Fashion, Clothing and Apparels
6.	Banking and Payment Services.
7.	Logistics, Transportation &Warehousing
8.	Travel and Tourism
9.	Beauty and Wellness
10.	Furniture and Furnishing.
11.	Healthcare

Role of Entrepreneurship and Skill development in empowerment of Women and Youth

The Union Government is carrying out varied programmes to make the women and youth of our country as self-reliant. These programmes not only help these sections in creating employment and business opportunities and assist them in availing required assistance also.

These programmes are providing assistance to Women Self-Help Groups and loans to youth are willing to set up new businesses in order to create new employment opportunities and eradication of the poverty, but these processes are marked by some of the institutional and non-institution barriers. Now, in order to address this problem, global entrepreneurs, summit was jointly organised by NITI Ayog and the US government in the year 2017 in Hyderabad, Telangana state with an idea to establish a women entrepreneur platform was conceived. This platform was officially launched by Narandra Modi, the PM of India on March 2018.

This platform has ensured to increase the numbers of the women Participation in social entrepreneurship, and awareness about markets and financial planning and literacy. It is therefore, entrepreneurship and the skill development are not only to make the women and youth self-reliant but also developing the confidence, managerial skills, power of the decision-making and innovating goods and services with leading a dignified life too. In the precedent decade, the use of IT by the large numbers of the enterprises in delivering various goods and services has led to have a positive impact in our lives and simultaneously has benefitted them too. There are new ventures which are providing an adequate pace to the economic activities in the country and providing the employment opportunities to the unemployed youth. They are proving helpful to develop the confidence and the change the outlook on the concept of the self- employment and entrepreneurship among the common people as these small ventures are proving an important cog in the entire supply chain machinery.

Entrepreneurship & Skill Development, Sustainable Development Goals- 2030 and Rural India

The role of **Entrepreneurship & Skill Development** will be crucial in the forthcoming decade if we are to achieve SDG-2030. This is because **Entrepreneurship & Skill Development** are determining factors for social and economic growth of any nation. There are Sixteen Sustainable Development Goals as per the Agenda-2030. These include: Poverty Alleviation, Food security and nutrition, better healthcare facilities, Inclusive and quality based livelihood, women empowerment and Gender Equality, water and sanitary management, ensure the energy security, sustainable economic growth, Innovation, reducing inequality and a Peaceful and Inclusive

Entrepreneurship & Skill Development: The Integrated efforts of Government, Civil Society, Private Sector and other interest holders will act as directives and guidelines in order to achieve the SDG-2030 and ensure social, political, economic and cultural growth, strengthening and awakening of common people particularly in the Rural and Remote Areas. The time bound achievement of SDG will directly or indirectly depend upon **Entrepreneurship & Skill Development** because it is related to some important aspects of people's lives such as better means of livelihood, employment, healthcare etc. which are at the centre of SDGs. Also,

Entrepreneurship & Skill Development strengthens confidence and liberty in people by ensuring their economic independence.

Conclusion

Entrepreneurship & Skill Development are considered as the backbone of any country for achieving economic and social development. India is taking great efforts to promote Industries, businesses and other commercial activities and at the same time emerging entrepreneurs are being felicitated, attracted and provided assistance also. On the other hand, it is an opportunity to carry out the ground work which is required to interlink Education and Skill Development to Entrepreneurship, employment and self-employment so that we are able to provide quality and sustainable lifestyle to our future generations. In order to tap the hidden potential of the available work force, it becomes imperative to impart the innovative training through organising the periodic training programme, so that the human resource development may take place through effective resource planning at the different institutional hierarchy, demarcated for imparting the training for the technical and non-technical personnel. It requires a periodic adequate funding and the institutional support so that an effective and result oriented skill may be developed and may be proved conducive to transfer a layman or women in a result oriented human resources.

References

'Young Entrepreneurs turn Angels for Younger Start-Ups', Times of India, December 2019.

Entrepreneurship in India, NKC, 2019.

https://www.aicte-india.org.

National Skill Development Report, Ministry of Micro, Small & Medium Enterprises (MSME), GoI.

Sharma, Varun & Sharma, M.L. (2020). Entrepreneurship and Skill Development, *International Journal of Advance Research in Commerce, Management & Social Sciences*, 3 (2): 261-266.

Singh, Rishika & Maha Lakhmi (2018). Quality Enhancement: Vocational Skill Development & Entrepreneurship, *International Journal of Scientific Research & Management,* 6 (4).

Somraj & Sharma, Sunita (2022). Skill Development and Entrepreneurship: A Comparative study, *Journal of the Emerging technologies and Innovative Research,* 9 (11).

21

Skill Development: Prospects and Pitfalls of Indian Workforce

Shivani Arora[1], Sarika Walia[2], Pushpendra Gothwal[3], C.S. Yadav[4]

Abstract

The goals of this project are to bring attention to the need for skilled labour in India, which has been brought to the forefront by the government's "Make in India" programme and the rapid expansion of the "economy". The main objective of this study is to analyze vocational education and training as it is today and examine the vocational training models of developing nations. The 'Make in India' initiative provides a useful lens through which to examine India's skill development approach. Since they are both BRICS members and growing economies, China and Brazil's vocational training models are also examined here. The vocational education system in Singapore is analysed as a means of gaining knowledge that may be applied to the establishment of policies and programmes in the United States. Due to its young population, India enjoys a "demographic dividend" that makes it the world's most dynamic labour market. By comparison to China and the OECD, the country will have a significantly younger population and a lower median age. This indicates that India has the potential to become the world's

1. Assistant Professor, PDP Department, Graphic Era Hill University, Dehradun, Uttarakhand.
2. Assistant Professor, Department of Management Studies, Gurugram University, Gurugram.
3. Research Scholar, Amity Business School, Amity University, Gurgaon, Haryana.
4. Professor, Shivalik Institute of Professional Studies, Dehradun, Uttarakhand.

greatest supplier of human labour. However, India continues to struggle to find qualified workers to fill open positions. Furthermore, it highlights the challenge the government has in adequately matching employment openings to available talent. When it comes to training new generations of workers, India lags far behind China and Singapore. This research is helpful for analysing the nation's present skill shortages and identifying sectors with lots of room for hiring skilled workers. The report's stated objective is to "address the issues faced in development of skills in the country and highlight the job prospects developing in the various industries with emphasis on the Make in India campaign". The country has a lot of room to grow its skilled workforce and benefit from the so-called "demographic dividend." Public-private partnerships and branding efforts work together to increase the availability of qualified workers.

Keywords: Skill development, Vocational and Technical Education.

Introduction

In the first three months of 2016, the Indian economy expanded at a robust annual rate of 7.6 percent. Population trends in India bode well for the country's efforts to boost GDP. With 64.8 percent of the population in the labour force, India's economy is poised for rapid expansion. It's a boon to the economy and employment opportunities across the country. Because of rapid population ageing in the world's major economies, their share of the global workforce is shrinking rapidly. However, India will stand out as an outlier in the next years, becoming a global labour force leader. India will be the world's leading supplier of skilled labour, giving it an advantage in the labour market. Boston Consulting Group released a report in which it examined the global workforce demand and supply concerns. As many as 47 million fewer people could be in the world by 2020, the report warned. Meanwhile, India will have 56 million unemployed people to spare. If India can train its employees effectively, it will be able to take advantage of the country's growing labour force. In this light, investing in people's abilities stands out as an essential part of "economic strategy".

Objectives of the Study:

- An analysis of "Vocational Education", "Training", and "Skill Development" regulatory framework.
- To examine the models that countries like "China", "Brazil", and "Singapore" use.

- To understand problems related to implementation of "skill development" programmes.
- To evaluate the prospects for professional development and growth in India.

Literature Review

To get a better understanding of the Skill Development system, research has been done on the "Skill Development Model". The "skill development models" used by China, Brazil, and Singapore are being investigated with the goal of gaining an understanding of skill development from an international viewpoint. China and Brazil were selected for the study because, like India, they are both emerging economies on the global stage and are both members of the BRICS group of nations. In the year 2015-16, the United Nations Human Development Index classified Singapore as 2nd most highly skilled country in the world. Therefore, in order to gain a knowledge of the model of a country with a highly qualified workforce, the "Vocational and Technical Education model" of Singapore is thoroughly investigated.

Skill Development Model in India

India has a major competitive advantage in the global labour market due to its large "young workforce." The "Ministry of Skill Development and Entrepreneurship" was formed due to the increased demand for skilled labour on a worldwide scale. The announcement of the ministry's formation came in June of 2014. Because of the shifts in the job market, Indian Prime Minister Shri Narendra Modi decided to create a ministry dedicated to training and education. There was an emphasis on coordinating efforts with other departments to help with the massive shortage of trained personnel. Organisational efforts to foster skill development were coordinated through the establishment and laying down of uniform and standardised approaches to education. Additionally, it seeks to coordinate the efforts of other departments to improve people's abilities. It defines the goals, the outcomes desired, and the many institutions responsible for ensuring those aims are realised. Skills Development has a well-thought-out structure that takes into account the needs of all the primary players. It convenes numerous actors involved in the development of human capital in India. (Refer Figure 4). Towards this end, the Ministry maintains close ties with the "National Skill Development Corporation" (NSDC). It provides assistance in skill mapping, market research, and curriculum development for educational institutions. This plan's primary objective is to increase skill-development initiatives in order to rectify the significant talent supply and demand imbalance. ***In India, there are two main ways to learn a new skill: the formal education system and the informal economy.***

Providing this sort of formal education is a goal of both public and private organisations. Indian government is also considering the "Public-Private Partnership" (PPP) model. The government-sponsored "Industrial Training Institutes" (ITIs) are the primary access point for acquiring Vocational education and training in the country. As an alternative, there are vocational schools and Industrial Training Centers (ITCs), both of which are operated independently of government. As part of their technical education, students in India can take advantage of the apprenticeship programmes mandated by the country's labour laws. Although there is considerable involvement from the commercial sector in skill development, public sector initiatives are far more common. The informal route is less formal and can involve on-the-job training or hands-on experience to transmit knowledge.

India's central government devised a policy framework to improve the population's skill sets. The Apprentices Act of 1961 is a legal framework for formally learning new skills. Both the National Skills Qualification Framework and the National Skill Policy are a part of this. The former is a set of rules and regulations for improving skills, and the latter is a set of standards for evaluating those skills (NSQF). The Apprentice Act of 1961 mandates that employers take part in training their future workforce by providing students with apprenticeships. Experts in the field can provide students with effective instruction in the areas of skill acquisition and development.

The legislation's stated goal is to compel both public and private organisations to provide pupils with training. For students to be competitive in the employment market, the industry must give them with meaningful internships and apprenticeships.

In 2009, policymakers set out to bolster efforts across the country to develop people's skill sets by creating a "National Policy on Skill Development". This PPP idea is overseen by the "Ministry of Skill Development and Entrepreneurship." Putting in place the necessary infrastructure for vocational education of sufficient size and caliber was the impetus for its founding. Since India has a large population with high aspirations but no resources to provide adequate "vocational education and training", our government has enlisted the help of more private companies to implement this training model.

On December 27th, 2013, the "National Skills Qualifications Framework" (NSQF) became law. The framework is based on the most up-to-date idea of competences, which evaluates the specific sets of knowledge, abilities, and aptitudes required at each level of certification. There are 10 distinct levels, each with its own set of learning objectives, and the grades range from one to ten. It makes little difference if the abilities were obtained through formal, informal, or non-formal education. Competency modelling, used as the basis for this framework, is widely regarded as the most useful approach to identifying and documenting the set of abilities necessary to do a job successfully.

Key Bodies	Enablers	Implementing Bodies	Beneficiaries
• Ministry of Skill Development & Entrepreneurship • MHRD • Ministry of Rural Development (MoRD) • Other Central Ministries	• State Skill Development Mission (SSDM) • NSDC • NSDA • SSCs • NCVT • SCVT • Labour Laws • Minimum Wages Act • Financial Institutions • Apprenticeships Act	• ITIs • Training Providers • Captive Training by Employers • Schools • Universities • Assessment Companies	• Marginalized societies • Unemployed youth • Low income Group • School & College Students

Source: FCCI KPMG Skilling India Report.[3]

Figure 4. Indian Skills Development Eco-system.

Indian Skill Development Model

Our system for fostering talent is extensive, varied, and intricate. The people of India are vast and entirely diverse. There are two distinct types of expertise development in our nation: "Skill-based" and "vocational education and training", respectively. In our nation skill development follows a complex organizational framework, as seen in Figure 1.

"Ministry of Human Resource Development" is in charge of educational and occupational programs in India. It regulates public, private, and non-profit institutions of education across all levels. College education is the main focus of the Universities and Higher Education Centre's. Examples include the arts, business, and the sciences.

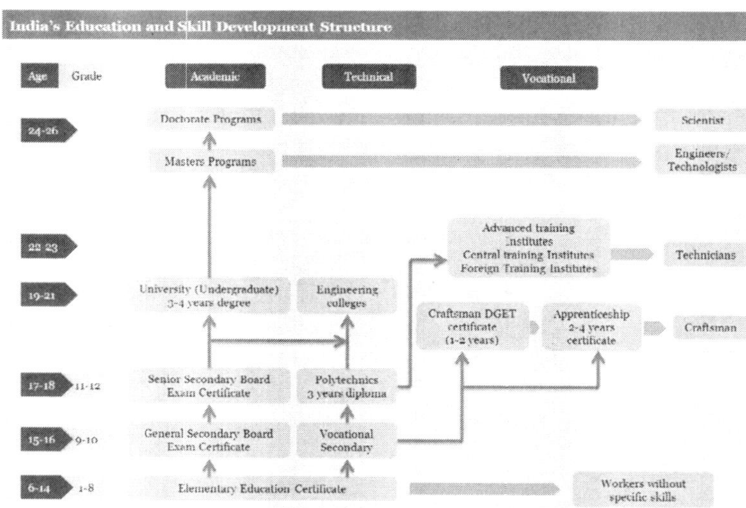

Source: National Skills Development Corporation[3]

Figure 1. Educational and Skill Development System in India.

Education in the technical fields is offered at universities, such as engineering and polytechnic schools. University and college operations are governed by the "University Grants Commission" (UGC). They finance, create, and guarantee the establishment of uniform standards for academic teaching and evaluation. The technical institutions and universities in India are governed by the "All India Council for Technical Education" (AICTE).

(A) "Public-Private Partnerships" (PPP) model

As a result of inadequate facilities and a lack of an industry-relevant curriculum, technical education in India has declined dramatically in recent years. The public-private partnership concept was introduced by the government with the goal of producing a more employable workforce. In 2005–2006, the government chose to use existing internal resources to modernise 100 ITIs. In order to improve 400 more ITIs, the World Bank was also brought in. The PPP model was prioritised for the development of the remaining ITIs. To that end, the "Ministry of Skill Development and Entrepreneurship" launched the "Skill Development Initiative" (SDI), with the goal of fostering more PPPs.

During the Scheme's five-year project span, one million persons will receive training. The plan is meant to equip participants with the necessary knowledge and abilities to carry out their duties successfully. Aside from its current staff and students, the initiative also targeted recent high school graduates and college underclassmen, with the goal of equipping them with marketable skills. By creating a pool of competent workers and so decreasing the supply and demand mismatch, the PPP model appeared promise. Training the trainers, the employees, and the faculty, as well as fostering a conducive atmosphere for learning, are all part of the programme's aims.

"Technical and Vocational Education and Training" System (TVET) of China

China has a sizable pool of educated workers. The "technical and vocational education and training" (TVET) system in China is extensive and successful. There are two types of educational facilities that offer TVET programmes in China. One seeks to provide students with a traditional academic education, while the other emphasises practical skills. The Ministry of Education (MOE) is responsible for compulsory education, while the "Ministry of Human Resources and Social Security" (MHRSS) is in charge of vocational education (MOHRSS) the school's vocational training programmes reflects an in-depth grasp of the theoretical principles and conceptual frameworks unique to each trade, which is a key component of the overall educational experience. Training individuals for work or further education is the goal of the other branch of the MOHRSS. Training in the workplace, as well as attempts to retrain school dropouts and the unemployed, place a premium on practical, on-the-job experience. China's Education Law of 1986 stipulates that students must attend school for nine years, the final three of which must be devoted to job training. Vocational education is offered in a variety of settings, including Technical/Skilled Worker Schools, which offer a wide range of programmes for workers at varying levels of experience, and community colleges, which focus on preparing students for entry-level positions.

As a result, students in their last year of secondary vocational education participate in a three-year vocational scheme education programmes (Refer Figure 2). By taking part in the TVET system as a whole, the business community is guaranteed a voice in the process.

China's reputation as a manufacturing powerhouse demands ready access to a highly trained labour force. They have a strong skill development model, with backing from the government, to satisfy the rising need for skilled workers in the country.

Vocational Education Law which was laid out in 1996 outlines China's framework for managing its "technical education" and "training system". It defines the duties of the "Ministry of Education" and the "Ministry of Human Resources and Social Security" in relation to vocational education. The legislation also covers the responsibilities of local, state, and federal governments, as well as the functions played by business, the private sector, and vocational schools in the nation's skill development process. Making education compulsory in primary school is one way, the government shows how important it is. The legislation is given the utmost consideration in order to ensure that skill development is carried out in the nation.

Companies in China provide substantial aid to training programmes. The occupational norms are laid forth, and there is solid coordination between the training and the economy. The industries are required by law to offer free vocational education and guaranteed employment.

China places a premium on ensuring that businesses contribute as much as possible to vocational education and training. Articles from the law that emphasize industry involvement and skill development are included below.

"Article 20: Businesses are expected to provide workers, employees, and prospective hires with well-thought-out vocational training programmes that take into account the company's unique circumstances.

Businesses have the option of establishing and operating their own vocational schools and vocational training institutes, or entrusting these schools with the vocational education of their employees and prospective hires.

Article 29: The local people's government at the province level or above shall order the enterprise to repair its failure to provide vocational education in line with Article 20 of this Law if the enterprise refuses to do so voluntarily.

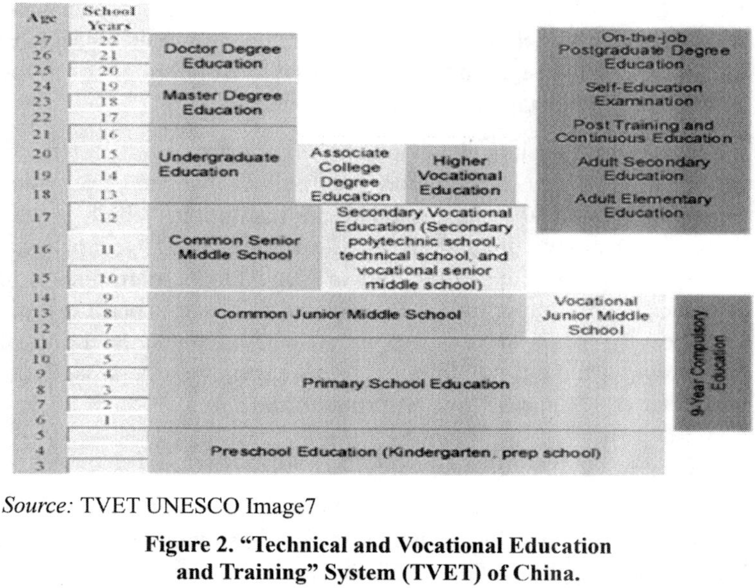

Source: TVET UNESCO Image7

Figure 2. "Technical and Vocational Education and Training" System (TVET) of China.

Vocational Educational Training Model: - Brazil

Continued "Formation courses: (FIC courses), "Technical Courses", and "Technological Courses" make up the present tiers of vocational education and training's structure. Courses in Initial or Continued Formation (FIC) serve the largest demographic. Everyone is welcome to join a programmes like this. Neither age nor education level are prerequisites. Their primary objective is to provide an entry-level credential to individuals with limited academic background or limited work experience. Students in secondary education and those who have completed secondary education can benefit from taking technical courses. There are three modes of operation for these lessons: I. Integrated - Made available to those who wish to pursue both General Education and Vocational Training at the same school. II. Concurrent: Open to anyone taking a General Sequence course, while the latter is restricted to high school grads.

Technology classes are the same level as college level work. Only high school graduates can enroll in these courses, which award a credential on par with that of a four-year college. Students must have finished high school, although not compulsarily a technical high school, in order to sign up for a tech class. Most programmes in the field of technology take three years to complete.

School-based skill development is a priority in Brazil. In particular, they focus on technical programmes that can be provided to students within the same educational institution. Which is why there are so many applications for the course. Their Occupational Education and Training Programme PRONATEC's main goal is to increase people's opportunities for social and economic participation. It is heavily based on social policy, with the stated intention of "promoting training possibilities to teenagers, workers, and the beneficiaries of the cash transfer programmes."

Vocational and Technical Education (VTE) model:- Singapore

The advancement of skills is highly valued in Singapore, hence the country spends a lot of money on VET programmes. If you're looking for a highly skilled staff, Singapore is a better option than India.

The approach is based on India's system and places an emphasis on the quality of technical education students receive. To encourage more students to pursue careers in technical fields, the plan prioritises providing a relevant education grounded in industry standards while also keeping the programme's overall cost low. The "Traineeship", "Approved Training Centres", and "Certified On-the-Job Training Programmes" are just a few examples of the many available options.

The government also wanted to increase awareness of these initiatives and so it took part in various campaigns including "using the hand," television-broadcast "Top of the Trade" competitions, and "Apprenticeship of the Year" award. The TVET model's main benefit is the transfer of applicable skills to the workforce12 thanks to the curriculum's design, which was informed by input from industry specialists.

The VTE has centres of excellence and works with other organisations to facilitate the sharing of training materials, member insights, and skill-building technological projects. Through the VTE model, the government invests in the education and training of both high school and college grads, as well as dropouts, so that the people can maintain their education and skills.

India's Current Skill Analysis

In comparison to the United Kingdom (68%), Germany (75%), the United States (52%), Japan (80%), and South Korea (96%), only 2.3 percent of India's workforce appears to have received formal skill training. Most of the Indian labour force is generally unemployable due to a lack of necessary job skills. A worrisome indicator for the world's youngest populace leader, India. India has a lot of room to grow in terms of training and educating its labour force.

According to the Planning Commission's 12th Five-Year Plan document, India's working population is undereducated. Eighty-five percent of the working population has a secondary school diploma or higher. Roughly 55 percent have attended primary school, whereas only 2 percent have completed any sort of formal vocational training. More students are being recruited for post-secondary education and technical programmes. The basis upon which numerous other initiatives, including "Make in India," "Digital India," and a slew of start-up-centric and venture-funding initiatives, rest is "Skilled India."

Presently, India has a rather bleak outlook in terms of available skills. The India Skills Report 2015 found that there was a significant void in the growth of Indians' skill sets.

Only around one-third of the students who applied for jobs in the labour market actually had the abilities that companies were looking for. Even while we have enough people to get the work done, not all of them have the right set of skills. Core engineering, retail, hotels, e-commerce, and finance are all growing sectors with a shortage of skilled applicants (Refer to Table 1). Considering the current status of the job market, the government has started taking action to solve this critical problem. The government has made improving one's skill set a top priority, and this issue will remain crucial for the next decade.

Figure 3 from The Skills Gap depicts the anticipated industry shortfall in 2022. The infrastructure industry will expand rapidly, followed by the automotive and parts industries. Large-scale efforts to improve education and training in India are required if the Make in India initiative is to be prioritised.

Challenges

With its current infrastructure and policy framework, India is confronting many obstacles. Below, we address some of the difficulties associated with skill acquisition:

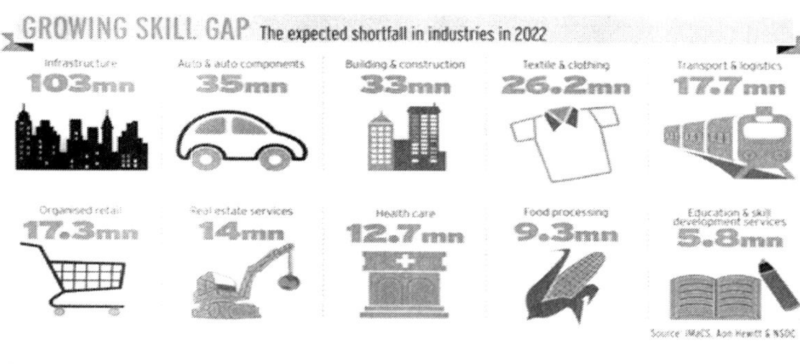

Source: Ministry of Skill Development and Entrepreneurship

Figure 3. Skill Gap 202215.

Limited capacity and insufficient scale

When compared to the massive need for new workers, the current educational infrastructure facilities provided are woefully inadequate. Unfortunately, qualified and experienced instructors are in short supply. It's indicative of the improper and inadequate infrastructure present in both large and small communities. The teaching staff requires encouragement and training before being trusted with further responsibility. Furthermore, the number of people who want to get trained should inform the size of the training infrastructure.

The 'Train the Trainers'16 initiative is also vital to the success of any training programme. As a result of the faculty's expertise, students may be assured that they will leave this course having gained all the necessary knowledge and having had a truly remarkable educational experience. Trainers should be able to gauge their pupils' requirements in light of the current job market. It also calls for the perfect combination of theoretical study and hands-on training. As a result, developing effective strategies for training trainers has become a priority.

Mobilisation

It is now a very difficult effort to get kids to enrol in vocational training programmes. Many persons involved in training have a highly conventional worldview. In light of the low wages and lack of prestige associated with technical crafts professions, the students would progress to managerial responsibilities. Some students simply cannot afford to participate in such activities, and others may be unaware of available financial aid or scholarship opportunities. As a blue collar occupation, skilled labour has historically been stigmatised as having low wages, few opportunities for advancement, and a lack of intellectual challenge. To attract a large number of people to training programmes, like in Singapore, our government should put significant effort into branding strategies for skill development.

Employer's buy-in

Professionals with either formal education or on-the-job experience are valued equally in the sector. In order to train their employees, several businesses build their own training facilities.

Although the Skill Development is centred on the P3 model, it requires significant work from both parties.

Scalability

Stakeholder buy-in is crucial for the achievement of any model's goals. There isn't much movement on these projects since the business world isn't on board. For a long time, the government did not make investing in people's abilities a top priority. High initial investment is a major turnoff for potential backers of this business. Challenges like a lack of available infrastructure and a delayed approval process for bank loans rarely discourage aspiring business owners from coming up with their own solutions. It's even trickier in rural areas, where people often aren't aware of the government's and other financial institutions' assistance for lending facilities and other financial aid programmes. High operational costs are just one of the many obstacles that prevent enterprises from venturing into urban regions.

Skills Mismatch

The gap between the skills desired by industry and those taught in schools and other training programmes is wide. The skill set doesn't meet the needs of employers since there isn't enough collaboration between academia and business. Even if the population has some level of expertise, it is not marketable to businesses. That's why it's crucial to involve actual professionals in the field when crafting courses.

Non-technical skills are not prioritised

Employers in India have expressed a need for employees to also have behavioural skills, while vocational schools in the country are solely teaching technical ones. According to the India Hiring Intent Survey, Indian employers highly value domain knowledge, communication, cultural compatibility, values of honesty and integrity, adaptability, focus on results, interpersonal competence, and a learning mentality. The development of these abilities is not a central focus of the training. This is a serious problem since it leads to a large pool of qualified people being out of work.

Conclusion

The growth of people's capabilities is crucial to the progress of any nation. A successful programmes requires collaboration between government bodies, community members, and students. If the reforms are implemented widely enough, it will improve the country's employment climate. India needs to take advantage of its expanding population, or "demographic dividend". Value will be added to the national economy, and the "Make in India" initiative's access to a trained labour force will be strengthened. Like in China, we need to incorporate vocational education into the formal education system. Development and improvement of abilities are greatly aided by the Public Private Partnership. The growth of public-private partnerships has helped NSDC enhance the private sector's training infrastructure. Over the past few years, this type of collaboration has grown in popularity. Partnerships of this sort are also being pushed for in more rural areas, where there are disproportionately many hopefuls. In order to maintain the model's quality and longevity, it is crucial to fortify ties with training institutions. The government should prioritise the development of non-technical skills in light of the anticipated high demand in the retail and hospitality industries. If the Skilled India initiatives are serious about increasing the country's employment rate, they must priorities and train more people in the art of entrepreneurship. If the government wants more people to take advantage of the "Start-up India" and "Stand up India programmes", it needs to do a better job of marketing them. If the Skill India programmes is going to be a success story, the NSDC needs to pay attention to the unorganised sector as well. As a result, "Koushal Bharat, Kushal Bharat" will be realised in India, and the "Make in India campaign" will be a success from a skill perspective.

References

FCCI and KPMG Report; Skilling India a look back at the progress, challenges and the way forward. Available from: https://www.kpmg.com/IN/en/.../FICCI-KPMG-GlobalSkills-Report-low.pdf Date accessed: 19/10/16

ICRA Management Consulting Services Limited. The Skill Development Landscape in India and Implementing Quality Skills Training; 3rd Global Skill Summit of the Federation of Indian Chambers of Commerce & Industry (FICCI). 2010 Aug.

India Skills Report. 2016. Available from: https://wheebox.com/logo/ISR-2016-small.pdf Date accessed: 16/10/16

Jaganatthan, S. Skill Development: Promises, Approaches in Developed Countries and Emerging Economies, ADB Briefs. 2013 Nov; (19):1–8

Kanth, A. K. Brief Note on Vocational / Educational Training in China. Available from: http://www.prayaschildren.org/pdf/Attachmentbrief_note_about_the_vocational_technical_education_in_china.pdf Date accessed: 14/10/16

Kuruvilla, S, Erickson, C, Hwang, A. An assessment of Singapore Skills Development System: Does it constitute a viable model for other developing nations? Cornell University; ILR School. 2001 May. Available from: http://digitalcommons.ilr.cornell.edu/articles/214 Date accessed: 15/10/16

Ministry of Skill Development and Entrepreneurship.(n.d.).Available from: http://www.skilldevelopment.gov.in/nationalskilldevelopmentcorporation.htmlDate accessed:10/10/16

National Skill Development Corporation. Available from:http://www.nsdcindia.org/Date accessed: 10/10/16

Patil, A. Skill Development in India: Challenges and Strategies, ISAS Working Paper. 2009 Sep.

Planning Commission, XII Five Year Plan, Employment and Skill Development.

Santosh Mehrotra, AG. Estimating the skill gap on a realistic basis for 2022. Institute of Applied Manpower Research. 2013 Feb.

Santosh Mehrotra, KD. Understanding Skill Development and Training in China: Lessons for India, Institute of Applied Manpower Research. 2013 Dec.

Souza, AP, Lima, L, Arbage, A et al. Vocational Education and Training in Brazil, Knowledge sharing forum on development experiences: Comparative Experiences of Korea and Latin America and Caribbean. 2015 Jun.

The World's Top Countries for high- skilled employment.(n.d.).Available from: http://www.forbes.com/sites/niallmccarthy/2015/06/01/the-worlds-top-countries-forhigh-skilled-employment-infographic/#796c442d31b0.Date accessed: 19/10/16

UNESCO TVET. Available from: http://www.sh-dz.net/ what-is-tvet-unesco-unevoc.html Date accessed: 13/10/16

Vocational Education Law of the People's Republic of China. (n.d.). Available from: http://www.china.org.cn/ english/education/184662.htm Date accessed: 14/10/16

Vocational Education Law of the People's Republic of China. Available from: http://www.china.org.cn/english/ education/184662.htm Date accessed: 14/10/16

Young, E. Knowledge paper on skill development in India: Learner first. Available from: http://www.ey.com/in/en/industries/india-sectors/education/knowledge-paper-onskill-development-in-india---where-are-we-on-skills Date accessed: 17/10/16.

22

A Study on Role and Importance of Self Help Groups

Sonia[1], Tripta[2]

Abstract

This study examines the role and importance of Self help groups. SHGs are voluntary organisations of people, that are formed to attain collective goals of people. People who share a common social background, caste, heritage, band together for a common purpose in order to raise the resources for the benefit of all the members of the group. SHGs are viewed as instruments for achieving goals such as developing leadership skills, empowering women and people in need, improving nutrition and birth control use and increasing school enrolment. They work to increase the functional capacity of its members in areas such as income generation and employment. They also provide loans that are collateral free to its members.

Introduction

A Self help group consists of 10-20 impoverished individuals from the same socioeconomic background who assemble deliberately and engage primarily in activities related to savings. SHGs are either registered or unregistered. Men, women or even a mixed group of

1. Associate Professor, Institute of Management Studies and Research, Maharshi Dayanand University, Rohtak.

2. Research Scholar, Institute of Management Studies and Research, Maharshi Dayanand University, Rohtak.

people can be included. SHGs are also known as DWARCA groups, which stands for "Development of Women and Children in Rural Areas", after an initiative that inspired them. Savings, loans, and loan repayments are handled collectively. These organisations are connected to a financial or microfinance institution through a third party to get extra funding and deposit savings. The major goal of SHGs is to instil a culture of banking, saving, and thrift to achieve economic success through credit. The organising and mobilisation of women toward the fundamental power of informality, solidarity, and collective action is the most crucial element of SHG.

Origin of SHGs

Self Help Groups (SHGs) were developed as a result of the Grameen Bank of Bangladesh's experiment with a novel method of rural financing in that country, which was started by Prof. Mohammed Yunus in 1975. Grameen bank provided loans without requesting that borrowers submit paperwork or offer collateral. NABARD started SHGs in the years 1986–1987 in India. However, the actual effort did not begin until SHGs were linked to banks. A Self help group is a small group of rural poor who deliberately agree to save a small sum of money on a regular basis. This money is then put in a shared account to cover members' emergency expenses and to offer loans without collateral as chosen by the group.

Features of Self Help Groups

- **Number of members-** A SHG is made up of 10 to 20 members from the same socio-economic background. These individuals make up the weakest and lowest segment of society. A separate SHG may be formed if there are more than 20 members. The size of the SHG is crucial since a big group size makes it difficult to maintain and monitor effectively. Less members mean poorer savings. Therefore, each group should consist of 10 to 20 people.
- **Regular meetings-** The SHG must hold weekly meetings on a regular basis. The location of the meeting is decided by the group as a whole. Members can exchange their ideas and feel a sense of belonging with one another with the support of regular gatherings. Regular gatherings enable participants

to learn about one other's personal and collective issues. The frequent meeting inspires them to take collective action, which may involve doing something for themselves or the community, or even fighting back against unjust and detrimental social norms.

- **Unique name-** Every SHG must have a distinctive name chosen by its members. The group's name conveys information about its mission. Members are free to choose any name in their native tongue, but it must be inspiring and encourage saving and depositing.
- **Savings-** Members are required to regularly save a specific amount. Weakly, biweekly, and monthly are all possible. All of the SHG members have saved money, which enables them to take advantage of loans when they need money. SHG members must make a small quantity of savings despite the fact that they are economically impoverished. Savings can be achieved by adding an extra activity, reducing spending, or doing both at once. Savings may be obtained through home expenses, any employment activity etc.
- **Members must have a bank account-** Each SHG is required to have a bank account in any service area bank under the group's name. Members can choose their bank signatories. A signatory should be the facilitator or a representative of the promoting organisation. If banks are difficult to reach, as they are in the majority of disadvantaged communities, that is not an issue. Members must learn to keep their money safely.
- **Members must have individual passbooks-** Members are required to have their own passbook. It is used by the bookkeeper to record all transactions, including borrowing, saving, and repaying loans, among others. Additionally, a SHG keeps track of attendance, membership, loans, minutes, accounts, saving registers, etc. The upkeep of these books is the duty of the bookkeeper. Even if everyone in a group is illiterate, they are nevertheless urged to keep records. Typically, they employ any literate worker to keep the books and registers.

- **Regular training programmes**- The members of SHGs receive a lot of training programmes and competence development which help them to increase their capacity. Most of these underprivileged members were not able to benefit from schooling when it was available. Members receive a variety of training programmes that cover topics like understanding SHGs and their advantages, understanding microfinance programme schemes, etc.

Adamsen & Soc (2002) assessed how SHGs helped people suffering from life threatening disease. Qualitative interviews were conducted to find how people experience in SHGs. The study included participants from 12 SHGs suffering from various diseases. The research design adopted in the study was Prospective, Exploratory and Descriptive and also non-experimental. The findings showed that participation in a SHG positively impacts the patients' ability to fight with the diseases but it was not proved that it also increases the survival rates.

Orok Orok-Duke et al., (2009) conducted a study to understand "Self-Help Groups Linkage Programme". Linkage Banking, objectives of SHGs linkage banking programme, reasons for dismal performance of SHGs linkage banking programme, the non-governmental organisations (NGOs) – SHGs – community bank linkage model and related recommendations has been discussed in this paper.

Mansuri (2010) examined the impact of SHGs. The results demonstrate that microfinance programmes are successful, but non-farm economic activities continue to pose a significant difficulty, and it is challenging to locate an economic activity that would generate the level of profit required to pay the loan's interest rate.

Kumar Mehta et al., (2011) studied the economic and social impact of microfinance and also the members empowerment during Pre-SHG and Post-SHG period. A descriptive study of SHGs promoted by Gramudyog Hastakala Kendra, an NGO that works for promotion of SHGs in Kathua District was conducted. For the present study, 10 SHGs have been selected through convenience sampling techniques. The results showed that after joining SHGs the communication level of members, Self Confidence, frequency of interaction with outsiders, access to amenities have increased and family violence has decreased, thus social impact of microfinance is positive and empowerment of SHGs members has also been increased. Beside this the economic impact of Microfinance was also positive.

Karimzadeh et al., (2011) carried out research to find the role played by Self Help Groups in Women empowerment, poverty alleviation and to also to find the growth of Self Help Groups and microfinance sector. Descriptive research was conducted and secondary data was collected for this purpose. Results showed that Micro-finance institutions provide credit to needy people for alleviating poverty and SHG bank linkage minimises the problems of inadequate banking facilities to the poor people.

Goswami et al., (2011) carried out research on "Impact of training on ornamental fish breeding and culture of fish farmers' self help group". Cooch Behar Krishi Vigyan Kendra of Uttar Banga Krishi Viswavidyalaya organised a three-day training course on "Ornamental Fish Breeding & Culture," after which the course's effects on 40 students was assessed. Prior to and after training, ornamental fish farmers' self-help group members' knowledge and attitudes regarding ornamental fish breeding and culture was compared. Participants showed a considerable improvement in knowledge and a more positive attitude. All of the trainees exhibited a supportive and creative approach toward the breeding and culture of ornamental fish.

Sivashankar & Khedgi (2011) examined the numerous proposals made by SHG members and the various challenges they faced, this study looked at the effect of training on the knowledge level of SHG members in animal husbandry. Sandur taluk was chosen from a list of SHG members who received training at Krishi Vigyan Kendra, Hagari. The respondents in the study were chosen using a simple random sampling method. To make conclusions, percentages, mean scores, 't' values and standard deviation was calculated. Based on the results of the current study, it can be said that the majority of respondents fell into the category of medium knowledge. As a result of the training, it can be assumed that respondents' knowledge levels have improved. Additionally, it is evident that there is a substantial disparity between respondents' knowledge levels before and after training.

Alam & Nizamuddin (2012) examined the socioeconomic status of SHG women, the motivations for joining SHGs, the structure, behaviour, and effectiveness of self-help groups, as well as the effects of SHGs on women. This study was analytical and data was collected through primary and secondary sources. To analyse the data in a way that was understandable, average and percentage analysis was done. The Garret ranking method was employed to determine the motivations behind joining the self-help group. The relationship between the variables that were observed is ascertained by factor analysis. The findings indicate that SHGs have a bigger effect on the beneficiaries' social and economic spheres.

Sahu & Singh (2012) assessed the role of Self-Help Groups in women empowerment in rural areas of Pondicherry. It was a Qualitative study. Content analysis was done manually and themes were generated. Findings of this study was divided into various domains like ability to make purchases, freedom of mobility, political awareness, household decisions, freedom from domination, economic security, etc. Results showed that SHGs should be promoted for women empowerment and development of the society.

C. (2012) determined the characteristics of SHGs and their members, the degree of empowerment attained by SHG members, the type and scope of problems experienced by SHG members, and to investigate the relationship between group features and empowerment. Exploratory research design was used for the study. Stratified, multi-stage and judgement sampling techniques were used for sample selection. Findings showed that the idea of SHGs for rural women's empowerment has not yet fully matured in achieving its goal.

Sarania (2014) investigated the effect of Self-Help Groups (SHGs) on rural residents' access to financial services. For this study, 180 respondents (90 participants and 90 nonparticipants) were chosen, and the overall findings showed that the SHG-Bank linkage programme increased the degree of financial inclusion among SHG households as compared with non-participants households.

Shah & Panigrahi (2015) identified the factors influencing loans borrowed by BPL households and to examine the determinants of credit delivery from formal and informal sources to women households who belong to below poverty line (BPL) in Ganjam district of Odisha. It also examined the determinants of women's participation in self-help groups (SHGs) to avail credit. The findings indicated that women's participation in SHGs to borrow credit was significantly influenced by factors including the number of children, education, age, caste, sources of income, their status as the head of the household, informal debt, migration, distance to banks, and household economic status.

Saravanan (2016) carried out research on "The impact of self-help groups on the socio-economic development of rural household women in Tamil Nadu - A Study". This study was carried out to examine the role played by self help groups in improving status of rural women and to study how SHG helps in promoting income generating activities in rural household women. Secondary sources of data collection were used in this study. The result showed that Self Help Groups help women not only for their development but also for meeting their needs holistically.

Singh & Mittal (2017) carried out a study on "Self help groups in Haryana : An analysis of trends and schemes". The Self Help Group trends and patterns in the State of Haryana was highlighted in this study. Government and non-government groups in the state are working on a microfinance programme and encouraging SHGs through various programmes and schemes run by several departments. SHGs are fostered in Haryana by the Women and Child Development Department through the Swayamsiddha and Programme for the Advancement of Gender Equity. The Swa-shakti project has received promotion from Women's Awareness & Management Academy. Under the Integrated Natural Resource Management and Poverty Reduction and Haryana Community Forest Project, the Forest Department has been supporting SHGs. Through the SHGs-Bank linkage Programme of NABARD, banks are promoting SHGs, while DRDA is promoting SHGs under the Swarnjayati Gram Swarajgar Yojana (Now National Rural Livelihoods Mission, NRLM).

Chakraborty et al., (2019) conducted a study to find the role of SHGs in women empowerment and to find the impact of those schemes on households and its role in poverty alleviation and also to find the effectiveness of various Government Schemes on SHGs. The present study was undertaken primarily in Gautam Buddh Nagar district of Uttar Pradesh. Few areas of Delhi – NCR have also been covered for the study. Both primary and secondary data was collected for this study. For collecting data, a self-constructed questionnaire was administered to 100 women associated with a self-help group in Delhi-NCR region. To measure the internal consistency and reliability of responses Cronbach alpha was used. The results revealed that SHGs contribute to improving the status of women in many aspects. Financial stability and social status of the respondents increased considerably due to the entrepreneurial activities of SHGs. Various Govt. schemes and easy access to microfinance also helped the SHGs to carry out their operations.

Benefits of microfinance for rural impoverished households

Although the phrases "micro credit" and "micro finance" are used frequently, it is critical to differentiate between the two. Micro credit means provision of credit services to clients with low income, in the form of loans for the development of their businesses and for gaining income from other sources. The Grameen Bank of Bangladesh's definition of micro credit is small loans given to extremely impoverished individuals for self-employment initiatives that create revenue, enabling them to take care of themselves and their families. As a result, the loans size and micro-entrepreneurs, particularly those from low-income households, are the main components to be considered. Typically, no collateral is required to obtain one of these loans. Microfinance, on the other hand, is a financial service provided by various financial institutions to the rural poor. All banking and financial services, such as credit, savings, money transfers, insurance leasing, equity transfers, etc., are included in these services. With the caveats that the consumer is poor and the transaction value is low, they are offered to customers in order to satisfy their needs and requirements. Self-help groups that provide microfinance to the underprivileged have helped the impoverished rise above their financial circumstances and, more importantly, break the dominance of predatory lenders.

Bank-SHG linkage Programme

The SHG-bank linkage programme was created by NABARD as a primary method that the Indian banking system could employ to broaden its reach to the underprivileged. The NABARD initiated this programme in 1992 to connect the unorganised sector with the formal banking sector. The main aim is to form poor people SHGs, that encourage them to pool their savings on a regular basis, and then the pooled savings are used to provide small interest-bearing loans to its members. NABARD viewed the marketing and bank connection of SHGs as part of a larger arrangement for providing financial services to the poor in a sustainable way that would result in the empowerment of the members of these SHGs rather than simply as a loan scheme.

Women empowerment

Entrepreneurship can promote women's empowerment and economic growth. Men and women both experience difficulties starting a microbusiness however, rural women face greater difficulties, as they don't have enough finances, resources, family support, and other factors. It is an effective tool for eliminating poverty and serves as a stimulus for the members' social growth.

Creating a micro business aids in the empowerment of women. Their ability to make decisions about how to spend their money, how to raise their children, how to travel freely, how to combat the ills of society, and how to have access to resources and property all contribute to their empowerment. SHGs acts as bridge between female entrepreneurs who want to start a business but lack the resources to do so and the funding they need. Small group of women join together and contribute money on a regular basis to form SHG. SHGs, which are becoming significant microfinance systems, serve as forums for women to unite around concerns of gender parity, nutrition, health, and gender justice. By increasing their abilities and providing them with the opportunity to participate in various entrepreneurial activities, SHGs have already significantly contributed to the development of entrepreneurial aptitudes among rural women. SHGs foster an environment where women entrepreneurs can grow their businesses by offering them microloans.

Spheres of Empowerment

There are basically four spheres of women empowerment:

- **Economic Empowerment-** Economic empowerment means improving the quality of life of someone in economic, monetary, and value terms. In India, women head approximately 10 percent of total households, and land and other property ownership is primarily in the name of male family members. As a result, women have little ownership of resources and decision-making autonomy. Women's Work-participation is a necessary condition, but it is not sufficient for economic empowerment of women.
- **Social Empowerment-** The process of improving women's quality of life in social aspects is referred to as social empowerment. It is the process of reducing gender discrimination based on superstitious beliefs, social functions, religious beliefs, customs, culture, and so on. Indian women are given less priority in education, are denied adequate food, and have limited access to health care. The social empowerment of women is a long and difficult process because it requires a shift in people's attitudes, which can only be accomplished by raising public awareness and enacting various legal measures to combat social discrimination.
- **Political Empowerment-** Political empowerment means increasing the quality of women's political participation. Despite the fact that women's political participation has been steadily increasing, the desired level has yet to be reached. This can be accomplished by emphasising the importance of women's education and enunciating legal measures such as power reservation policies, asset holding, and so on.
- **Psychological Empowerment-** The process of improving women's quality of life in terms of personal and psychological

considerations is known as psychological empowerment. This can only be accomplished by instilling motivation and self-confidence in women through the provision of orientation and decision-making opportunities.

Self Help Groups (SHGs) and Financial inclusion

Financial inclusion is the timely provision of banking and financial services to a sizable portion of society's underprivileged and low-income groups at a reasonable price. Payments, credit, insurance, savings and remittance services are among the different financial services. Although other services are included, credit takes precedence in India's definition of financial inclusion. This is because the disadvantaged sectors of the population have limited resources; they need credit at regular intervals at a reasonable borrowing cost through which they can purchase more resources. In India, meeting the needs of poor people is a very challenging phenomenon. To attain complete financial inclusion prior to the Indian formal banking system, this presents the biggest hurdle. To meet the needs of people, it was considered that new delivery mechanisms, alternative policies, systems, and procedures, savings and loan products, and additional services were needed. In 1992, NABARD began the self-help group bank linkage initiative. In India, SHG promotes various types of financial transactions between informal Self Help Groups (SHGs) and the official banking system, which consists of various banks.

Poverty Alleviation- Formation of SHGs have enabled members to save a portion of their earnings. It has increased its assets and income while also creating new job opportunities. There has been a significant shift from using loans for personal purposes and now these loans are used to generate income. The members' combined savings had made them financially secure. This has enabled them to break free from the cycle of poverty and unemployment.

Human Resource development- Members' financial security encourages them to invest more in their children's education. Member households observed that attendance of students in schools has increased and school dropout rates have decreased. Improved maternal health, lower child mortality, housing, good nutrition, and health - particularly among women and children - have all resulted from financial stability. Thus, SHGs help in human resource development as it provides financial security to its members.

Training and capacity building-Through various government schemes and some microfinance institutions various training programmes are regularly being organised for members of SHGs and its leaders.

Basically two types of training are provided: (a) Entrepreneurial training (For example, Accounting, basic book-keeping) that is used to set up a small business, and (b) Technical training that is required for some particular business.

SHGs Provides healthcare services- The main challenge for India is to achieve healthcare universally so as to cover everyone, by protecting them from unnecessary costs of healthcare. In this way, they act as a bridge between poor communities and institutions providing healthcare. SHGs can help provide health services to rural poor communities in a more decentralised way. Various Self Help Groups are providing services like, Newborn care, children's health, teaching home-based maternal, family planning methods, waste management and household water treatment.

Conclusion

SHGs are the key instruments in women's empowerment, it empowers the status and position of women in the family as well as society. A woman as a part of a successful SHG can be financially independent and lead to success in issues like gender equality. SHGs helps in poverty alleviation, human resource development, it provides training to its members, it provides microfinance that helped the impoverished rise above their financial circumstances and, more importantly, break the dominance of predatory lenders, it provides timely formal credit at a reasonable cost of borrowing that enables its members to develop resources, besides this SHGs also provides healthcare facilities to rural poor people.

References

Adamsen, L., & Soc, M. (n.d.). "From victim to agent": the clinical and social significance of self-help group participation for people with life-threatening diseases.

Alam, P., & Nizamuddin, S. (2012). Role of Micro Finance & Self Help Groups in Women Empowerment: A Case Study of District Mewat. *International Journal of Entrepreneurship & Business Environment Perspectives,* 1(2).

C., M. (2012). Empowering rural women in Kerala: A study on the role of Self Help Groups (SHGs). *International Journal of Sociology and Anthropology,* 4(9), 270–280. https://doi.org/10.5897/ijsa12.003

Chakraborty, A., Sharma, P., & Chaturvedi, C. (2019). Increasing Impact of Self-Help Groups on Women Empowerment and Poverty Alleviation: A Study of Reliability. *SSRN Electronic Journal.* https://doi.org/10.2139/ssrn.3407126

Goswami, B., Banga, U., & Vishwavidyalaya, K. (2011). Impact Of Training On Ornamental Fish Breeding And Culture Of Fish Farmers' Self Help Group. *J. Aqua Trop,* 26, 191–196. https://doi.org/10.13140/RG.2.2.15927.21928

Karimzadeh, M., Princess, G., & Scholar, M. (2011). Role of Self Help Groups through Micro-finance for poverty alleviation and Micro-Entrepreneurship of women "Impact of Micro Finance on Living Standard Empowerment and Poverty Alleviation of Poor W… Role of Self Help Groups through Micro-finance for poverty alleviation and Micro-Entrepreneurship of women. In Banaras Hindu University.

Kumar Mehta, S., Govind Mishra, H., Singh, A., & Professor, A. (n.d.). *Role of Self Help Groups in Socio-Economic Change of Vulnerable Poor of Jammu Region.*

Mansuri, B. B. (n.d.). *Microfinancing through self help Groups-A Case Study Of Bank Linkage Programme of Nabard.* https://www.researchgate.net/publication/267836298

Orok Orok-Duke, by E., Edu, B., & Akpan Ekott, G. (n.d.). *Linkage Banking Programme in Nigeria Concept, Relevance and Implementation (A Case Study Of Self-Help Groups).* http://ssrn.com/abstract=1404362

Sahu, L., & Singh, S. K. (2012). Qualitative Study on Role of Self Help Group in Women Empowerment in Rural Pondicherry, India. In *National Journal of Community Medicine,* Volume (Vol. 3, Issue 3). www.njcmindia.org

Sarania, R. (2014). Volume-I, Issue-III Self Help Groups (SHGs) and Financial Inclusion-A Case Study in Baksa District of Assam. In *International Journal of Humanities & Social Science Studies* (IJHSSS) A Peer-Reviewed Bi-monthly Bi-lingual Research Journal. Online.

Saravanan, M. (2016). The Impact of Self-Help Groups on the Socio-Economic Development of Rural Household Women in Tamil Nadu - A Study. International Journal of Research -Granthaalayah, 4(7(SE)), 22–31. https://doi.org/10.29121/granthaalayah.v4.i7(se).2016.2624

Shah, D., & Panigrahi, S. (2015). Determinants of participation of women in Self-Help Groups (SGHs) and credit delivery from formal and informal sources to BPL households in Odisha. *Indian Journal of Agricultural Economics,* 70(902-2016-68380), 405-416.

Singh, T., & Mittal, P. (2017). Self Help Groups in Haryana: An Analysis of Trends and Schemes. *Management insight,* 13(1), 54-68.

Sivashankar, N., & Khedgi, K. (2011). Influence of Trainings on the Knowledge Level of Self Help Group Members. *Studies on Home and Community Science,* 5(3), 135–140. https://doi.org/10.1080/09737189.2011.11885340

23

The Impact of CSR on Entrepreneurship and Start-Up Movement in India

Taruna Sharma[1], Shivani Arora[2], Sarika Walia[3], C.S. Yadav[4]

Abstract

In this day and age of globalisation, new businesses are taking off and contributing significantly to the expansion of the economy. In addition to this, there was an epidemic of COVID-19 as well as several other obstacles, such as a budget deficit, a dearth of novel ideas, a scarcity of appropriate space and infrastructure, etc. In addition, a start-up company is unable to develop its mentorship and connections to the market because incubators do not have consistent inflows of funding. In addition, the Companies Act of 2013 was recently amended. Moreover, as part of the concept of "Corporate Social Responsibility" (CSR), firms are now obligated to invest two percent of their net earnings over the previous three fiscal years on social welfare endeavours, as outlined in Schedule VII of the Act.

---

1. Research Scholar, University of Engineering and Technology Roorkee, Haridwar, Uttarakhand.
2. Assistant Professor, PDP Department, Graphic Era Hill University, Dehradun, Uttarakhand.
3. Assistant Professor, Department of Management Studies, Gurugram University, Gurugram.
4. Professor, Shivalik Institute of Professional Studies, Dehradun, Uttarakhand.

The research set out to learn more about the importance of corporate social responsibility (CSR) contributions to new businesses, the circumstances under which corporate funds would qualify as CSR, the importance of starting new enterprises and the current laws and regulations in India that are set up to facilitate their launch. The research found that corporations may help finance start-ups by combining corporate social responsibility funds with the knowledge and connections of established businesses.

Keywords: Start-ups, Incubators, Corporate Social Responsibility (CSR), Skill-building for Entrepreneurship, Innovation.

Introduction

In the age of globalisation, new businesses are playing an important part in addressing the myriad of problems confronting society. In addition to its already terrible impacts, the COVID-19 Pandemic, there is a growing demand for cutting-edge technology and novel approaches to the development of medications and immunisations. As a result, the importance of assisting newly established businesses has become even clearer. Taking into consideration this reality, India has set its sights on becoming a "start-up nation" by making the most of the country's young population and its high level of entrepreneurial zeal.

It is important to keep in mind that in order for start-ups to realise their full potential, they require an atmosphere that is supportive of that potential. Business incubators have shown themselves to be the best option for helping new enterprises get off the ground and tapping into the innovative spirit of today's youth. This is because incubators facilitate the process described above. Incubators of this kind are therefore performing an extremely important function in the development of our nation's ecosystem for start-up businesses.

The "Government of India" (GOI) has made many steps to foster start-up businesses and promote social entrepreneurship. The Ministry of Science and Technology has launched a number of programmes to help aspiring business owners realise their goals, including the creation of Technology Business Incubators (TBIs) and the legal requirement, within the bounds of CSR (Corporate Social Responsibility) in the Co's Act, 2013, for corporations to make donations to TBIs and NGOs that have been vetted and registered.

India has many community-owned enterprises since the 1950s, such as Amul and Fab India, that promote social development and entrepreneurship (British Committee, 2016). India is a centre of creativity and new business ideas, but new ideas need help to "productise" and a supportive environment to thrive. A start-up business needs a well-planned structure to succeed. In this regard, incubators may be important. The Companies Act, 2013 modification, which urged firms to promote India's incubation ecosystem, was the most important action to inspire business expansion and country prosperity. This was the biggest step to get the business sector involved in national development. CSR money may also help start-ups overcome financial challenges and scale up their operations, enabling them to benefit society.

Objectives of the Study

This study aims to examine the following topics:

- To get an understanding of the significance of Corporate Social Responsibility (CSR) activities in relation to the encouragement of Entrepreneurship in India.
- To do research into the importance of entrepreneurialism in countries like India, which have economies that are rising at the quickest rates.
- To gather information about the current state of start-ups through a review of the relevant literature.
- To make suggestions for moving forward and offer a path forward.

Research Methodology

The secondary mode of data collecting was utilised throughout the course of the research project. It was decided to conduct some rapid desk research of the current literature around start-ups and then assess the results of that research. In addition, annual reports of corporations that fund start-ups, journals, research publications, magazine articles, news articles stories were used to collect the data together.

Review of Literature

On January 16, 2016, the Government of India launched a programme called "Start-up India," with the intention of fostering an entrepreneurial mindset among young people and imparting to them the required skill sets. Anitha (2017) claims that the government's "Start-up India" initiative is an excellent policy choice for motivating and developing the country's young people. The country's economy and the youth's entrepreneurial spirit would both benefit from this action. In addition, those who want to pursue their aspirations of being entrepreneurs can find a wealth of chances in a variety of industries, such as textiles, the media, healthcare, event planning, tourism, automobile ventures, and others. On the other hand, There are a number of factors working against the development of the start-up, including a deficiency in infrastructure, fears associated with starting a business, and a shortage of qualified employees. According to the study's conclusions, new businesses and the government may work together to mitigate the consequences of these problems.

Jain (2020) carried out research in order to investigate how a public health emergency such as COVID-19 will affect employment opportunities. It was discovered, during the course of the research process, that there would be continued ambiguity surrounding the rate of job creation as well as the employment levels in the subsequent year. The author also predicted a rise in joblessness as a consequence of the pandemic. Nonetheless, the present pandemic crisis may lead to a rise in the number of start-ups, as more people seek out new enterprises as a means of survival. It was concluded that while the post-covid scenario may be difficult with respect to the creation of new jobs, the entrepreneurial environment would rapidly advance.

There is a growing population of young and driven businesspeople in India; nevertheless, more than 90 percent of the country's new businesses fail due to a lack of innovation, a dearth of competent workers, and insufficient capital "Institute for Business Value" (IBV, 2018).

Starting a business may be challenging, and the difficulties you encounter will increase as your company grows. The study by Adhana and Kumar (2020) lists a number of problems, some of which include legal complications, the viability of businesses, different degrees of awareness, and so on. In this respect, incubators have the potential to play a very important role in assisting new businesses in getting off the ground. The paper went on to describe further aspects of the larger ecosystem that encourages entrepreneurial endeavours in the form of various policy initiatives of the government, and other types of relaxations. One such initiative is the India Aspiration Fund, while others include the Mudra Yojana, the Start-up India Learning Programme, and the Pradhan Mantri Laghu Udyog Yojana 2016. There are also a number of other relaxations, such as tax exemptions, ease in bidding through government procurement, an easier departure plan within a period of ninety days, and so on. To further assist newly established businesses, the government has established a fund with a total value of ₹ 10,000 Cr. that will be available over a period of four years. According to a survey by the IBM Institute for Business Value and Oxford Economics, around 90 percent of entrepreneurial companies fail after five years due to a lack of innovation, despite the fact that such beneficial initiatives have been initiated. Despite the fact that such excellent measures have been halted, this conclusion was reached. Start-ups in the nation need to be successful, therefore it's important to focus the available skill pool on things like market research and strategic development. This is required for the success of the nation's start-ups.

Start-up, according to the Outlook study for 2019, India has been identified as a desirable location for start-up businesses to establish themselves and experience success. This is due to the fact that transportation costs are reduced as a consequence of the close proximity of various service providers and customers. In addition, India has a tremendously enormous market, and after surpassing China in terms of the number of people who use the internet, it now has the second largest base of Internet users in the entire globe (Adhana & Kumar, 2020).

India's Legal Requirement for Corporate Social Responsibility (CSR)

Regulations and requirements of CSR can be found outlined in Section 135 and Schedule VII of the Companies Act of 2013 in addition to the Companies (Corporate Social Responsibility) Rules of 2021.

Applicability	Requirement
• Annual Revenue of More Than One Billion Indian Rupees (INR); • Total Net Worth of More Than Five Hundred Million Indian Rupees (INR); • Annual Net Profit of More Than Five Billion Indian Rupees (INR)	Two percent of the average net earnings made during the previous three fiscal years should be spent (Act Section 198 must be used to determine the amount of profit).
Responsibility	**Execution**
• Disclosing individuals who make up the CSR committee. • It is required by law for the board to provide its approval to the CSR Policy. • Allocate funds for initiatives related to corporate social responsibility in accordance with Schedule VII of the statute. • You are required to report any violations or deficiencies. • Carry out studies of both the need assessment and the effect evaluation.	• It is recommended that a CSR committee be established, with a minimum of three directors serving, and at least one of those members being an independent non-executive director. • It is mandated for the CSR Committee to: Create a Corporate Social Responsibility (CSR) policy and yearly action plan, then present to the board. Establish a strategy for spending corporate social responsibility money. Project tools for implementation, tracking, and reporting.

Source: (KPMG India, 2017).

CSR Funding for Incubators

During the typical period of two years that start-up companies spend working with an incubator, the incubators offer start-ups a variety of services, including providing a place to work and basic support services, as well as the provision of expert insights and guidance from industry professionals. In addition, research laboratories and several other forms of technical support are provided as part of the infrastructure support that is provided (Menon & Malik, 2016).

The following requirements must be met for a corporation's contributions to a fund that has been established to assist in the launch of new businesses in order for those contributions to be considered an acceptable form of corporate social responsibility (CSR) spending:

- Government funding is channelled through "Technology-based Incubators" (TBIs) of government-sanctioned educational institutions like the "Indian Institutes of Technology" (IITs), "National Laboratories," and several other Autonomous Bodies funded by the "Indian Council for Agricultural Research" (ICAR), publicly funded

Universities, and the "Council of Scientific and Industrial Research" (CSIR) (The Economic Times, 2019).

- Providing financial support to non-governmental organisations (NGOs) that are duly recognised by the law and registered under Sec 8 of the Co's Act an Association or Trust. These organisations are often referred to as (Start-up Supporting Entities) SSE.

Even given the constraints we've explored, a TBI may help any kind of start-up by utilising its existing expertise, tools, and resources. Contrarily, Start-up Supporting Entities (SSEs) are limited to assisting start-ups in the industries listed in Schedule VII.

There is a gradual increase in the number of start-up businesses, and incubators have the potential to play a significant role in supporting these businesses. Start-ups need infrastructure, funding, and markets, but incubators may also provide mentoring and assistance that is hard to get elsewhere. More than 120 TBIs are currently being promoted in India by the Department of Science and Technology (DST), the Ministry of Information and Communication Technology (MICT), as well as a variety of other commercial organisations, institutions, and banks, as well as numerous government departments (Department of Science and Technology).

Connecting Corporate Social Responsibility and New Businesses

According to a report that was published by KPMG India in 2017, the legal mandates for CSR contributions towards incubators were documented in detail in the report. The report also detailed the ways in which incubators can support start-up businesses by providing skill-building opportunities, mentorship programmes, and financial assistance. In addition, the study analysed and tallied the CSR projects that were carried out by corporations to provide assistance for incubators and the impact that these programmes had. Villgro, the Centre for Innovation Incubation and Entrepreneurship (CIIE), and the Society for Innovation and Entrepreneurship are a few examples of Incubators that were mentioned in the report. SAP, Tata Motors, Bajaj Electricals, Castrol, and Mahindra & Mahindra Financial Services sponsor incubators (SINE). The study noted that section 135 of the Companies Act does not require contributions to technological incubators or big corporations. The report gave this information. The law only requires companies to pay 2 percent of their sales to Schedule VII social welfare programmes. Because of this, corporations can spend 2 percent of their revenues however they want, which means they can support incubators with all or part of their CSR spending. Corporations may sponsor an incubator or start-up firm without restriction. Thus, companies may fund incubators. However, the law mandates businesses to publish their contributions in yearly reports.

The survey concluded that because start-ups conduct such in-depth market research, they have the ability to boost the country's innovation and development. As a result, there is a requirement for collaboration between corporations and start-ups due to the mutual benefits that would result: corporations would gain access to the start-ups' innovative ideas and market knowledge, while start-ups would gain access to the corporate expertise, business sense, and CSR funds of corporations.

British Council (2016) performed study on India's current social, political, and economic environment for ethical businesses and published their findings. In addition, a literature analysis was undertaken on social entrepreneurs and the various sorts of organisations that support them, regardless of whether this support is voluntary or mandated by various government-enacted laws and policies. This study's primary research was conducted on 256 distinct social enterprises. This was done in order for the researchers to obtain a deeper grasp of the current situation of social entrepreneurship. According to the results, the most influential groups in India's business community include those involved in innovation and acceleration, influence investing, multilateral institutions and financing agencies, firms, business chambers, organisations, forums, and networks. New business projects have received more support throughout the years, according to the survey, but social enterprises still don't have widespread name recognition or funding. In a recent survey, we found that 32 percent of people felt that banks didn't fully grasp the concept of social entrepreneurship. Most social entrepreneurs don't fully grasp the potential of debt financing and investments, thus they don't take use of such avenues to raise capital. In addition, the recently created Start-up India initiative by the Indian government does not let social enterprises to participate.

As it stands, only non-governmental organisations (NGOs) are able to receive corporate social responsibility (CSR) funds for the purpose of carrying out social welfare projects. This money is off-limits to both the government and nonprofits. Therefore, it is necessary for the government to encourage businesses and other organisations to invest in social enterprises.

The presence of a large number of young people in a population that has a significant deficit of experienced workers is one of the most significant challenges that the private sector of entrepreneurship faces today. India is a country in which half of the population is under the age of 35, and the country has the potential to generate a very productive workforce. In addition, many social companies engage young people in their work, with an estimated 89 percent of these businesses planning to increase their workforce in the near future. Nonetheless, there was a deficiency in capabilities; more than 31 percent of respondents noted a lack of managerial skills, 24 percent of respondents indicated a lack of technical skills, and over 26 percent of respondents said employing junior staff was a severe challenge. Furthermore, though woman social enterprises have better gender parity than mainstream industry (for instance, there are roughly 24 percent female leaders in female-run social enterprises), the gap between the sexes in leadership positions is still quite wide, whereas there are approximately 8.9 percent female leaders in the general business market), there is still a significant gender gap in the business world. In addition, the research showed that female business leaders of social enterprises have a difficult time obtaining funding and are frequently questioned about their families, maternity leaves, and maintain a healthy work-life balance so that you can accurately assess their abilities and potential. According to the research, in order to have a larger effect, retain talent, influence legislation for the benefit of society, and attract foreign investment, India's social companies require more financing from industry leaders. Teaching young people about social entrepreneurship and encouraging schools and institutions to instil an entrepreneurial mindset are both necessary for the government to achieve its goal of social change.

The significance of business partnerships with non-profit organisations was investigated in the following report titled "Bala Vikasa International Center (BVIC), 2015," which was published in 2015. Even though there have been numerous instances in the past in which partnerships between corporations and social enterprises have been extremely successful, there is a significant lack of awareness in India regarding the potential advantages that could result from such collaborations. One such cooperation is that which exists between the Abdul Latif Jameel Group and the Grameen Foundation. When it comes to distributing Toyota goods, the Abdul Latif Jameel Group is a major player.

As a result of this collaboration, the Grameen-Jameel network was established to provide assistance to microfinance intermediaries in the Middle East region. It's possible that the CSR standards stated in the Companies Act of 2013 could also be useful to such small enterprises in their quest for help from larger corporations. The most potential advantage should be derived by social entrepreneurs from CSR money, hence it is crucial that CSR programmes designed to aid social enterprises be carried out with minimal overhead.

In addition, providing financial support to social enterprises can result in improved relations with the local community, as well as a decreased likelihood of unrest and mistrust on the part of the local populace. This has the potential to result in a number of positive outcomes for corporations. In addition, consumers are more likely to buy from corporations that are associated with a good cause (41 percent of consumers in one study said they were more likely to buy from a corporation if it was associated with a cause), and the public's perception of a corporation as a socially responsible organisation can have a positive impact on the company's bottom line. Aside from that, customers will show more favour toward businesses who are active in the communities they serve. To boost earnings and have a beneficial impact on the communities where they operate, companies are also looking into the idea of selling their products in the BOP market.

As a result, corporations have the intention of working together with social enterprises and non-governmental organisations (NGOs) to create sustainable change, rather than simply participating in charity-based programmes. In its conclusion, the paper emphasised the relevance of the partnership between corporations and social enterprises at a time when corporations are under great scrutiny about their engagement in socially responsible projects that can benefit the community at large, the planet, and civilisation as a whole.

Discussion

CSR aid to incubators may assist start-ups to fill in the gaps in their infrastructure and financing. In addition, start-ups may obtain guidance from seasoned professionals, and funding can be made available to help with the creation of R&D facilities. The number of privately owned firms in India has increased as a direct result of this trend.

The exchange of knowledge about current and future trends in different sectors as well as the assistance of existing firms in extending their area of influence are two further benefits of collaboration between established businesses (corporations) and young businesses (start-ups). In addition, forming partnerships with newly established businesses can result in increased interaction between established corporations and a variety of other stakeholders.

Corporations are able to provide assistance to start-up companies by putting their skilled employees in touch with those companies so that those employees can share the industry knowledge they have gained. In addition, employees of established companies can offer some of their spare time to new businesses in order to provide them with initial support and assistance. The goal and vision of the start-up can be matched with the expertise of corporate employees, and incubators can act as a go-between to facilitate this process. This helps to ensure that the start-up and the corporation are a good fit for one another.

Even though the number of new businesses opening their doors across the country is on the rise, many of them are still having trouble getting their operations off the ground. There could be a number of reasons for this, including insufficient funding, a lack of innovation, and inadequate means of collaboration. Access to both financial resources and physical infrastructure is an absolute necessity, however, if one wishes to ensure the long-term viability of the start-up ecosystem in India.

In addition, incubators have been demonstrated to be the most effective method of providing support for new businesses, despite the fact that these incubators do not receive sufficient amounts of funding. In this regard, corporations have the potential to play a significant role by lending financial assistance to business incubators in the form of CSR funds. With the assistance of these funds, business incubators will be able to address a wide variety of problems relating to the economy, society, and the environment.

With the participation of corporations, there would also be an increase in the rate of innovation as well as an increase in the number of opportunities that are available to start-up businesses. Additionally, this would open up opportunities for corporations to supply a wide variety of goods and services. In addition, establishing corporate entities as socially responsible entities can be accomplished by providing financial assistance to newly established businesses that have a focus on economic development.

In addition, participating in new ventures that are founded on original concepts and solid market analysis can assist established businesses get up and running quickly and adapt to the ever-changing needs of consumers. Globally recognised business leaders have warned that "corporations would die if they did not innovate." Therefore, businesses are teaming up with new ventures to acquire access to cutting-edge research, tools, and processes that may be used to create better products.

Thus, engagement with start-ups would benefit firms financially and through industry research and development that generates new ideas. Corporations would benefit in many ways. In conclusion, corporations' CSR money can help entrepreneurs and corporations grow the economy.

References

British Council, The State of Social Enterprise in Bangladesh, Ghana, India, and Pakistan: The state of social enterprise in India, 2016.

D.Adhana & A. Kumar, Start-Up Ecosystem in India: A Study With Focus on Entrepreneurship and University Business Incubators, *Aegaeum Journal,* 2020.

Ely, R. T. and Hess, R. H. (1937). *Outlines of Economics*, 6th Ed. (New York: Mac Milan), pp. 488.

Fernando, A.C. *Business Ethics and Corporate Governance*, 2nd edition, Pearson education.

Ferrell, O.C., Fraedrich John and Ferrell, *Business Ethics: Ethical Decision Making & Cases,* 10th edition, Cengage Learning.

Gupta, C. B. and Khanka, S.S. (2010), *Entrepreneurship and Small Business Management,* 4th edition, New Delhi: Sultan Chand & Sons.

Hisrich, D. Robert and Peters, P. Michael, *Entrepreurship* 6th edition, Tata Mc Graw Hill edition.

IICA, White paper on India & Corporate Incubation: Annual Report, 2015.

India Entrepreneurship Report, 2014 by Amway and Indicus Analytics, www.amwayentrepreneurshipreport.com

Jacobs, J.(1969), *The Economy of Cities*, New York: Vintage Books.

K. A. Anitha. Start-up India: opportunities and challenges. *Academica-An International Multidisciplinary Research Journal,* 2017.

K. Menon & G. Malik, *Funding options for startups: A conceptual framework and practical guide,* Notion Press, 2016.

KPMG India, Handbook on Leveraging CSR Contribution for Supporting Start-Ups/Social Enterprises. New Delhi: Deutsche Gesellschaft für Internationale Zusammenarbeit (GIZ) GmbH, 2017.

M. Das, Rangarajan & G. Dutta. Corporate sustainability in SMEs: an Asian perspective. *Journal of Asia Business Studies,* 2020.

MSME Report (2012), MSME Policy, retrieved from http://msme.gov.in/WriteReadData/DocumentFile/ANNUALREPORT-MSME-2013-14P.pdf

Naidu, N.V.R. and Rao, T.K. (2008), *Management and Entrepreneurship,* New Delhi: I.K International Publishing House, pg. 179.

Onuoha, G., (2007) Entrepreneurship, *AIST International Journal* 10, pp. 20-32.

P. Aggarwal & A. K. Singh, CSR and sustainability reporting practices in India: an in-depth content analysis of top-listed companies, *Social Responsibility Journal,* 2019.

Palmer (1971), The application of psychological testing to entrepreneurial potential, *California Management Review,* 13, pp. 32-38 Electronic copy available at: https://ssrn.com/abstract=2761878

R. Malpani & A. Ghosh, Corporate Social Responsibility Practices: A Strategy for Indian Startups to Sustain, *Business Perspectives and Research,* 2022.

Ronstadt, R.C. (1984). *Entrepreneurship,* Dover, MA: Lord Publishing Co., pp. 28

Sanjeev Rinku and Khanna, Parul (2008), *Ethics and Values in Business Management,* Ane Books India, New Delhi.

Say, J.B (1827). *Production, Distribution and Consumption of Wealth*, John Grigg, Philadelphia, pp. 28-286.

Schumpeter, J. (1952), *Can Capitalism survive,* New York: Harper and Row, 1952, p. 72.

Stanwick, P.A. Stanwick, S.D., 2009. *Understanding Business Ethics,* 1st Edition, Pearson, 5 New York.

Timmons, J.A. 1994. *New Venture Creation: Entrepreneurship for the 21st Century.* Fourth edition. Irwin Press, Burr Ridge, IL.

Velasquez, M.G., 2006. *Business Ethics Concept and Cases,* 6th Edition, Pearson, New York.

Vesper, K. (1980). *New Venture Strategies,* Englewood Cliffs, NJ: Prentice Hall, pp. 2.

Vikasa International Center, Social Enterprise: The new Model of CSR. Hyderabad: *Global Affairs Canada & SOPAR,* 2015.

Weiss, J.W., 2006. *Business Ethics: A Stakeholder and Issues Management Approach,* 4th Edition, Thomson-South Western, Ohio.

Wicks, A. & Freeman, E. (2010). *Business ethics.* Upper Saddle River, Pearson Education Inc.